OpenCV 4 with Python Blueprints
Second Edition

Build creative computer vision projects with the latest version of OpenCV 4 and Python 3

Dr. Menua Gevorgyan
Arsen Mamikonyan
Michael Beyeler

BIRMINGHAM - MUMBAI

OpenCV 4 with Python Blueprints
Second Edition

Commissioning Editor: Richa Tripathi
Acquisition Editor: Denim Pinto
Content Development Editor: Rosal Colaco
Senior Editor: Afshaan Khan
Technical Editor: Ketan Kamble
Copy Editor: Safis Editing
Project Coordinator: Francy Puthiry
Proofreader: Safis Editing
Indexer: Priyanka Dhadke
Production Designer: Aparna Bhagat

First published: October 2015
Second edition: March 2020

Production reference: 1190320

Published by Packt Publishing Ltd.
Livery Place
35 Livery Street
Birmingham
B3 2PB, UK.

ISBN 978-1-78980-181-1

www.packt.com

Packt.com

Subscribe to our online digital library for full access to over 7,000 books and videos, as well as industry leading tools to help you plan your personal development and advance your career. For more information, please visit our website.

Why subscribe?

- Spend less time learning and more time coding with practical eBooks and Videos from over 4,000 industry professionals

- Improve your learning with Skill Plans built especially for you

- Get a free eBook or video every month

- Fully searchable for easy access to vital information

- Copy and paste, print, and bookmark content

Did you know that Packt offers eBook versions of every book published, with PDF and ePub files available? You can upgrade to the eBook version at www.packt.com and as a print book customer, you are entitled to a discount on the eBook copy. Get in touch with us at customercare@packtpub.com for more details.

At www.packt.com, you can also read a collection of free technical articles, sign up for a range of free newsletters, and receive exclusive discounts and offers on Packt books and eBooks.

Contributors

About the authors

Dr. Menua Gevorgyan is an experienced researcher with a demonstrated history of working in the information technology and services industry. He is skilled in computer vision, deep learning, machine learning, and data science as well as having a lot of experience with OpenCV and Python programming. He is interested in machine perception and machine understanding problems, and wonders if it is possible to make a machine perceive the world as a human does.

I would like to thank Rosal Colaco, for the dedicated work to improve the book's quality, as well as Sandeep Mishra, for proposing the book.

Arsen Mamikonyan is an experienced machine learning specialist with demonstrated work experience in Silicon Valley and London, and teaching experience at the American University of Armenia. He is skilled in applied machine learning and data science and has built real-life applications using Python and OpenCV, among others. He holds a master's degree in engineering (MEng) with a concentration on artificial intelligence from the Massachusetts Institute of Technology.

I would like to thank my wife, Lusine, and my parents, Gayane and Andranik, for encouraging and putting up with me while I was writing this book. I would like to thank my coauthor, Menua, for bearing with my hectic work schedule and keeping my motivation high while we worked on this project.

Michael Beyeler is a postdoctoral fellow in neuroengineering and data science at the University of Washington, where he is working on computational models of bionic vision in order to improve the perceptual experience of blind patients implanted with a retinal prosthesis (bionic eye).

His work lies at the intersection of neuroscience, computer engineering, computer vision, and machine learning. He is also an active contributor to several open source software projects, and has professional programming experience in Python, C/C++, CUDA, MATLAB, and Android. Michael received a PhD in computer science from the University of California, Irvine, and an MSc in biomedical engineering and a BSc in electrical engineering from ETH Zurich, Switzerland.

About the reviewer

Sri Manikanta Palakollu is an undergraduate student pursuing his bachelor's degree in computer science and engineering at SICET under JNTUH. He is a founder of the OpenStack Developer Community in his college.

He started his journey as a competitive programmer. He loves to solve problems related to the data science field. His interests include data science, app development, web development, cybersecurity, and technical writing. He has published many articles on data science, machine learning, programming, and cybersecurity with publications such as Hacker Noon, freeCodeCamp, Towards Data Science, and DDI.

Packt is searching for authors like you

If you're interested in becoming an author for Packt, please visit `authors.packtpub.com` and apply today. We have worked with thousands of developers and tech professionals, just like you, to help them share their insight with the global tech community. You can make a general application, apply for a specific hot topic that we are recruiting an author for, or submit your own idea.

Table of Contents

Preface

The goal of this book is to get you hands-on with a wide range of intermediate to advanced projects using the latest version of the **OpenCV 4** framework and the **Python 3.8** language instead of only covering the core concepts of computer vision in theoretical lessons.

This updated second edition has increased the depth of the concepts we tackle with OpenCV. It will guide you through working on independent hands-on projects that focus on essential computer vision concepts such as image processing, 3D scene reconstruction, object detection, and object tracking. It will also cover, with real-life examples, statistical learning and deep neural networks.

You will begin by understanding concepts such as image filters and feature matching, as well as using custom sensors such as the **Kinect depth sensor**. You will also learn how to reconstruct and visualize a scene in 3D, how to align images, and how to combine multiple images into a single one. As you advance through the book, you will learn how to recognize traffic signs and emotions on faces and detect and track objects in video streams using neural networks, even if they disappear for short periods of time.

By the end of this OpenCV and Python book, you will have hands-on experience and be proficient at developing your own advanced computer vision applications according to specific business needs. Throughout the book, you will explore multiple machine learning and computer vision models such as **Support Vector Machines (SVMs)** and convolutional neural networks.

Who this book is for

This book is aimed at computer vision enthusiasts in pursuit of mastering their skills by developing advanced practical applications using OpenCV and other machine learning libraries.

Basic programming skills and Python programming knowledge is assumed.

What this book covers

Chapter 1, *Fun with Filters*, explores a number of interesting image filters (such as a black-and-white pencil sketch, warming/cooling filters, and a cartoonizer effect), and we'll apply them to the video stream of a webcam in real time.

Chapter 2, *Hand Gesture Recognition Using a Kinect Depth Sensor*, helps you develop an app to detect and track simple hand gestures in real time using the output of a depth sensor, such as Microsoft Kinect 3D Sensor or Asus Xtion.

Chapter 3, *Finding Objects via Feature Matching and Perspective Transforms*, helps you develop an app to detect an arbitrary object of interest in the video stream of a webcam, even if the object is viewed from different angles or distances, or under partial occlusion.

Chapter 4, *3D Scene Reconstruction Using Structure from Motion*, shows you how to reconstruct and visualize a scene in 3D by inferring its geometrical features from camera motion.

Chapter 5, *Using Computational Photography with OpenCV*, helps you develop command-line scripts that take images as input and produce panoramas or **High Dynamic Range (HDR)** images. The scripts will either align the images so that there is a pixel-to-pixel correspondence or stitch them creating a panorama, which is an interesting application of image alignment. In a panorama, the two images are not that of a plane but that of a 3D scene. In general, 3D alignment requires depth information. However, when the two images are taken by rotating the camera about its optical axis (as in the case of panoramas), we can align two images of a panorama.

Chapter 6, *Tracking Visually Salient Objects*, helps you develop an app to track multiple visually salient objects in a video sequence (such as all the players on the field during a soccer match) at once.

Chapter 7, *Learning to Recognize Traffic Signs*, shows you how to train a support vector machine to recognize traffic signs from the **German Traffic Sign Recognition Benchmark (GTSRB)** dataset.

Chapter 8, *Learning to Recognize Facial Emotions*, helps you develop an app that is able to both detect faces and recognize their emotional expressions in the video stream of a webcam in real time.

Chapter 9, *Learning to Recognize Facial Emotions*, walks you through developing an app for real-time object classification with deep convolutional neural networks. You will modify a classifier network to train on a custom dataset with custom classes. You will learn how to train a Keras model on a dataset and how to serialize and save your Keras model to a disk. You will then see how to classify new input images using your loaded Keras model. You will train a convolutional neural network using the image data you have to get a good classifier that will have very high accuracy.

Chapter 10, *Learning to Detect and Track Objects*, guides you as you develop an app for real-time object detection with deep neural networks, connecting it to a tracker. You will learn how object detectors work and how they are trained. You will implement a Kalman filter-based tracker, which will use object position and velocity to predict where it is likely to be. After completing this chapter, you will be able to build your own real-time object detection and tracking applications.

Appendix A, *Profiling and Accelerating Your Apps*, covers how to find bottlenecks in an app and achieve CPU- and CUDA-based GPU acceleration of existing code with Numba.

Appendix B, *Setting Up a Docker Container*, walks you through replicating the environment that we have used to run the code in this book.

To get the most out of this book

All of our code use **Python 3.8**, which is available on a variety of operating systems, such as **Windows**, **GNU Linux**, **macOS**, and others. We have made an effort to use only libraries that are available on these three operating systems. We will go over the exact versions of each of the dependencies we have used, which can be installed using pip (Python's dependency management system). If you have trouble getting any of these working, we have Dockerfiles available with which we have tested all the code in this book, which we cover in Appendix B, *Setting Up a Docker Container*.

Here is a list of dependencies that we have used, with the chapters they were used in:

Software required	Version	Chapter number	Download links to the software
Python	3.8	All	https://www.python.org/downloads/
OpenCV	4.2	All	https://opencv.org/releases/
NumPy	1.18.1	All	http://www.scipy.org/scipylib/download.html

wxPython	4.0		1, 4, 8	http://www.wxpython.org/download.php
matplotlib	3.1		4, 5, 6, 7	http://matplotlib.org/downloads.html
SciPy	1.4		1, 10	http://www.scipy.org/scipylib/download.html
rawpy	0.14		5	https://pypi.org/project/rawpy/
ExifRead	2.1.2		5	https://pypi.org/project/ExifRead/
TensorFlow	2.0		7, 9	https://www.tensorflow.org/install

In order to run the codes, you will need a regular laptop or Personal Computer (PC). Some chapters require a webcam, which can be either an embedded laptop camera or an external one. Chapter 2, *Hand Gesture Recognition Using a Kinect Depth Sensor* also requires a depth sensor that can be either a **Microsoft 3D Kinect sensor** or any other sensor, which is supported either by the libfreenect library or OpenCV, such as **ASUS Xtion**.

We have tested this using **Python 3.8** and **Python 3.7**, on **Ubuntu 18.04**.

If you already have Python on your computer, you can just get going with running the following on your terminal:

```
$ pip install -r requirements.txt
```

Here, requirements.txt is provided in the GitHub repository of the project, and has the following contents (which is the previously given table in a text file):

```
wxPython==4.0.5
numpy==1.18.1
scipy==1.4.1
matplotlib==3.1.2
requests==2.22.0
opencv-contrib-python==4.2.0.32
opencv-python==4.2.0.32
rawpy==0.14.0
ExifRead==2.1.2
tensorflow==2.0.1
```

Alternatively, you can follow the instructions in Appendix B, *Setting Up a Docker Container*, to get everything working with a Docker container.

Download the example code files

You can download the example code files for this book from your account at
www.packt.com. If you purchased this book elsewhere, you can visit
www.packtpub.com/support and register to have the files emailed directly to you.

You can download the code files by following these steps:

1. Log in or register at www.packt.com.
2. Select the **Support** tab.
3. Click on **Code Downloads**.
4. Enter the name of the book in the **Search** box and follow the onscreen instructions.

Once the file is downloaded, please make sure that you unzip or extract the folder using the latest version of:

- WinRAR/7-Zip for Windows
- Zipeg/iZip/UnRarX for Mac
- 7-Zip/PeaZip for Linux

The code bundle for the book is also hosted on GitHub at https://github.com/
PacktPublishing/OpenCV-4-with-Python-Blueprints-Second-Edition. In case there's an update to the code, it will be updated on the existing GitHub repository.

We also have other code bundles from our rich catalog of books and videos available at https://github.com/PacktPublishing/. Check them out!

Code in Action

Code in Action videos for this book can be viewed at http://bit.ly/2xcjKdS.

Download the color images

We also provide a PDF file that has color images of the screenshots/diagrams used in this book. You can download it here: http://static.packt-cdn.com/downloads/
9781789801811_ColorImages.pdf.

Conventions used

There are a number of text conventions used throughout this book.

CodeInText: Indicates code words in text, database table names, folder names, filenames, file extensions, pathnames, dummy URLs, user input, and Twitter handles. Here is an example: "We will use argparse as we want our script to accept arguments."

A block of code is set as follows:

```
import argparse

import cv2
import numpy as np

from classes import CLASSES_90
from sort import Sort
```

Any command-line input or output is written as follows:

```
$ python chapter8.py collect
```

Bold: Indicates a new term, an important word, or words that you see onscreen. For example, words in menus or dialog boxes appear in the text like this. Here is an example: "Select **System info** from the **Administration** panel."

Warnings or important notes appear like this.

Tips and tricks appear like this.

Get in touch

Feedback from our readers is always welcome.

General feedback: If you have questions about any aspect of this book, mention the book title in the subject of your message and email us at customercare@packtpub.com.

Errata: Although we have taken every care to ensure the accuracy of our content, mistakes do happen. If you have found a mistake in this book, we would be grateful if you would report this to us. Please visit www.packtpub.com/support/errata, selecting your book, clicking on the Errata Submission Form link, and entering the details.

Piracy: If you come across any illegal copies of our works in any form on the Internet, we would be grateful if you would provide us with the location address or website name. Please contact us at copyright@packt.com with a link to the material.

If you are interested in becoming an author: If there is a topic that you have expertise in and you are interested in either writing or contributing to a book, please visit authors.packtpub.com.

Reviews

Please leave a review. Once you have read and used this book, why not leave a review on the site that you purchased it from? Potential readers can then see and use your unbiased opinion to make purchase decisions, we at Packt can understand what you think about our products, and our authors can see your feedback on their book. Thank you!

For more information about Packt, please visit packt.com.

1
Fun with Filters

The goal of this chapter is to develop a number of image processing filters and then apply them to the video stream of a webcam in real time. These filters will rely on various OpenCV functions to manipulate matrices through splitting, merging, arithmetic operations, and applying lookup tables for complex functions.

We will cover the following three effects, which will help familiarize you with OpenCV, and we will build on these effects in future chapters of this book:

- **Warming and cooling filters**: We will implement our own **curve filters** using a lookup table.
- **Black-and-white pencil sketch**: We will make use of two image-blending techniques, known as **dodging** and **burning**.
- **Cartoonizer**: We will combine a bilateral filter, a median filter, and adaptive thresholding.

OpenCV is an advanced toolchain. It often raises the question, that is, not how to implement something from scratch, but which precanned implementation to choose for your needs. Generating complex effects is not hard if you have a lot of computing resources to spare. The challenge usually lies in finding an approach that not only gets the job done but also gets it done in time.

Instead of teaching the basic concepts of image manipulation through theoretical lessons, we will take a practical approach and develop a single end-to-end app that integrates a number of image filtering techniques. We will apply our theoretical knowledge to arrive at a solution that not only works but also speeds up seemingly complex effects so that a laptop can produce them in real time.

In this chapter, you will learn how to do the following using OpenCV:

- Creating a black-and-white pencil sketch
- Applying pencil sketch transformation
- Generating a warming and cooling filter
- Cartoonizing an image
- Putting it all together

Learning this will allow you to familiarize yourself with loading images into OpenCV and applying different transformations to those images using OpenCV. This chapter will help you learn the basics of how OpenCV operates, so we can focus on the internals of the algorithms in the following chapters.

Now, let's take a look at how to get everything up and running.

Getting started

All of the code in this book is targeted for **OpenCV 4.2** and has been tested on **Ubuntu 18.04**. Throughout this book, we will make extensive use of the NumPy package (http://www.numpy.org).

Additionally, this chapter requires the UnivariateSpline module of the SciPy package (http://www.scipy.org) and the **wxPython 4.0 Graphical User Interface** (**GUI**) (http://www.wxpython.org/download.php) for cross-platform GUI applications. We will try to avoid further dependencies where possible.

For more book-level dependencies, see Appendix A, *Profiling and Accelerating Your Apps*, and Appendix B, *Setting Up a Docker Container*.

You can find the code that we present in this chapter at our GitHub repository here: https://github.com/PacktPublishing/OpenCV-4-with-Python-Blueprints-Second-Edition/tree/master/chapter1.

Let's begin by planning the application we are going to create in this chapter.

Planning the app

The final app must consist of the following modules and scripts:

- `wx_gui.py`: This module is our implementation of a basic GUI using `wxpython`. We will make extensive use of this file throughout the book. This module includes the following layouts:
    - `wx_gui.BaseLayout`: This is a generic layout class from which more complicated layouts can be built.
- `chapter1.py`: This is the main script for this chapter. It contains the following functions and classes:
    - `chapter1.FilterLayout`: This is a custom layout based on `wx_gui.BaseLayout`, which displays the camera feed and a row of radio buttons that allows the user to select from the available image filters to be applied to each frame of the camera feed.
    - `chapter1.main`: This is the main routine function for starting the GUI application and accessing the webcam.
- `tools.py`: This is a Python module and has a lot of helper functions that we use in this chapter, which you can reuse for your projects.

The next section demonstrates how to create a black-and-white pencil sketch.

Creating a black-and-white pencil sketch

In order to obtain a pencil sketch (that is, a black-and-white drawing) of the camera frame, we will make use of two image-blending techniques, known as **dodging** and **burning**. These terms refer to techniques employed during the printing process in traditional photography; here, photographers would manipulate the exposure time of a certain area of a darkroom print in order to lighten or darken it. Dodging *lightens* an image, whereas burning *darkens* it. Areas that were not supposed to undergo changes were protected with a **mask**.

Today, modern image editing programs, such as **Photoshop** and **Gimp**, offer ways to mimic these effects in digital images. For example, masks are still used to mimic the effect of changing the exposure time of an image, wherein areas of a mask with relatively intense values will *expose* the image more, thus lightening the image. OpenCV does not offer a native function to implement these techniques; however, with a little insight and a few tricks, we will arrive at our own efficient implementation that can be used to produce a beautiful pencil sketch effect.

If you search on the internet, you might stumble upon the following common procedure to achieve a pencil sketch from an **RGB** (**red**, **green**, and **blue**) color image:

1. First, convert the color image to grayscale.
2. Then, invert the grayscale image to get a negative.
3. Apply a **Gaussian blur** to the negative from *step 2*.
4. Blend the grayscale image (from *step 1*) with the blurred negative (from *step 3*) by using **color dodge**.

Whereas *steps 1 to 3* are straightforward, *step 4* can be a little tricky. Let's get that one out of the way first.

 OpenCV 3 came with a pencil sketch effect right out of the box. The `cv2.pencilSketch` function uses a domain filter introduced in the 2011 paper, *Domain Transform for Edge-Aware Image and Video Processing*, by Eduardo Gastal and Manuel Oliveira. However, for the purposes of this book, we will develop our own filter.

The next section shows you how to implement dodging and burning in OpenCV.

Understanding approaches for using dodging and burning techniques

Dodging decreases the exposure for areas of the image that we wish to make lighter (than before) in an image, A. In image processing, we usually select or specify areas of the image that need to be altered using masks. A mask, B, is an array of the same dimensions as the image on which it can be applied (think of it as a sheet of paper you use to cover the image that has holes in it). "Holes" in the sheet of paper are represented with 255 (or ones if we are working on the 0-1 range) in an opaque region with zeros.

In modern image editing tools, such as Photoshop, the color dodging of the image A with the mask B is implemented by using the following ternary statement that acts on every pixel using the index i:

```
((B[i] == 255) ? B[i] :
    min(255, ((A[i] << 8) / (255 - B[i])))))
```

The previous code essentially divides the value of the A[i] image pixel by the inverse of the B[i] mask pixel value (which are in the range of 0-255), while making sure that the resulting pixel value will be in the range of (0, 255) and that we do not divide by 0.

We could translate the previous complex-looking expression or code into the following naive Python function, which accepts two OpenCV matrices (`image` and `mask`) and returns the blended image:

```
def dodge_naive(image, mask):
    # determine the shape of the input image
    width, height = image.shape[:2]

    # prepare output argument with same size as image
    blend = np.zeros((width, height), np.uint8)

    for c in range(width):
        for r in range(height):

            # shift image pixel value by 8 bits
            # divide by the inverse of the mask
            result = (image[c, r] << 8) / (255 - mask[c, r])

            # make sure resulting value stays within bounds
            blend[c, r] = min(255, result)
    return blend
```

As you might have guessed, although the previous code might be functionally correct, it will undoubtedly be horrendously slow. Firstly, the function uses the `for` loops, which are almost always a bad idea in Python. Secondly, the NumPy arrays (the underlying format of OpenCV images in Python) are optimized for the array calculations, so accessing and modifying each `image[c, r]` pixel separately will be really slow.

Instead, we should realize that the `<<8` operation is the same as multiplying the pixel value with the number 2^8 (**=256**), and that pixel-wise division can be achieved with the `cv2.divide` function. Thus, an improved version of our `dodge` function that takes advantage of matrix multiplication (which is faster) looks like this:

```
import cv2

def dodge(image, mask):
    return cv2.divide(image, 255 - mask, scale=256)
```

Here, we have reduced the `dodge` function to a single line! The new `dodge` function produces the same result as `dodge_naive`, but it is orders of magnitude faster than the naive version. In addition to this, `cv2.divide` automatically takes care of the division by zero, making the result zero, where `255 - mask` is zero.

Here is a dodged version of `Lena.png` where we have dodges in the square with pixels in the range of (**100:300, 100:300**):

Image credit—"Lenna" by Conor Lawless is licensed under CC BY 2.0

As you can see, the lightened region is very obvious in the right photograph because the transition is very sharp. There are ways to correct this, one of which we will take a look at in the next section.

Let's learn how to obtain a Gaussian blur by using two-dimensional convolution next.

Implementing a Gaussian blur with two-dimensional convolution

A Gaussian blur is implemented by convolving the image with a kernel of Gaussian values. Two- dimensional convolution is something that is used very widely in image processing. Usually, we have a big picture (let's look at a 5 x 5 subsection of that particular image), and we have a kernel (or filter) that is another matrix of a smaller size (in our example, 3 x 3).

In order to get the convolution values, let's suppose that we want to get the value at *location (2, 3)*. We place the kernel centered at the *location (2, 3)*, and we calculate the pointwise product of the overlay matrix (highlighted area, in the following image (red color)) with the kernel and take the overall sum. The resulting value (that is, **158.4**) is the value we write on the other matrix at the *location (2, 3)*.

We repeat this process for all elements, and the resulting matrix (the matrix on the right) is the convolution of the kernel with the image. In the following diagram, on the left, you can see the original image with the pixel values in the boxes (values higher than 100). We also see an orange filter with values in the bottom right of each cell (a collection of **0.1** or **0.2** that sum to **1**). In the matrix on the right, you see the values when the filter is applied to the image on the left:

	0	1	2	3	4
0	143	145	148	146	149
1	143	151	153 (0.1)	150 (0.1)	152 (0.1)
2	153	151	161 (0.1)	157 (0.2)	162 (0.1)
3	161	157	164 (0.1)	167 (0.1)	161 (0.1)
4	155	165	164	170	157

	0	1	2	3	4
0	149.5	146.7	146.8	147.3	148.1
1	147.5	149.9	151.5	152.8	152.4
2	150.2	154.5	157.2	158.4	157.1
3	154.6	158.8	162.0	163.0	159.2
4	157.8	163.8	167.0	165.7	159.4

Note that, for points on the boundaries, the kernel is not aligned with the matrix, so we have to figure out a strategy to give values for those points. There is no single good strategy that works for everything; some of the approaches are to either extend the border with zeros or extend with border values.

Let's take a look at how to transform a normal picture into a pencil sketch.

Applying pencil sketch transformation

With the tricks that we learned from the previous sections in our bag, we are now ready to take a look at the entire procedure.

 The final code can be found in the `convert_to_pencil_sketch` function within the `tools.py` file.

The following procedure shows you how to convert a color image into grayscale. After that, we aim to blend the grayscale image with its blurred negative:

1. First, we convert an RGB image (`imgRGB`) into grayscale:

   ```
   img_gray = cv2.cvtColor(img_rgb, cv2.COLOR_RGB2GRAY)
   ```

   As you can see, we have used `cv2.COLOR_RGB2GRAY` as a parameter to the `cv2.cvtColor` function, which changes the color spaces. Note that it does not matter whether the input image is RGB or BGR (which is the default for OpenCV); we will get a nice grayscale image in the end.

2. Then, we invert the image and blur it with a large Gaussian kernel of size `(21,21)`:

   ```
   inv_gray = 255 - gray_image
   blurred_image = cv2.GaussianBlur(inv_gray, (21, 21), 0, 0)
   ```

3. We use `dodge` to blend the original grayscale image with the blurred inverse:

   ```
   gray_sketch = cv2.divide(gray_image, 255 - blurred_image,
   scale=256)
   ```

The resulting image looks like this:

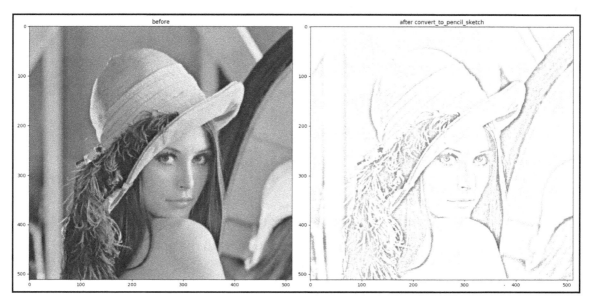

Image credit—"Lenna" by Conor Lawless is licensed under CC BY 2.0

Did you notice that our code can be optimized further? Let's take a look at how to optimize with OpenCV next.

Using an optimized version of a Gaussian blur

A Gaussian blur is basically a convolution with a Gaussian function. Well, one of the features of convolutions is their associative property. This means that it does not matter whether we first invert the image and then blur it, or first blur the image and then invert it.

If we start with a blurred image and pass its inverse to the dodge function, then within that function the image will be inverted again (the 255-mask part), essentially yielding the original image. If we get rid of these redundant operations, the optimized convert_to_pencil_sketch function will look like this:

```
def convert_to_pencil_sketch(rgb_image):
    gray_image = cv2.cvtColor(rgb_image, cv2.COLOR_RGB2GRAY)
    blurred_image = cv2.GaussianBlur(gray_image, (21, 21), 0, 0)
    gray_sketch = cv2.divide(gray_image, blurred_image, scale=256)
    return cv2.cvtColor(gray_sketch, cv2.COLOR_GRAY2RGB)
```

For kicks and giggles, we want to lightly blend our transformed image (`img_sketch`) with a background image (`canvas`) that makes it look as though we drew the image on a canvas. So, before returning, we would like to blend with `canvas` if it exists:

```
if canvas is not None:
    gray_sketch = cv2.multiply(gray_sketch, canvas, scale=1 / 256)
```

We name our final function `pencil_sketch_on_canvas`, and it looks like this (together with optimizations):

```
def pencil_sketch_on_canvas(rgb_image, canvas=None):
    gray_image = cv2.cvtColor(rgb_image, cv2.COLOR_RGB2GRAY)
    blurred_image = cv2.GaussianBlur(gray_image, (21, 21), 0, 0)
    gray_sketch = cv2.divide(gray_image, blurred_image, scale=256)
    if canvas is not None:
        gray_sketch = cv2.multiply(gray_sketch, canvas, scale=1 / 256)
    return cv2.cvtColor(gray_sketch, cv2.COLOR_GRAY2RGB)
```

This is just our `convert_to_pencil_sketch` function, with the optional `canvas` argument that can add an artistic touch to the pencil sketch.

And we're done! The final output looks like this:

Let's take a look at how to generate a warming and cooling filter in the next section, where you'll learn how to use **lookup tables** for image manipulation.

Generating a warming and cooling filter

When we perceive images, our brain picks up on a number of subtle clues to infer important details about the scene. For example, in broad daylight, highlights may have a slightly yellowish tint because they are in direct sunlight, whereas shadows may appear slightly bluish because of the ambient light of the blue sky. When we view an image with such color properties, we might immediately think of a sunny day.

This effect is not a mystery to photographers, who sometimes purposely manipulate the white balance of an image to convey a certain mood. Warm colors are generally perceived as more pleasant, whereas cool colors are associated with night and drabness.

To manipulate the perceived color temperature of an image, we will implement a curve filter. These filters control how color transitions appear between different regions of an image, allowing us to subtly shift the color spectrum without adding an unnatural-looking overall tint to the image.

In the next section, we'll look at how to manipulate color using curve shifting.

Using color manipulation via curve shifting

A curve filter is essentially a function, $y = f(x)$, that maps an input pixel value, x, to an output pixel value, y. The curve is parameterized by a set of $n + 1$ anchor points, as follows:

$$\{(x_0, y_0), (x_1, y_1), \cdots, (x_n, y_n)\}$$

Here, each anchor point is a pair of numbers that represent the input and output pixel values. For example, the pair (30, 90) means that an input pixel value of 30 is increased to an output value of 90. Values between anchor points are interpolated along a smooth curve (hence, the name curve filter).

Such a filter can be applied to any image channel, be it a single grayscale channel or the **R** (**red**), **G** (**green**), and **B** (**blue**) channels of an RGB color image. Therefore, for our purposes, all values of x and y must stay between 0 and 255.

For example, if we wanted to make a grayscale image slightly brighter, we could use a curve filter with the following set of control points:

$$\{(0,0), (128,192), (255,255)\}$$

This would mean that all input pixel values except **0** and **255** would be increased slightly, resulting in an overall brightening effect on the image.

If we want such filters to produce natural-looking images, it is important to respect the following two rules:

- Every set of anchor points should include **(0,0)** and **(255,255)**. This is important in order to prevent the image from appearing as if it has an overall tint, as black remains black and white remains white.
- The *f(x)* function should be monotonously increasing. In other words, by increasing *x*, *f(x)* either stays the same or increases (that is, it never decreases). This is important for making sure that shadows remain shadows and highlights remain highlights.

The next section demonstrates how to implement a curve filter using lookup tables.

Implementing a curve filter using lookup tables

Curve filters are computationally expensive because the values of *f(x)* must be interpolated whenever *x* does not coincide with one of the prespecified anchor points. Performing this computation for every pixel of every image frame that we encounter would have dramatic effects on performance.

Instead, we make use of a lookup table. Since there are only 256 possible pixel values for our purposes, we need to calculate *f(x)* only for all the 256 possible values of *x*. Interpolation is handled by the `UnivariateSpline` function of the `scipy.interpolate` module, as shown in the following code snippet:

```
from scipy.interpolate import UnivariateSpline

def spline_to_lookup_table(spline_breaks: list, break_values: list):
    spl = UnivariateSpline(spline_breaks, break_values)
    return spl(range(256)
```

The `return` argument of the function is a list of 256 elements that contains the interpolated *f(x)* values for every possible value of *x*.

All we need to do now is to come up with a set of anchor points, (x_i, y_i), and we are ready to apply the filter to a grayscale input image (`img_gray`):

```
import cv2
import numpy as np

x = [0, 128, 255]
y = [0, 192, 255]
myLUT = spline_to_lookup_table(x, y)
img_curved = cv2.LUT(img_gray, myLUT).astype(np.uint8)
```

The result looks like this (the original image is on the *left*, and the transformed image is on the *right*):

In the next section, we'll design the warming and cooling effect. You will also learn how to apply lookup tables to colored images, and how warming and cooling effects work.

Designing the warming and cooling effect

With the mechanism to quickly apply a generic curve filter to any image channel in place, we can now turn to the question of how to manipulate the perceived color temperature of an image. Again, the final code will have its own function in the `tools` module.

If you have a minute to spare, I advise you to play around with the different curve settings for a while. You can choose any number of anchor points and apply the curve filter to any image channel you can think of (red, green, blue, hue, saturation, brightness, lightness, and so on). You could even combine multiple channels, or decrease one and shift another to the desired region. *What will the result look like?*

However, if the number of possibilities dazzles you, take a more conservative approach. First, by making use of our `spline_to_lookup_table` function developed in the preceding steps, let's define two generic curve filters: one that (by trend) increases all the pixel values of a channel and one that generally decreases them:

```
INCREASE_LOOKUP_TABLE = spline_to_lookup_table([0, 64, 128, 192, 256],
                                               [0, 70, 140, 210, 256])
DECREASE_LOOKUP_TABLE = spline_to_lookup_table([0, 64, 128, 192, 256],
                                               [0, 30, 80, 120, 192])
```

Now, let's examine how we could apply lookup tables to an RGB image. OpenCV has a nice function called `cv2.LUT` that takes a lookup table and applies it to a matrix. So, first, we have to decompose the image into different channels:

```
c_r, c_g, c_b = cv2.split(rgb_image)
```

Then, we apply a filter to each channel if desired:

```
if green_filter is not None:
    c_g = cv2.LUT(c_g, green_filter).astype(np.uint8)
```

Doing this for all the three channels in an RGB image, we get the following helper function:

```
def apply_rgb_filters(rgb_image, *,
                      red_filter=None, green_filter=None,
blue_filter=None):
    c_r, c_g, c_b = cv2.split(rgb_image)
    if red_filter is not None:
        c_r = cv2.LUT(c_r, red_filter).astype(np.uint8)
    if green_filter is not None:
        c_g = cv2.LUT(c_g, green_filter).astype(np.uint8)
    if blue_filter is not None:
        c_b = cv2.LUT(c_b, blue_filter).astype(np.uint8)
    return cv2.merge((c_r, c_g, c_b))
```

The easiest way to make an image appear as if it was taken on a hot, sunny day (maybe close to sunset) is to increase the reds in the image and make the colors appear vivid by increasing the color saturation. We will achieve this in two steps:

1. Increase the pixel values in the **R channel** (from RGB image) and decrease the pixel values in the **B channel** of an RGB color image using `INCREASE_LOOKUP_TABLE` and `DECREASE_LOOKUP_TABLE`, respectively:

```
        interim_img = apply_rgb_filters(rgb_image,
    red_filter=INCREASE_LOOKUP_TABLE,
    blue_filter=DECREASE_LOOKUP_TABLE)
```

2. Transform the image into the **HSV** color space (**H** means **hue**, **S** means **saturation**, and **V** means **value**), and increase the **S channel** using `INCREASE_LOOKUP_TABLE`. This can be achieved with the following function, which expects an RGB color image and a lookup table to apply (similar to the `apply_rgb_filters` function) as input:

```
def apply_hue_filter(rgb_image, hue_filter):
    c_h, c_s, c_v = cv2.split(cv2.cvtColor(rgb_image,
cv2.COLOR_RGB2HSV))
    c_s = cv2.LUT(c_s, hue_filter).astype(np.uint8)
    return cv2.cvtColor(cv2.merge((c_h, c_s, c_v)),
cv2.COLOR_HSV2RGB)
```

The result looks like this:

Analogously, we can define a cooling filter that increases the pixel values in the B channel, decreases the pixel values in the R channel of an RGB image, converts the image into the HSV color space, and decreases color saturation via the S channel:

```
def _render_cool(rgb_image: np.ndarray) -> np.ndarray:
    interim_img = apply_rgb_filters(rgb_image,
                                    red_filter=DECREASE_LOOKUP_TABLE,
                                    blue_filter=INCREASE_LOOKUP_TABLE)
    return apply_hue_filter(interim_img, DECREASE_LOOKUP_TABLE)
```

Now the result looks like this:

Let's explore how to cartoonize an image in the next section, where we'll learn what a bilateral filter is and much more.

Cartoonizing an image

Over the past few years, professional cartoonizer software has popped up all over the place. In order to achieve a basic cartoon effect, all we need is a **bilateral filter** and some **edge detection**.

The bilateral filter will reduce the color palette or the numbers of colors that are used in the image. This mimics a cartoon drawing, wherein a cartoonist typically has few colors to work with. Then, we can apply edge detection to the resulting image to generate bold silhouettes. The real challenge, however, lies in the computational cost of bilateral filters. We will, therefore, use some tricks to produce an acceptable cartoon effect in real time.

We will adhere to the following procedure to transform an RGB color image into a cartoon:

1. First, apply a bilateral filter to reduce the color palette of the image.
2. Then, convert the original color image into grayscale.
3. After that, apply a **median blur** to reduce image noise.
4. Use **adaptive thresholding** to detect and emphasize the edges in an edge mask.
5. Finally, combine the color image from *step 1* with the edge mask from *step 4*.

In the upcoming sections, we will learn about the previously mentioned steps in detail. First, we'll learn how to use a bilateral filter for edge-aware smoothing.

Using a bilateral filter for edge-aware smoothing

A strong bilateral filter is ideally suitable for converting an RGB image into a color painting or a cartoon, because it smoothens the flat regions while keeping the edges sharp. The only drawback of this filter is its computational cost—it is orders of magnitude slower than other smoothing operations, such as a Gaussian blur.

The first measure to take when we need to reduce the computational cost is to perform an operation on an image of low resolution. In order to downscale an RGB image (imgRGB) to a quarter of its size (that is, reduce the width and height to half), we could use cv2.resize:

```
img_small = cv2.resize(img_rgb, (0, 0), fx=0.5, fy=0.5)
```

A pixel value in the resized image will correspond to the pixel average of a small neighborhood in the original image. However, this process may produce image artifacts, which is also known as **aliasing**. While image aliasing is a big problem on its own, the negative effect might be enhanced by subsequent processing, for example, edge detection.

A better alternative might be to use the **Gaussian pyramid** for downscaling (again to a quarter of the original size). The Gaussian pyramid consists of a blur operation that is performed before the image is resampled, which reduces any aliasing effects:

```
downsampled_img = cv2.pyrDown(rgb_image)
```

However, even at this scale, the bilateral filter might still be too slow to run in real time. Another trick is to repeatedly (say, five times) apply a small bilateral filter to the image instead of applying a large bilateral filter once:

```
for _ in range(num_bilaterals):
    filterd_small_img = cv2.bilateralFilter(downsampled_img, 9, 9, 7)
```

The three parameters in cv2.bilateralFilter control the diameter of the pixel neighborhood (d=9) and the standard deviation of the filter in the color space (sigmaColor=9) and coordinate space (sigmaSpace=7).

So, the final code to run the bilateral filter that we use is as follows:

1. Downsample the image using multiple pyrDown calls:

```
downsampled_img = rgb_image
for _ in range(num_pyr_downs):
    downsampled_img = cv2.pyrDown(downsampled_img)
```

2. Then, apply multiple bilateral filters:

```
for _ in range(num_bilaterals):
    filterd_small_img = cv2.bilateralFilter(downsampled_img, 9,
9, 7)
```

3. And finally, upsample it to the original size:

```
filtered_normal_img = filterd_small_img
for _ in range(num_pyr_downs):
    filtered_normal_img = cv2.pyrUp(filtered_normal_img)
```

The result looks like a blurred color painting of a creepy programmer, as follows:

The next section shows you how to detect and emphasize prominent edges.

Detecting and emphasizing prominent edges

Again, when it comes to edge detection, the challenge often does not lie in how the underlying algorithm works, but instead lies in which particular algorithm to choose for the task at hand. You might already be familiar with a variety of edge detectors. For example, **Canny edge detection** (cv2.Canny) provides a relatively simple and effective method to detect edges in an image, but it is susceptible to noise.

The **Sobel** operator (cv2.Sobel) can reduce such artifacts, but it is not rotationally symmetric. The **Scharr** operator (cv2.Scharr) was targeted at correcting this but only looks at the first image derivative. If you are interested, there are even more operators for you, such as the **Laplacian ridge operator** (which includes the second derivative), but they are far more complex. And in the end, for our specific purposes, they might not look better, perhaps because they are as susceptible to lighting conditions as any other algorithm.

For the purposes of this project, we will choose a function that might not even be associated with conventional edge detection—cv2.adaptiveThreshold. Like cv2.threshold, this function uses a threshold pixel value to convert a grayscale image into a binary image. That is, if a pixel value in the original image is above the threshold, then the pixel value in the final image will be 255. Otherwise, it will be 0.

However, the beauty of adaptive thresholding is that it does not look at the overall properties of the image. Instead, it detects the most salient features in each small neighborhood independently, without regard to the global image characteristics. This makes the algorithm extremely robust to lighting conditions, which is exactly what we want when we seek to draw bold black outlines around objects, and people in a cartoon.

However, it also makes the algorithm susceptible to noise. To counteract this, we will preprocess the image with a median filter. A median filter does what its name suggests: it replaces each pixel value with the median value of all the pixels in a small pixel neighborhood. Therefore, to detect edges, we follow this short procedure:

1. We first convert the RGB image (rgb_image) into grayscale (img_gray) and then apply a median blur with a seven-pixel local neighborhood:

```
# convert to grayscale and apply median blur
img_gray = cv2.cvtColor(rgb_image, cv2.COLOR_RGB2GRAY)
img_blur = cv2.medianBlur(img_gray, 7)
```

2. After reducing the noise, it is now safe to detect and enhance the edges using adaptive thresholding. Even if there is some image noise left, the cv2.ADAPTIVE_THRESH_MEAN_C algorithm with blockSize=9 will ensure that the threshold is applied to the mean of a 9 x 9 neighborhood minus C=2:

```
gray_edges = cv2.adaptiveThreshold(img_blur, 255,
                          cv2.ADAPTIVE_THRESH_MEAN_C,
                          cv2.THRESH_BINARY, 9, 2)
```

The result of the adaptive thresholding looks like this:

Next, let's look at how to combine colors and outlines to produce a cartoon in the following section.

Combining colors and outlines to produce a cartoon

The last step is to combine the two previously achieved effects. Simply fuse the two effects together into a single image using `cv2.bitwise_and`. The complete function is as follows:

```
def cartoonize(rgb_image, *,
               num_pyr_downs=2, num_bilaterals=7):
    # STEP 1 -- Apply a bilateral filter to reduce the color palette of
    # the image.
    downsampled_img = rgb_image
    for _ in range(num_pyr_downs):
        downsampled_img = cv2.pyrDown(downsampled_img)

    for _ in range(num_bilaterals):
        filterd_small_img = cv2.bilateralFilter(downsampled_img, 9, 9, 7)

    filtered_normal_img = filterd_small_img
    for _ in range(num_pyr_downs):
        filtered_normal_img = cv2.pyrUp(filtered_normal_img)

    # make sure resulting image has the same dims as original
    if filtered_normal_img.shape != rgb_image.shape:
        filtered_normal_img = cv2.resize(
```

```
                filtered_normal_img, rgb_image.shape[:2])

    # STEP 2 -- Convert the original color image into grayscale.
    img_gray = cv2.cvtColor(rgb_image, cv2.COLOR_RGB2GRAY)
    # STEP 3 -- Apply amedian blur to reduce image noise.
    img_blur = cv2.medianBlur(img_gray, 7)

    # STEP 4 -- Use adaptive thresholding to detect and emphasize the edges
    # in an edge mask.
    gray_edges = cv2.adaptiveThreshold(img_blur, 255,
                                    cv2.ADAPTIVE_THRESH_MEAN_C,
                                    cv2.THRESH_BINARY, 9, 2)
    # STEP 5 -- Combine the color image from step 1 with the edge mask
    # from step 4.
    rgb_edges = cv2.cvtColor(gray_edges, cv2.COLOR_GRAY2RGB)
    return cv2.bitwise_and(filtered_normal_img, rgb_edges)
```

The result looks like this:

In the next section, we'll set up the main script and design a GUI application.

Putting it all together

In the previous sections, we implemented a couple of nice filters that show how we can get nice effects with OpenCV. In this section, we want to build an interactive application that will allow you to apply these filters in real time to your laptop camera.

So, we need to write a **user interface** (**UI**) that will allow us to capture the camera stream and have some buttons so that you can select which filter you want to apply. We will start by setting up the camera capture with OpenCV. Then, we will build a nice interface around it using wxPython.

Running the app

To run the application, we will turn to the chapter1.py script. Follow these steps to do so:

1. We first start by importing all the necessary modules:

```
import wx
import cv2
import numpy as np
```

2. We will also have to import a generic GUI layout (from wx_gui) and all the designed image effects (from tools):

```
from wx_gui import BaseLayout
from tools import apply_hue_filter
from tools import apply_rgb_filters
from tools import load_img_resized
from tools import spline_to_lookup_table
from tools import cartoonize
from tools import pencil_sketch_on_canvas
```

3. OpenCV provides a straightforward way to access a computer's webcam or camera device. The following code snippet opens the default camera ID (0) of a computer using cv2.VideoCapture:

```
def main():
    capture = cv2.VideoCapture(0)
```

4. In order to give our application a fair chance to run in real time, we will limit the size of the video stream to 640 x 480 pixels:

```
capture.set(cv2.CAP_PROP_FRAME_WIDTH, 640)
capture.set(cv2.CAP_PROP_FRAME_HEIGHT, 480)
```

5. Then, the `capture` stream can be passed to our GUI application, which is an instance of the `FilterLayout` class:

```
# start graphical user interface
app = wx.App()
layout = FilterLayout(capture, title='Fun with Filters')
layout.Center()
layout.Show()
app.MainLoop()
```

After we create `FilterLayout`, we center the layout, so it appears in the center of the screen. And we call `Show()` to actually show the layout. Finally, we call `app.MainLoop()`, so the application starts working, receiving, and processing events.

The only thing left to do now is to design the said GUI.

Mapping the GUI base class

The `FilterLayout` GUI will be based on a generic, plain layout class called `BaseLayout`, which we will be able to use in subsequent chapters as well.

The `BaseLayout` class is designed as an **abstract base class**. You can think of this class as a blueprint or recipe that will apply to all the layouts that we are yet to design, that is, a skeleton class that will serve as the backbone for all of our future GUI code.

We start the file by importing the packages that we will use—the `wxPython` module, which we use to create the GUI; `numpy`, which we use to do matrix manipulations; and OpenCV (of course):

```
import numpy as np
import wx
import cv2
```

The class is designed to be derived from the blueprint or skeleton, that is, the `wx.Frame` class:

```
class BaseLayout(wx.Frame):
```

Later on, when we write our own custom layout (`FilterLayout`), we will use the same notation to specify that the class is based on the `BaseLayout` blueprint (or skeleton) class, for example, in `class FilterLayout(BaseLayout):`. But for now, let's focus on the `BaseLayout` class.

An abstract class has at least one abstract method. We are going to make the method abstract by ensuring that if the method stays unimplemented, the application will not run and we throw an exception:

```
class BaseLayout(wx.Frame):
    ...
    ...
    ...
    def process_frame(self, frame_rgb: np.ndarray) -> np.ndarray:
        """Process the frame of the camera (or other capture device)

        :param frame_rgb: Image to process in rgb format, of shape (H, W,
3)
        :return: Processed image in rgb format, of shape (H, W, 3)
        """
        raise NotImplementedError()
```

Then, any class that is derived from it, such as `FilterLayout`, must specify a full implementation of that method. This will allow us to create custom layouts, as you will see in a moment.

But first, let's proceed to the GUI constructor.

Understanding the GUI constructor

The `BaseLayout` constructor accepts an ID (-1), a title string (`'Fun with Filters'`), a video capture object, and an optional argument that specifies the number of frames per second. Then, the first thing to do in the constructor is to try to read a frame from the captured object in order to determine the image size:

```
def __init__(self,
             capture: cv2.VideoCapture,
             title: str = None,
             parent=None,
             window_id: int = -1,  # default value
             fps: int = 10):
    self.capture = capture
    _, frame = self._acquire_frame()
    self.imgHeight, self.imgWidth = frame.shape[:2]
```

We will use the image size to prepare a buffer that will store each video frame as a bitmap and to set the size of the GUI. Because we want to display a bunch of control buttons below the current video frame, we set the height of the GUI to `self.imgHeight + 20`:

```
super().__init__(parent, window_id, title,
                 size=(self.imgWidth, self.imgHeight + 20))
self.fps = fps
self.bmp = wx.Bitmap.FromBuffer(self.imgWidth, self.imgHeight,
frame)
```

In the next section, we will build a basic layout for our application with a video stream and some buttons using `wxPython`.

Learning about a basic GUI layout

The most basic layout consists of only a large black panel that provides enough room to display the video feed:

```
self.video_pnl = wx.Panel(self, size=(self.imgWidth,
self.imgHeight))
self.video_pnl.SetBackgroundColour(wx.BLACK)
```

In order for the layout to be extendable, we add it to a vertically arranged `wx.BoxSizer` object:

```
# display the button layout beneath the video stream
self.panels_vertical = wx.BoxSizer(wx.VERTICAL)
self.panels_vertical.Add(self.video_pnl, 1, flag=wx.EXPAND |
wx.TOP,
                         border=1)
```

Next, we specify an abstract method, `augment_layout`, for which we will not fill in any code. Instead, any user of our base class can make their own custom modifications to the basic layout:

```
self.augment_layout()
```

Then, we just need to set the minimum size of the resulting layout and center it:

```
self.SetMinSize((self.imgWidth, self.imgHeight))
self.SetSizer(self.panels_vertical)
self.Centre()
```

The next section shows you how to handle video streams.

Handling video streams

The video stream of the webcam is handled by a series of steps that begin with the __init__ method. These steps might appear overly complicated at first, but they are necessary in order to allow the video to run smoothly, even at higher frame rates (that is, to counteract flickering).

The wxPython module works with events and callback methods. When a certain event is triggered, it can cause a certain class method to be executed (in other words, a method can *bind* to an event). We will use this mechanism to our advantage and display a new frame every so often using the following steps:

1. We create a timer that will generate a wx.EVT_TIMER event whenever 1000./self.fps milliseconds have passed:

```
self.timer = wx.Timer(self)
self.timer.Start(1000. / self.fps)
```

2. Whenever the timer is up, we want the _on_next_frame method to be called. It will try to acquire a new video frame:

```
self.Bind(wx.EVT_TIMER, self._on_next_frame)
```

3. The _on_next_frame method will process the new video frame and store the processed frame in a bitmap. This will trigger another event, wx.EVT_PAINT. We want to bind this event to the _on_paint method, which will paint the display of the new frame. So, we create a placeholder for the video and bind wx.EVT_PAINT to it:

```
self.video_pnl.Bind(wx.EVT_PAINT, self._on_paint)
```

The _on_next_frame method grabs a new frame and, once done, sends the frame to another method, process_frame, for further processing (which is an abstract method and should be implemented by the child class):

```
def _on_next_frame(self, event):
    """
    Capture a new frame from the capture device,
    send an RGB version to `self.process_frame`, refresh.
    """
    success, frame = self._acquire_frame()
    if success:
        # process current frame
        frame = self.process_frame(cv2.cvtColor(frame,
cv2.COLOR_BGR2RGB))
        ...
```

The processed frame (`frame`) is then stored in a bitmap buffer (`self.bmp`). Calling `Refresh` triggers the aforementioned `wx.EVT_PAINT` event, which binds to `_on_paint`:

```
...
# update buffer and paint (EVT_PAINT triggered by Refresh)
self.bmp.CopyFromBuffer(frame)
self.Refresh(eraseBackground=False)
```

The `paint` method then grabs the frame from the buffer and displays it:

```
def _on_paint(self, event):
    """ Draw the camera frame stored in `self.bmp` onto
`self.video_pnl`.
    """
    wx.BufferedPaintDC(self.video_pnl).DrawBitmap(self.bmp, 0, 0)
```

The next section shows you how to create a custom filter layout.

Drafting a custom filter layout

Now we are almost done! If we want to use the `BaseLayout` class, we need to provide code for the two methods that were previously left blank, which are as follows:

- `augment_layout`: This is where we can make task-specific modifications to the GUI layout.
- `process_frame`: This is where we perform task-specific processing on each captured frame of the camera feed.

We also need to change the constructor to initialize any parameters we will need—in this case, the canvas background for the pencil sketch:

```
def __init__(self, *args, **kwargs):
    super().__init__(*args, **kwargs)
    color_canvas = load_img_resized('pencilsketch_bg.jpg',
                                    (self.imgWidth, self.imgHeight))
    self.canvas = cv2.cvtColor(color_canvas, cv2.COLOR_RGB2GRAY)
```

To customize the layout, we arrange a number of radio buttons horizontally—one button per image effect mode. Here, the `style=wx.RB_GROUP` option makes sure that only one of `radio buttons` can be selected at a time. And to make these changes visible, `pnl` needs to be added to a list of existing panels—`self.panels_vertical`:

```
def augment_layout(self):
    """ Add a row of radio buttons below the camera feed. """
```

```
# create a horizontal layout with all filter modes as radio buttons
pnl = wx.Panel(self, -1)
self.mode_warm = wx.RadioButton(pnl, -1, 'Warming Filter', (10,
10),
                                 style=wx.RB_GROUP)
self.mode_cool = wx.RadioButton(pnl, -1, 'Cooling Filter', (10,
10))
self.mode_sketch = wx.RadioButton(pnl, -1, 'Pencil Sketch', (10,
10))
self.mode_cartoon = wx.RadioButton(pnl, -1, 'Cartoon', (10, 10))
hbox = wx.BoxSizer(wx.HORIZONTAL)
hbox.Add(self.mode_warm, 1)
hbox.Add(self.mode_cool, 1)
hbox.Add(self.mode_sketch, 1)
hbox.Add(self.mode_cartoon, 1)
pnl.SetSizer(hbox)

# add panel with radio buttons to existing panels in a vertical
# arrangement
self.panels_vertical.Add(pnl, flag=wx.EXPAND | wx.BOTTOM | wx.TOP,
                         border=1
```

The last method to be specified is `process_frame`. Recall that this method is triggered whenever a new camera frame is received. All that we need to do is pick the right image effect to be applied, which depends on the radio button configuration. We simply check which of the buttons is currently selected and call the corresponding `render` method:

```
def process_frame(self, frame_rgb: np.ndarray) -> np.ndarray:
    """Process the frame of the camera (or other capture device)

    Choose a filter effect based on the which of the radio buttons
    was clicked.

    :param frame_rgb: Image to process in rgb format, of shape (H, W,
3)
    :return: Processed image in rgb format, of shape (H, W, 3)
    """
    if self.mode_warm.GetValue():
        return self._render_warm(frame_rgb)
    elif self.mode_cool.GetValue():
        return self._render_cool(frame_rgb)
    elif self.mode_sketch.GetValue():
        return pencil_sketch_on_canvas(frame_rgb, canvas=self.canvas)
    elif self.mode_cartoon.GetValue():
        return cartoonize(frame_rgb)
    else:
        raise NotImplementedError()
```

And we're done! The following screenshot shows us the output pictures with different filters:

The preceding screenshot shows all of the four filters that we created applied to a single image.

Summary

In this chapter, we explored a number of interesting image processing effects. We used dodging and burning to create a black-and-white pencil sketch effect, explored lookup tables to arrive at an efficient implementation of curve filters, and got creative to produce a cartoon effect.

One of the techniques used was two-dimesional convolution, which takes a filter and an image and creates a new image. In this chapter, we provided the filters to get the results we wanted, but we don't always have the filters that are necessary to produce the results we want. Recently, deep learning has emerged, which tries to learn the values for different filters to help it get the results it wants.

In the next chapter, we will shift gears a bit and explore the use of depth sensors, such as **Microsoft Kinect 3D**, to recognize hand gestures in real time.

Attributions

`Lenna.png`—the image of Lenna is available at `http://www.flickr.com/photos/15489034@N00/3388463896` by Conor Lawless under the generic CC 2.0 attribution.

2
Hand Gesture Recognition Using a Kinect Depth Sensor

The goal of this chapter is to develop an app that detects and tracks simple hand gestures in real time, using the output of a depth sensor, such as that of a **Microsoft Kinect 3D sensor** or an **ASUS Xtion sensor**. The app will analyze each captured frame to perform the following tasks:

- **Hand region segmentation**: The user's hand region will be extracted in each frame by analyzing the **depth map** output of the Kinect sensor, which is done by **thresholding**, applying some **morphological operations**, and finding **connected components**.
- **Hand shape analysis**: The shape of the segmented hand region will be analyzed by determining **contours**, **convex hull**, and **convexity defects**.
- **Hand gesture recognition**: The number of extended fingers will be determined based on the hand contour's **convexity defects**, and the gesture will be classified accordingly (with no extended fingers corresponding to a fist, and five extended fingers corresponding to an open hand).

Gesture recognition is an ever-popular topic in computer science. This is because it not only enables humans to communicate with machines (**Human-Machine Interaction** (**HMI**)) but also constitutes the first step for machines to begin understanding human body language. With affordable sensors such as Microsoft Kinect or Asus Xtion and open source software such as **OpenKinect** and **OpenNI**, it has never been easier to get started in the field yourself. *So, what shall we do with all this technology?*

In this chapter, we will cover the following topics:

- Planning the app
- Setting up the app
- Tracking hand gestures in real time
- Understanding hand region segmentation
- Performing hand shape analysis
- Performing hand gesture recognition

The beauty of the algorithm that we are going to implement in this chapter is that it works well for many hand gestures, yet it is simple enough to run in real time on a generic laptop. Also, if we want, we can easily extend it to incorporate more complicated hand-pose estimations.

Once you complete the app, you will understand how to use depth sensors in your own apps. You will learn how to compose shapes of interest with OpenCV from the depth information, as well as understanding how to analyze shapes with OpenCV, using their geometric properties.

Getting started

This chapter requires you to have a Microsoft Kinect 3D sensor installed. Alternatively, you may install an Asus Xtion sensor or any other depth sensor for which OpenCV has built-in support.

First, install OpenKinect and **libfreenect** from
`http://www.openkinect.org/wiki/Getting_Started`. You can find the code that we present in this chapter at our GitHub repository: `https://github.com/PacktPublishing/OpenCV-4-with-Python-Blueprints-Second-Edition/tree/master/chapter2`.

Let's first plan the application we are going to create in this chapter.

Planning the app

The final app will consist of the following modules and scripts:

- `gestures`: This is a module that consists of an algorithm for recognizing hand gestures.

- `gestures.process`: This is a function that implements the entire process flow of hand gesture recognition. It accepts a single-channel depth image (acquired from the Kinect depth sensor) and returns an annotated **Blue, Green, Red (BGR)** color image with an estimated number of extended fingers.
- `chapter2`: This is the main script for the chapter.
- `chapter2.main`: This is the main function routine that iterates over frames acquired from a depth sensor that uses `.process` gestures to process frames, and then illustrates results.

The end product looks like this:

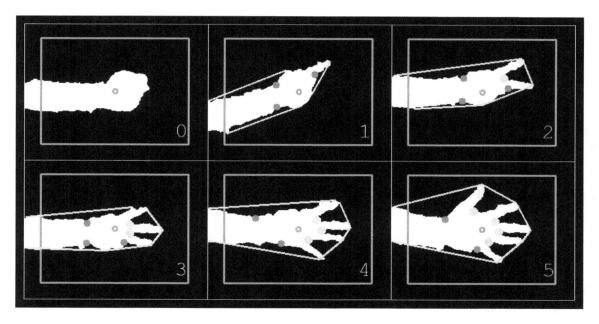

No matter how many fingers of a hand are extended, the algorithm correctly segments the hand region (white), draws the corresponding convex hull (the green line surrounding the hand), finds all convexity defects that belong to the spaces between fingers (large green points) while ignoring others (small red points), and infers the correct number of extended fingers (the number in the bottom-right corner), even for a fist.

Now, let's set up the application in the next section.

Setting up the app

Before we can get down to the nitty-gritty of our gesture recognition algorithm, we need to make sure that we can access the depth sensor and display a stream of depth frames. In this section, we will cover the following things that will help us set up the app:

- Accessing the Kinect 3D sensor
- Utilizing OpenNI-compatible sensors
- Running the app and main function routine

First, we will look at how to use the Kinect 3D sensor.

Accessing the Kinect 3D sensor

The easiest way to access a Kinect sensor is by using an `OpenKinect` module called `freenect`. For installation instructions, take a look at the preceding section.

The `freenect` module has functions such as `sync_get_depth()` and `sync_get_video()`, used to obtain images synchronously from the depth sensor and camera sensor respectively. For this chapter, we will need only the Kinect depth map, which is a single-channel (grayscale) image in which each pixel value is the estimated distance from the camera to a particular surface in the visual scene.

Here, we will design a function that will read a frame from the sensor and convert it to the desired format, and return the frame together with a success status, as follows:

```
def read_frame(): -> Tuple[bool,np.ndarray]:
```

The function consists of the following steps:

1. Grab a `frame`; terminate the function if a frame was not acquired, like this:

```
frame, timestamp = freenect.sync_get_depth()
if frame is None:
    return False, None
```

The `sync_get_depth` method returns both the depth map and a timestamp. By default, the map is in an 11-bit format. The last 10 bits of the sensor describes the depth, while the first bit states that the distance estimation was not successful when it's equal to 1.

2. It is a good idea to standardize the data into an 8-bit precision format, as an 11-bit format is inappropriate to be visualized with `cv2.imshow` right away, as well as in the future. We might want to use some different sensor that returns in a different format, as follows:

```
np.clip(depth, 0, 2**10-1, depth)
depth >>= 2
```

In the previous code, we have first clipped the values to 1,023 (or `2**10-1`) to fit in 10 bits. Such clipping results in the assignment of the undetected distance to the farthest possible point. Next, we shift 2 bits to the right to fit the distance in 8 bits.

3. Finally, we convert the image into an 8-bit unsigned integer array and `return` the result, as follows:

```
return True, depth.astype(np.uint8)
```

Now, the `depth` image can be visualized as follows:

```
cv2.imshow("depth", read_frame()[1])
```

Let's see how to use OpenNI-compatible sensors in the next section.

Utilizing OpenNI-compatible sensors

To use an OpenNI-compatible sensor, you must first make sure that **OpenNI2** is installed and that your version of OpenCV was built with the support of OpenNI. The build information can be printed as follows:

```
import cv2
print(cv2.getBuildInformation())
```

If your version was built with OpenNI support, you will find it under the `Video I/O` section. Otherwise, you will have to rebuild OpenCV with OpenNI support, which is done by passing the `-D WITH_OPENNI2=ON` flag to `cmake`.

After the installation process is complete, you can access the sensor similarly to other video input devices, using cv2.VideoCapture. In this app, in order to use an OpenNI-compatible sensor instead of a Kinect 3D sensor, you have to cover the following steps:

1. Create a video capture that connects to your OpenNI-compatible sensor, like this:

```
device = cv2.cv.CV_CAP_OPENNI
capture = cv2.VideoCapture(device)
```

If you want to connect to Asus Xtion, the device variable should be assigned to the cv2.CV_CAP_OPENNI_ASUS value instead.

2. Change the input frame size to the standard **Video Graphics Array (VGA)** resolution, as follows:

```
capture.set(cv2.cv.CV_CAP_PROP_FRAME_WIDTH, 640)
capture.set(cv2.cv.CV_CAP_PROP_FRAME_HEIGHT, 480)
```

3. In the previous section, we designed the read_frame function, which accesses the Kinect sensor using freenect. In order to read depth images from the video capture, you have to change that function to the following one:

```
def read_frame():
    if not capture.grab():
        return False,None
    return capture.retrieve(cv2.CAP_OPENNI_DEPTH_MAP)
```

You will note that we have used the grab and retrieve methods instead of the read method. The reason is that the read method of cv2.VideoCapture is inappropriate when we need to synchronize a set of cameras or a multi-head camera, such as a Kinect.

For such cases, you grab frames from multiple sensors at a certain moment in time with the grab method and then retrieve the data of the sensors of interest with the retrieve method. For example, in your own apps, you might also need to retrieve a BGR frame (standard camera frame), which can be done by passing cv2.CAP_OPENNI_BGR_IMAGE to the retrieve method.

So, now that you can read data from your sensor, let's see how to run the application in the next section.

Running the app and main function routine

The `chapter2.py` script is responsible for running the app, and it first imports the following modules:

```
import cv2
import numpy as np
from gestures import recognize
from frame_reader import read_frame
```

The `recognize` function is responsible for recognizing a hand gesture, and we will compose it later in this chapter. We have also placed the `read_frame` method that we composed in the previous section in a separate script, for convenience.

In order to simplify the segmentation task, we will instruct the user to place their hand in the center of the screen. To provide a visual aid for this, we create the following function:

```
def draw_helpers(img_draw: np.ndarray) -> None:
    # draw some helpers for correctly placing hand
    height, width = img_draw.shape[:2]
    color = (0,102,255)
    cv2.circle(img_draw, (width // 2, height // 2), 3, color, 2)
    cv2.rectangle(img_draw, (width // 3, height // 3),
                  (width * 2 // 3, height * 2 // 3), color, 2)
```

The function draws a rectangle around the image center and highlights the center pixel of the image in orange.

All the heavy lifting is done by the `main` function, shown in the following code block:

```
def main():
    for _, frame in iter(read_frame, (False, None)):
```

The function iterates over grayscale frames from Kinect, and, in each iteration, it covers the following steps:

1. Recognize hand gestures using the `recognize` function, which returns the estimated number of extended fingers (`num_fingers`) and an annotated BGR color image, as follows:

    ```
    num_fingers, img_draw = recognize(frame)
    ```

2. Call the `draw_helpers` function on the annotated BGR image in order to provide a visual aid for hand placement, as follows:

```
draw_helpers(img_draw)
```

3. Finally, the `main` function draws the number of fingers on the annotated `frame`, displays results with `cv2.imshow`, and sets termination criteria, as follows:

```
# print number of fingers on image
cv2.putText(img_draw, str(num_fingers), (30, 30),
        cv2.FONT_HERSHEY_SIMPLEX, 1, (255, 255, 255))
cv2.imshow("frame", img_draw)
# Exit on escape
if cv2.waitKey(10) == 27:
    break
```

So, now that we have the main script, you will note that the only function that we are missing is the `recognize` function. In order to track hand gestures, we need to compose this function, which we will do in the next section.

Tracking hand gestures in real time

Hand gestures are analyzed by the `recognize` function; this is where the real magic takes place. This function handles the entire process flow, from the raw grayscale image to a recognized hand gesture. It returns the number of fingers and the illustration frame. It implements the following procedure:

1. It extracts the user's hand region by analyzing the depth map (`img_gray`), and returns a hand region mask (`segment`), like this:

```
def recognize(img_gray: np.ndarray) -> Tuple[int,np.ndarray]:
    # segment arm region
    segment = segment_arm(img_gray)
```

2. It performs `contour` analysis on the hand region mask (`segment`). Then, it returns the largest contour found in the image (`contour`) and any convexity defects (`defects`), as follows:

```
# find the hull of the segmented area, and based on that find the
# convexity defects
contour, defects = find_hull_defects(segment)
```

3. Based on the contour found and the convexity defects, it detects the number of extended fingers (num_fingers) in the image. Then, it creates an illustration image (img_draw) using (segment) image as a template, and annotates it with contour and defect points, like this:

```
img_draw = cv2.cvtColor(segment, cv2.COLOR_GRAY2RGB)
num_fingers, img_draw = detect_num_fingers(contour,
                                    defects, img_draw)
```

4. Finally, the estimated number of extended fingers (num_fingers), as well as the annotated output image (img_draw), are returned, as follows:

```
return num_fingers, img_draw
```

In the next section, let's learn how to accomplish hand region segmentation, which we used at the beginning of the procedure.

Understanding hand region segmentation

The automatic detection of an arm—and later, the hand region—could be designed to be arbitrarily complicated, maybe by combining information about the shape and color of an arm or hand. However, using skin color as a determining feature to find hands in visual scenes might fail terribly in poor lighting conditions or when the user is wearing gloves. Instead, we choose to recognize the user's hand by its shape in the depth map.

Allowing hands of all sorts to be present in any region of the image unnecessarily complicates the mission of the present chapter, so we make two simplifying assumptions:

- We will instruct the user of our app to place their hand in front of the center of the screen, orienting their palm roughly parallel to the orientation of the Kinect sensor so that it is easier to identify the corresponding depth layer of the hand.
- We will also instruct the user to sit roughly 1 to 2 meters away from the Kinect and to slightly extend their arm in front of their body so that the hand will end up in a slightly different depth layer than the arm. However, the algorithm will still work even if the full arm is visible.

In this way, it will be relatively straightforward to segment the image based on the depth layer alone. Otherwise, we would have to come up with a hand detection algorithm first, which would unnecessarily complicate our mission. If you feel adventurous, feel free to do this on your own.

Let's see how to find the most prominent depth of the image center region in the next section.

Finding the most prominent depth of the image center region

Once the hand is placed roughly in the center of the screen, we can start finding all image pixels that lie on the same depth plane as the hand. This is done by following these steps:

1. First, we simply need to determine the most prominent depth value of the center region of the image. The simplest approach would be to look only at the depth value of the center pixel, like this:

```
width, height = depth.shape
center_pixel_depth = depth[width/2, height/2]
```

2. Then, create a mask in which all pixels at a depth of center_pixel_depth are white and all others are black, as follows:

```
import numpy as np

depth_mask = np.where(depth == center_pixel_depth, 255,
    0).astype(np.uint8)
```

However, this approach will not be very robust, because there is the chance that it will be compromised by the following:

- Your hand will not be placed perfectly parallel to the Kinect sensor.
- Your hand will not be perfectly flat.
- The Kinect sensor values will be noisy.

Therefore, different regions of your hand will have slightly different depth values.

The segment_arm method takes a slightly better approach—it looks at a small neighborhood in the center of the image and determines the median depth value. This is done by following these steps:

1. First, we find the center region (for example, 21 x 21 pixels) of the image frame, like this:

```
def segment_arm(frame: np.ndarray, abs_depth_dev: int = 14) ->
np.ndarray:
```

```
height, width = frame.shape
# find center (21x21 pixels) region of imageheight frame
center_half = 10 # half-width of 21 is 21/2-1
center = frame[height // 2 - center_half:height // 2 +
center_half,
                width // 2 - center_half:width // 2 +
center_half]
```

2. Then, we determine the median depth value, med_val, as follows:

```
med_val = np.median(center)
```

We can now compare med_val with the depth value of all pixels in the image and create a mask in which all pixels whose depth values are within a particular range [med_val-abs_depth_dev, med_val+abs_depth_dev] are white, and all other pixels are black.

However, for reasons that will become clear in a moment, let's paint the pixels gray instead of white, like this:

```
frame = np.where(abs(frame - med_val) <= abs_depth_dev,
                128, 0).astype(np.uint8)
```

3. The result will look like this:

You will note that the segmentation mask is not smooth. In particular, it contains holes at points where the depth sensor failed to make a prediction. Let's learn how to apply morphological closing to smoothen the segmentation mask, in the next section.

Applying morphological closing for smoothening

A common problem with segmentation is that a hard threshold typically results in small imperfections (that is, holes, as in the preceding image) in the segmented region. These holes can be alleviated by using morphological opening and closing. When it is opened, it removes small objects from the foreground (assuming that the objects are bright on a dark foreground), whereas closing removes small holes (dark regions).

This means that we can get rid of the small black regions in our mask by applying morphological closing (dilation followed by erosion) with a small 3 x 3-pixel kernel, as follows:

```
kernel = np.ones((3, 3), np.uint8)
frame = cv2.morphologyEx(frame, cv2.MORPH_CLOSE, kernel)
```

The result looks a lot smoother, as follows:

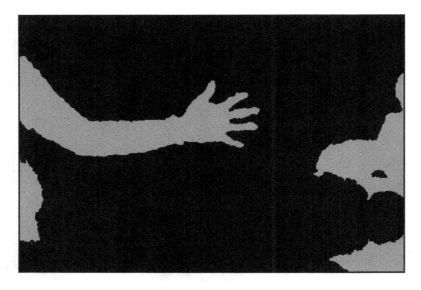

Notice, however, that the mask still contains regions that do not belong to the hand or arm, such as what appears to be one of the knees on the left and some furniture on the right. These objects just happen to be on the same depth layer of my arm and hand. If possible, we could now combine the depth information with another descriptor, maybe a texture- or skeleton-based hand classifier that would weed out all non-skin regions.

An easier approach is to realize that most of the time, hands are not connected to knees or furniture. Let's learn how to find connected components in a segmentation mask.

Finding connected components in a segmentation mask

We already know that the center region belongs to the hand. For such a scenario, we can simply apply `cv2.floodfill` to find all the connected image regions.

Before we do this, we want to be absolutely certain that the seed point for the flood fill belongs to the right mask region. This can be achieved by assigning a grayscale value of `128` to the seed point. However, we also want to make sure that the center pixel does not, by any coincidence, lie within a cavity that the morphological operation failed to close.

So, let's set a small 7 x 7-pixel region with a grayscale value of `128` instead, like this:

```
small_kernel = 3
frame[height // 2 - small_kernel:height // 2 + small_kernel,
      width // 2 - small_kernel:width // 2 + small_kernel] = 128
```

As **flood filling** (as well as morphological operations) is potentially dangerous, OpenCV requires the specification of a mask that avoids *flooding* the entire image. This mask has to be 2 pixels wider and taller than the original image and has to be used in combination with the `cv2.FLOODFILL_MASK_ONLY` flag.

It can be very helpful to constrain the flood filling to a small region of the image or a specific contour so that we need not connect two neighboring regions that should never have been connected in the first place. *It's better to be safe than sorry, right?*

Nevertheless, today, we feel courageous! Let's make the `mask` entirely black, like this:

```
mask = np.zeros((height + 2, width + 2), np.uint8)
```

Then, we can apply the flood fill to the center pixel (the seed point), and paint all the connected regions white, as follows:

```
flood = frame.copy()
cv2.floodFill(flood, mask, (width // 2, height // 2), 255,
              flags=4 | (255 << 8))
```

At this point, it should be clear why we decided to start with a gray mask earlier. We now have a mask that contains white regions (arm and hand), gray regions (neither arm nor hand, but other things in the same depth plane), and black regions (all others). With this setup, it is easy to apply a simple binary `threshold` to highlight only the relevant regions of the pre-segmented depth plane, as follows:

```
ret, flooded = cv2.threshold(flood, 129, 255, cv2.THRESH_BINARY)
```

This is what the resulting mask looks like:

The resulting segmentation mask can now be returned to the `recognize` function, where it will be used as an input to the `find_hull_defects` function, as well as a canvas for drawing the final output image (`img_draw`). The function analyzes the shape of a hand in order to detect the defects of a hull that corresponds to the hand. Let's learn how to perform hand shape analysis in the next section.

Performing hand shape analysis

Now that we know (roughly) where the hand is located, we aim to learn something about its shape. In this app, we will make a decision on which exact gesture is shown, based on convexity defects of a contour corresponding to the hand.

Let's move on and learn how to determine the contour of the segmented hand region in the next section, which will be the first step in our hand shape analysis.

Determining the contour of the segmented hand region

The first step involves determining the contour of the segmented hand region. Luckily, OpenCV comes with a pre-canned version of such an algorithm—cv2.findContours. This function acts on a binary image and returns a set of points that are believed to be part of the contour. As there might be multiple contours present in the image, it is possible to retrieve an entire hierarchy of contours, as follows:

```
def find_hull_defects(segment: np.ndarray) -> Tuple[np.ndarray,
np.ndarray]:
    contours, hierarchy = cv2.findContours(segment, cv2.RETR_TREE,
                                    cv2.CHAIN_APPROX_SIMPLE)
```

Furthermore, because we do not know which contour we are looking for, we have to make an assumption to clean up the contour result, since it is possible that some small cavities are left over even after the morphological closing. However, we are fairly certain that our mask contains only the segmented area of interest. We will assume that the largest contour found is the one that we are looking for.

Thus, we simply traverse the list of contours, calculate the contour area (cv2.contourArea), and store only the largest one (max_contour), like this:

```
max_contour = max(contours, key=cv2.contourArea)
```

The contour that we found might still have too many corners. We approximate the contour with a similar contour that does not have sides that are less than 1 percent of the perimeter of the contour, like this:

```
epsilon = 0.01 * cv2.arcLength(max_contour, True)
max_contour = cv2.approxPolyDP(max_contour, epsilon, True)
```

Let's learn how to find the convex hull of a contour area, in the next section.

Finding the convex hull of a contour area

Once we have identified the largest contour in our mask, it is straightforward to compute the convex hull of the contour area. The convex hull is basically the envelope of the contour area. If you think of all the pixels that belong to the contour area as a set of nails poking out of a board, then a tight rubber band encircles all the nails forming the convex hull shape. We can get the convex hull directly from our largest contour (`max_contour`), like this:

```
hull = cv2.convexHull(max_contour, returnPoints=False)
```

As we now want to look at convexity deficits in this hull, we are instructed by the OpenCV documentation to set the `returnPoints` optional flag to `False`.

The convex hull drawn in yellow around a segmented hand region looks like this:

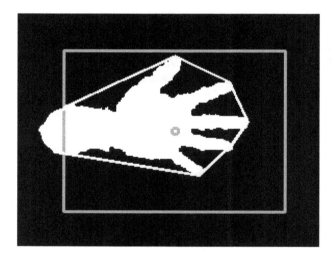

As mentioned previously, we will determine a hand gesture based on convexity defects. Let's move on and learn how to find the convexity defects of a convex hull in the next section, which will bring us one step closer to recognizing hand gestures.

Finding the convexity defects of a convex hull

As is evident from the preceding screenshot, not all points on the convex hull belong to the segmented hand region. In fact, all the fingers and the wrist cause severe *convexity defects*—that is, points of the contour that are far away from the hull.

We can find these defects by looking at both the largest contour (`max_contour`) and the corresponding convex hull (`hull`), as follows:

```
defects = cv2.convexityDefects(max_contour, hull)
```

The output of this function (`defects`) is a NumPy array containing all defects. Each defect is an array of four integers that are `start_index` (index of the point in the contour where the defect begins), `end_index` (index of the point in the contour where the defect ends), `farthest_pt_index` (the index of the farthest point from the convex hull within the defect), and `fixpt_depth` (the distance between the farthest point and the convex hull).

We will make use of this information in just a moment when we try to estimate the number of extended fingers.

For now, though, our job is done. The extracted contour (`max_contour`) and convexity defects (`defects`) can be returned to `recognize`, where they will be used as inputs to `detect_num_fingers`, as follows:

```
return max_contour, defects
```

So, now that we have found the defects, let's move on and learn how to perform hand gesture recognition using the convexity defects, which will bring us toward the completion of the app.

Performing hand gesture recognition

What remains to be done is to classify the hand gesture based on the number of extended fingers. For example, if we find five extended fingers, we assume the hand to be open, whereas no extended fingers implies a fist. All that we are trying to do is count from zero to five, and make the app recognize the corresponding number of fingers.

This is actually trickier than it might seem at first. For example, people in **Europe** might count to three by extending their *thumb, index finger,* and *middle finger*. If you do that in the **US**, people there might get horrendously confused, because they do not tend to use their thumbs when signaling the number two.

This might lead to frustration, especially in restaurants (trust me). If we could find a way to generalize these two scenarios—maybe by appropriately counting the number of extended fingers, we would have an algorithm that could teach simple hand gesture recognition to not only a machine but also (maybe) to a person of average intellect.

As you might have guessed, the answer is related to convexity defects. As mentioned earlier, extended fingers cause defects in the convex hull. However, the inverse is not true; that is, not all convexity defects are caused by fingers! There might be additional defects caused by the wrist, as well as the overall orientation of the hand or the arm. *How can we distinguish between these different causes of defects?*

Let's distinguish between different cases of convexity defects, in the next section.

Distinguishing between different causes of convexity defects

The trick is to look at the angle between the farthest point from the convex hull point within the defect (`farthest_pt_index`) and the start and endpoints of the defect (`start_index` and `end_index`, respectively), as illustrated in the following screenshot:

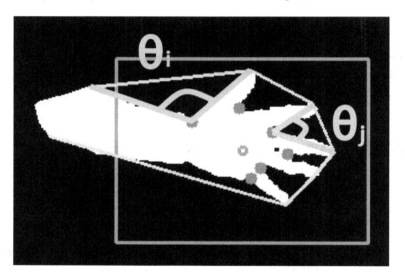

In the previous screenshot, the orange markers serve as a visual aid to center the hand in the middle of the screen, and the convex hull is outlined in green. Each red dot corresponds to *the point farthest from the convex hull* (`farthest_pt_index`) for every convexity defect detected. If we compare a typical angle that belongs to two extended fingers (such as θ_j) to an angle that is caused by general hand geometry (such as θ_i), we notice that the former is much smaller than the latter.

This is obviously because humans can spread their fingers only a little, thus creating a narrow angle made by the farthest defect point and the neighboring fingertips. Therefore, we can iterate over all convexity defects and compute the angle between the said points. For this, we will need a utility function that calculates the angle (in radians) between two arbitrary—a list like vectors, v1 and v2, as follows:

```
def angle_rad(v1, v2):
    return np.arctan2(np.linalg.norm(np.cross(v1, v2)),
        np.dot(v1, v2))
```

This method uses the cross product to compute the angle, rather than doing it in the standard way. The standard way of calculating the angle between two vectors v1 and v2 is by calculating their dot product and dividing it by the norm of v1 and the norm of v2. However, this method has two imperfections:

- You have to manually avoid division by zero if either the norm of v1 or the norm of v2 is zero.
- The method returns relatively inaccurate results for small angles.

Similarly, we provide a simple function to convert an angle from degrees to radians, illustrated here:

```
def deg2rad(angle_deg):
    return angle_deg/180.0*np.pi
```

In the next section, we'll see how to classify hand gestures based on the number of extended fingers.

Classifying hand gestures based on the number of extended fingers

What remains to be done is to actually classify the hand gesture based on the number of instances of extended fingers. The classification is done using the following function:

```
def detect_num_fingers(contour: np.ndarray, defects: np.ndarray,
                       img_draw: np.ndarray, thresh_deg: float = 80.0) ->
Tuple[int, np.ndarray]:
```

The function accepts the detected contour (contour), the convexity defects (defects), a canvas to draw on (img_draw), and a cutoff angle that can be used as a threshold to classify whether convexity defects are caused by extended fingers or not (thresh_deg).

Except for the angle between the thumb and the index finger, it is rather hard to get anything close to 90 degrees, so anything close to that number should work. We do not want the cutoff angle to be too high, because that might lead to errors in classifications. The complete function will return the number of fingers and the illustration frame, and consists of the following steps:

1. First, let's focus on special cases. If we do not find any convexity `defects`, it means that we possibly made a mistake during the convex hull calculation, or there are simply no extended fingers in the frame, so we return 0 as the number of detected fingers, as follows:

```
if defects is None:
    return [0, img_draw]
```

2. However, we can take this idea even further. Due to the fact that arms are usually slimmer than hands or fists, we can assume that the hand geometry will always generate at least two convexity defects (which usually belong to the wrists). So, if there are no additional defects, it implies that there are no extended fingers:

```
if len(defects) <= 2:
    return [0, img_draw]
```

3. Now that we have ruled out all special cases, we can begin counting real fingers. If there is a sufficient number of defects, we will find a defect between every pair of fingers. Thus, in order to get the number right (`num_fingers`), we should start counting at 1, like this:

```
num_fingers = 1
```

4. Then, we start iterating over all convexity defects. For each defect, we extract the three points and draw its hull for visualization purposes, as follows:

```
# Defects are of shape (num_defects,1,4)
for defect in defects[:, 0, :]:
    # Each defect is an array of four integers.
    # First three indexes of start, end and the furthest
    # points respectively
    start, end, far = [contour[i][0] for i in defect[:3]]
    # draw the hull
    cv2.line(img_draw, tuple(start), tuple(end), (0, 255, 0), 2)
```

5. Then, we compute the angle between the two edges from `far` to `start` and from `far` to `end`. If the angle is smaller than `thresh_deg` degrees, it means that we are dealing with a defect that is most likely caused by two extended fingers. In such cases, we want to increment the number of detected fingers (`num_fingers`) and draw the point with `green`. Otherwise, we draw the point with `red`, as follows:

```
# if angle is below a threshold, defect point belongs to two
# extended fingers
if angle_rad(start - far, end - far) < deg2rad(thresh_deg):
    # increment number of fingers
    num_fingers += 1

    # draw point as green
    cv2.circle(img_draw, tuple(far), 5, (0, 255, 0), -1)
else:
    # draw point as red
    cv2.circle(img_draw, tuple(far), 5, (0, 0, 255), -1)
```

6. After iterating over all convexity defects, we `return` the number of detected fingers and the assembled output image, like this:

```
return min(5, num_fingers), img_draw
```

Computing the minimum will make sure that we do not exceed the common number of fingers per hand.

The result can be seen in the following screenshot:

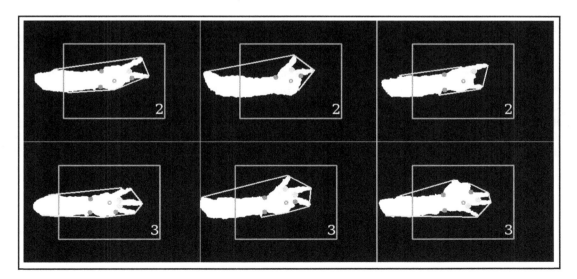

Interestingly, our app is able to detect the correct number of extended fingers in a variety of hand configurations. Defect points between extended fingers are easily classified as such by the algorithm, and others are successfully ignored.

Summary

This chapter showed a relatively simple—and yet surprisingly robust—way of recognizing a variety of hand gestures by counting the number of extended fingers.

The algorithm first shows how a task-relevant region of the image can be segmented using depth information acquired from a Microsoft Kinect 3D sensor, and how morphological operations can be used to clean up the segmentation result. By analyzing the shape of the segmented hand region, the algorithm comes up with a way to classify hand gestures based on the types of convexity effects found in the image.

Once again, mastering our use of OpenCV to perform the desired task did not require us to produce a large amount of code. Instead, we were challenged to gain an important insight that made us use the built-in functionality of OpenCV in an effective way.

Gesture recognition is a popular but challenging field in computer science, with applications in a large number of areas, such as **Human-Computer Interaction** (**HCI**), video surveillance, and even the video game industry. You can now use your advanced understanding of segmentation and structure analysis to build your own state-of-the-art gesture recognition system. Another approach you might want to use for hand gesture recognition is to train a deep image classification network on hand gestures. We will discuss deep networks for image classifications in Chapter 9, *Learning to Classify and Localize Objects*.

In the next chapter, we will continue to focus on detecting objects of interest in visual scenes, but we will assume a much more complicated case: viewing the object from an arbitrary perspective and distance. To do this, we will combine perspective transformations with scale-invariant feature descriptors to develop a robust feature-matching algorithm.

3
Finding Objects via Feature Matching and Perspective Transforms

In the previous chapter, you learned how to detect and track a simple object (the silhouette of a hand) in a very controlled environment. To be more specific, we instructed the user of our app to place the hand in the central region of the screen and then made assumptions about the size and shape of the object (the hand). In this chapter, we want to detect and track objects of arbitrary sizes, possibly viewed from several different angles or under partial occlusion.

For this, we will make use of feature descriptors, which are a way of capturing the important properties of our object of interest. We do this so that the object can be located even when it is embedded in a busy visual scene. We will apply our algorithm to the live stream of a webcam and do our best to keep the algorithm robust yet simple enough to run in real time.

In this chapter, we will cover the following topics:

- Listing the tasks performed by the app
- Planning the app
- Setting up the app
- Understanding the process flow
- Learning feature extraction
- Looking at feature detection

- Understanding feature descriptors
- Understanding feature matching
- Learning feature tracking
- Seeing the algorithm in action

The goal of this chapter is to develop an app that can detect and track an object of interest in the video stream of a webcam—even if the object is viewed from different angles or distances or under partial occlusion. Such an object can be the cover image of a book, a drawing, or anything else that has a sophisticated surface structure.

Once the template image is provided, the app will be able to detect that object, estimate its boundaries, and then track it in the video stream.

Getting started

This chapter has been tested with **OpenCV 4.1.1**.

 Note that you might have to obtain the so-called extra modules from `https://github.com/Itseez/opencv_contrib`.

We install OpenCV with `OPENCV_ENABLE_NONFREE` and the `OPENCV_EXTRA_MODULES_PATH` variable set in order to get **Speeded-Up Robust Features (SURF)** and the **Fast Library for Approximate Nearest Neighbors (FLANN)** installed. You can also use the Docker files available in the repository, which contain all the required installations.

Additionally, note that you may have to obtain a license to use **SURF** in commercial applications.

The code for this chapter can be found in the GitHub book repository available at `https://github.com/PacktPublishing/OpenCV-4-with-Python-Blueprints-Second-Edition/tree/master/chapter3`.

Listing the tasks performed by the app

The app will analyze each captured frame to perform the following tasks:

- **Feature extraction**: We will describe an object of interest with **Speeded-Up Robust Features** (**SURF**), which is an algorithm used to find distinctive keypoints in an image that are both scale-invariant and rotation invariant. These keypoints will help us to make sure that we are tracking the right object over multiple frames because the appearance of the object might change from time to time. It is important to find keypoints that do not depend on the viewing distance or viewing angle of the object (hence, the scale and rotation invariance).

- **Feature matching**: We will try to establish a correspondence between keypoints using the **Fast Library for Approximate Nearest Neighbors** (**FLANN**) to see whether a frame contains keypoints similar to the keypoints from our object of interest. If we find a good match, we will mark the object on each frame.

- **Feature tracking**: We will keep track of the located object of interest from frame to frame using various forms of **early outlier detection** and **outlier rejection** to speed up the algorithm.

- **Perspective transform**: We will then reverse any translations and rotations that the object has undergone by **warping the perspective** so that the object appears upright in the center of the screen. This creates a cool effect in which the object seems frozen in a position while the entire surrounding scene rotates around it.

An example of the first three steps, namely, the feature extraction, matching, and tracking is shown in the following screenshot:

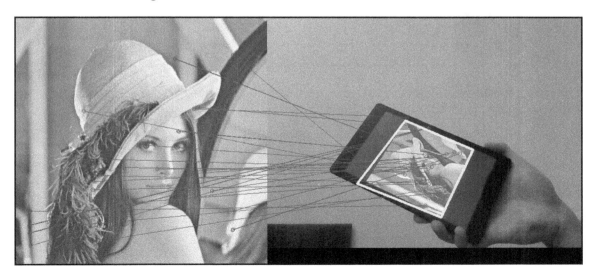

The screenshot contains a template image of our object of interest on the left and a handheld printout of the template image on the right. Matching features in the two frames are connected with blue lines, and the located object is outlined in green on the right.

The last step is to transform the located object so that it is projected onto the frontal plane, as depicted in the following photograph:

The image looks roughly like the original template image, appearing close-up, while the entire scene seems to warp around it.

Let's first plan the application that we are going to create in this chapter.

Planning the app

The final app will consist of a Python class for detecting, matching, and tracking image features, as well as a script that accesses the webcam and displays each processed frame.

The project will contain the following modules and scripts:

- `feature_matching`: This module contains an algorithm for feature extraction, feature matching, and feature tracking. We separate this algorithm from the rest of the application so that it can be used as a standalone module.
- `feature_matching.FeatureMatching`: This class implements the entire feature-matching process flow. It accepts a **Blue, Green, Red (BGR)** camera frame and tries to locate an object of interest in it.
- `chapter3`: This is the main script for the chapter.
- `chapter3.main`: This is the main function routine for starting the application, accessing the camera, sending each frame for processing to an instance of the `FeatureMatching` class, and for displaying results.

Let's set up the application before going into the details of the feature-matching algorithm.

Setting up the app

Before we can get down to the nitty-gritty of our feature-matching algorithm, we need to make sure that we can access the webcam and display the video stream.

Let's learn how to run the application in the next section.

Running the app – the main() function routine

To run our app, we will need to execute the `main()` function routine. The following steps show us the execution of `main()` routine:

1. The function first accesses the webcam with the `VideoCapture` method by passing `0` as an argument, which is a reference to the default webcam. If it can not access the webcam, the app will be terminated:

```
import cv2 as cv
from feature_matching import FeatureMatching

def main():
    capture = cv.VideoCapture(0)
    assert capture.isOpened(), "Cannot connect to camera"
```

2. Then, the desired frame size and frame per second of the video stream is set. The following snippet shows the code for setting the frame size and frame per second of the video:

```
capture.set(cv.CAP_PROP_FPS, 10)
capture.set(cv.CAP_PROP_FRAME_WIDTH, 640)
capture.set(cv.CAP_PROP_FRAME_HEIGHT, 480)
```

3. Next, an instance of the `FeatureMatching` class is initialized with a path to a template (or training) file that depicts the object of interest. The following code shows the `FeatureMatching` class:

```
matching = FeatureMatching(train_image='train.png')
```

4. After that, to process the frames from the camera, we create an iterator from the `capture.read` function, which will terminate when the function fails to return frame (`(False,None)`). This can be seen in the following code block:

```
for success, frame in iter(capture.read, (False, None)):
    cv.imshow("frame", frame)
    match_succsess, img_warped, img_flann =
matching.match(frame)
```

In the previous code block, the `FeatureMatching.match` method processes the **BGR** image (`capture.read` returns `frame` in BGR format). If the object is detected in the current frame, the `match` method will report `match_success=True` and return the warped image as well as the image that illustrates the matches—`img_flann`.

Let's move on and display the results in which our match method will return.

Displaying results

In fact, we can display the results only if the `match` method returns a result, right? This can be seen in the following block:

```
if match_succsess:
    cv.imshow("res", img_warped)
    cv.imshow("flann", img_flann)
if cv.waitKey(1) & 0xff == 27:
    break
```

Displaying images in OpenCV is straightforward and is done by the `imshow` method, which accepts the name of a window and an image. Additionally, loop termination criteria on the *Esc* keypress are set.

Now that we have set up our app, let's take a look at the process flow in the next section.

Understanding the process flow

Features are extracted, matched, and tracked by the `FeatureMatching` class—especially by the public `match` method. However, before we can begin analyzing the incoming video stream, we have some homework to do. It might not be clear right away what some of these things mean (especially for SURF and FLANN), but we will discuss these steps in detail in the following sections.

For now, we only have to worry about initialization:

```
class FeatureMatching:
    def __init__(self, train_image: str = "train.png") -> None:
```

The following steps cover the initialization process:

1. The following line sets up a SURF detector, which we will use for detecting and extracting features from images (see the *Learning feature extraction* section for further details), with a Hessian threshold between 300 and 500, that is, `400`:

   ```
   self.f_extractor = cv.xfeatures2d_SURF.create(hessianThreshold=400)
   ```

2. We load a template of our object of interest (`self.img_obj`), or print an error if it cannot be found:

   ```
   self.img_obj = cv.imread(train_image, cv.CV_8UC1)
   assert self.img_obj is not None, f"Could not find train image {train_image}"
   ```

3. Also, we store the shape of the image (`self.sh_train`) for convenience:

   ```
   self.sh_train = self.img_obj.shape[:2]
   ```

We will call the template image the **train image**, as our algorithm will be trained to find this image, and every incoming frame a **query image**, as we will use these images to query the **train image**. The following photograph is the train image:

Image credit—Lenna.png by Conor Lawless is licensed under CC BY 2.0

The previous train image has a size of 512 x 512 pixels and will be used to train the algorithm.

4. Next, we apply SURF to the object of interest. This can be done with a convenient function call that returns both a list of keypoints and the descriptor (you can refer to the *Learning feature extraction* section for further explanation):

```
self.key_train, self.desc_train = \
    self.f_extractor.detectAndCompute(self.img_obj, None)
```

We will do the same with each incoming frame and then compare lists of features across images.

5. Now, we set up a FLANN object that will be used to match the features of the train and query images (refer to the *Understanding feature matching* section for further details). This requires the specification of some additional parameters via dictionaries, such as which algorithm to use and how many trees to run in parallel:

```
index_params = {"algorithm": 0, "trees": 5}
search_params = {"checks": 50}
self.flann = cv.FlannBasedMatcher(index_params, search_params)
```

6. Finally, initialize some additional bookkeeping variables. These will come in handy when we want to make our feature tracking both faster and more accurate. For example, we will keep track of the latest computed homography matrix and of the number of frames we have spent without locating our object of interest (refer to the *Learning feature tracking* section for more details):

```
self.last_hinv = np.zeros((3, 3))
self.max_error_hinv = 50.
self.num_frames_no_success = 0
self.max_frames_no_success = 5
```

Then, the bulk of the work is done by the `FeatureMatching.match` method. This method follows the procedure elaborated here:

1. It extracts interesting image features from each incoming video frame.
2. It matches features between the template image and the video frame. This is done in `FeatureMatching.match_features`. If no such match is found, it skips to the next frame.
3. It finds the corner points of the template image in the video frame. This is done in the `detect_corner_points` function. If any of the corners lie (significantly) outside the frame, it skips to the next frame.
4. It calculates the area of the quadrilateral that the four corner points span. If the area is either too small or too large, it skips to the next frame.
5. It outlines the corner points of the template image in the current frame.
6. It finds the perspective transform that is necessary to bring the located object from the current frame to the `frontoparallel` plane. If the result is significantly different from the result we got recently for an earlier frame, it skips to the next frame.
7. It warps the perspective of the current frame to make the object of interest appear centered and upright.

In the following sections, we will discuss the previous steps in detail.

Let's first take a look at the feature extraction step in the next section. This step is the core of our algorithm. It will find informative areas in the image and represent them in a lower dimensionality so that we can use those representations afterward to decide whether two images contain similar features.

Learning feature extraction

Generally speaking, in machine learning, feature extraction is a process of dimensionality reduction of the data that results in an informative description of a data element.

In computer vision, a feature is usually an *interesting area* of an image. It is a measurable property of an image that is very informative about what the image represents. Usually, the grayscale value of an individual pixel (that is, the *raw data*) does not tell us a lot about the image as a whole. Instead, we need to derive a property that is more informative.

For example, knowing that there are patches in the image that look like eyes, a nose, and a mouth will allow us to reason about how likely it is that the image represents a face. In this case, the number of resources required to describe the data is drastically reduced. The data refers to, for example, whether we are seeing an image of a face. Does the image contain two eyes, a nose, or a mouth?

More low-level features, such as the presence of edges, corners, blobs, or ridges, may be more informative generally. Some features may be better than others, depending on the application.

Once we have made up our mind about what is our favorite feature, we first need to come up with a way to check whether or not the image contains such features. Additionally, we need to find out where it contains them and then create a descriptor of the feature. Let's learn how to detect features in the next section.

Looking at feature detection

In computer vision, the process of finding areas of interest in an image is called feature detection. Under the hood, for each point of the image, a feature detection algorithm decides whether an image point contains a feature of interest. OpenCV provides a whole range of feature detection (and description) algorithms.

In OpenCV, the details of the algorithms are encapsulated and all of them have similar APIs. Here are some of the algorithms:

- **Harris corner detection**: We know that edges are areas with high-intensity changes in all directions. Harris and Stephens came up with this algorithm, which is a fast way of finding such areas. This algorithm is implemented as `cv2.cornerHarris` in OpenCV.
- **Shi-Tomasi corner detection**: Shi and Tomasi developed a corner detection algorithm, and this algorithm is usually better than Harris corner detection by finding the *N* strongest corners. This algorithm is implemented as `cv2.goodFeaturesToTrack` in OpenCV.
- **Scale-Invariant Feature Transform** (**SIFT**): Corner detection is not sufficient when the scale of the image changes. To this end, David Lowe developed a method to describe keypoints in an image that are independent of orientation and size (hence the term **scale-invariant**). The algorithm is implemented as `cv2.xfeatures2d_SIFT` in OpenCV2 but has been moved to the *extra* modules in OpenCV3 since its code is proprietary.
- **SURF**: SIFT has proven to be really good, but it is not fast enough for most applications. This is where SURF comes in, which replaces the expensive Laplacian of a Gaussian (function) from SIFT with a box filter. The algorithm is implemented as `cv2.xfeatures2d_SURF` in OpenCV2, but, like SIFT, it has been moved to the *extra* modules in OpenCV3 since its code is proprietary.

OpenCV has support for even more feature descriptors, such as **Features from Accelerated Segment Test** (**FAST**), **Binary Robust Independent Elementary Features** (**BRIEF**), and **Oriented FAST and Rotated BRIEF** (**ORB**), the latter being an open source alternative to SIFT or SURF.

In the next section, we'll learn how to use SURF to detect features in an image.

Detecting features in an image with SURF

In the remainder of this chapter, we will make use of the SURF detector. The SURF algorithm can be roughly divided into two distinct steps, which are detecting points of interest and formulating a descriptor.

SURF relies on the Hessian corner detector for interest point detection, which requires the setting of a minimal `minhessianThreshold`. This threshold determines how large the output from the Hessian filter must be in order for a point to be used as an interesting point.

When the value is larger, fewer interest points are obtained, but they are theoretically more salient and vice versa. Feel free to experiment with different values.

In this chapter, we will choose a value of `400`, as we did earlier in `FeatureMatching.__init__`, where we created a SURF descriptor with the following code snippet:

```
self.f_extractor = cv2.xfeatures2d_SURF.create(hessianThreshold=400)
```

The keypoints in the image can be obtained in a single step, which is given as follows:

```
key_query = self.f_extractor.detect(img_query)
```

Here, `key_query` is a list of instances of `cv2.KeyPoint` and has the length of the number of detected keypoints. Each `KeyPoint` contains information about the location (`KeyPoint.pt`), the size (`KeyPoint.size`), and other useful information about our point of interest.

We can now easily draw the keypoints using the following function:

```
img_keypoints = cv2.drawKeypoints(img_query, key_query, None,
    (255, 0, 0), 4)
cv2.imshow("keypoints",img_keypoints)
```

Depending on an image, the number of detected keypoints can be very large and unclear when visualized; we check it with `len(keyQuery)`. If you care only about drawing the keypoints, try setting `min_hessian` to a large value until the number of returned keypoints provides a good illustration.

 Note that SURF is protected by patent laws. Therefore, if you wish to use SURF in a commercial application, you will be required to obtain a license.

In order to complete our feature extraction algorithm, we need to obtain descriptors for our detected keypoints, which we will do in the next section.

Obtaining feature descriptors with SURF

The process of extracting features from an image with OpenCV using SURF is also a single step. It is done by the `compute` method of our feature extractor. The latter accepts an image and the keypoints of the image as arguments:

```
key_query, desc_query = self.f_extractor.compute(img_query, key_query)
```

Here, `desc_query` is a NumPY ndarray with shape `(num_keypoints, descriptor_size)`. You can see that each descriptor is a vector in an n-dimensional space (n-length array of numbers). Each vector describes the corresponding key point and provides some meaningful information about our complete image.

Hence, we have completed our feature extraction algorithm that had to provide meaningful information about our image in reduced dimensionality. It's up to the creator of the algorithm to decide what kind of information is contained in the descriptor vector, but at the very least the vectors should be such that they are closer to similar keypoints than for keypoints that appear different.

Our feature extraction algorithm also has a convenient method to combine the processes of feature detection and descriptor creation:

```
key_query, desc_query = self.f_extractor.detectAndCompute (img_query, None)
```

It returns both keypoints and descriptors in a single step and accepts a mask of an area of interest, which, in our case, is the complete image.

As we have extracted our features, the next step is to query and train images that contain similar features, which is accomplished by a feature matching algorithm. So, let's learn about feature matching in the next section.

Understanding feature matching

Once we have extracted features and their descriptors from two (or more) images, we can start asking whether some of these features show up in both (or all) images. For example, if we have descriptors for both our object of interest (`self.desc_train`) and the current video frame (`desc_query`), we can try to find regions of the current frame that look like our object of interest.

This is done by the following method, which makes use of FLANN:

```
good_matches = self.match_features(desc_query)
```

The process of finding frame-to-frame correspondences can be formulated as the search for the nearest neighbor from one set of descriptors for every element of another set.

The first set of descriptors is usually called the **train set**, because, in machine learning, these descriptors are used to train a model, such as the model of the object that we want to detect. In our case, the train set corresponds to the descriptor of the template image (our object of interest). Hence, we call our template image the **train image** (self.img_train).

The second set is usually called the **query set** because we continually ask whether it contains our train image. In our case, the query set corresponds to the descriptor of each incoming frame. Hence, we call a frame the **query image** (img_query).

Features can be matched in any number of ways, for example, with the help of a brute-force matcher (cv2.BFMatcher) that looks for each descriptor in the first set and the closest descriptor in the second set by trying each one (an exhaustive search).

In the next section, we'll learn how to match features across images with FLANN.

Matching features across images with FLANN

The alternative is to use an approximate **k-nearest neighbor** (**kNN**) algorithm to find correspondences, which is based on the fast third-party library, FLANN. A FLANN match is performed with the following code snippet, where we use kNN with k=2:

```
def match_features(self, desc_frame: np.ndarray) -> List[cv2.DMatch]:
    matches = self.flann.knnMatch(self.desc_train, desc_frame, k=2)
```

The result of flann.knnMatch is a list of correspondences between two sets of descriptors, both contained in the matches variable. These are the train set, because it corresponds to the pattern image of our object of interest, and the query set, because it corresponds to the image in which we are searching for our object of interest.

Now that we have found the nearest neighbors of our features, let's move ahead and find out how we can remove outliers in the next section.

Testing the ratio for outlier removal

The more correct matches that are found (which means that more pattern-to-image correspondences exist), the higher the chance that the pattern is present in the image. However, some matches might be false positives.

A well-known technique for removing outliers is called the ratio test. Since we performed kNN-matching with k=2, the two nearest descriptors are returned for each match. The first match is the closest neighbor and the second match is the second-closest neighbor. Intuitively, a correct match will have a much closer first neighbor than its second-closest neighbor. On the other hand, the two closest neighbors will be at a similar distance from an incorrect match.

Therefore, we can find out how good a match is by looking at the difference between the distances. The ratio test says that the match is good only if the distance ratio between the first match and the second match is smaller than a given number (usually around 0.5). In our case, this number is chosen to be 0.7. The following snippet finds good matches:

```
# discard bad matches, ratio test as per Lowe's paper
good_matches = [ x[0] for x in matches
    if x[0].distance < 0.7 * x[1].distance]
```

To remove all matches that do not satisfy this requirement, we filter the list of matches and store the good matches in the good_matches list.

Then, we pass the matches we found to FeatureMatching.match so that they can be processed further:

```
return good_matches
```

However, before elaborating on our algorithm, let's first visualize our matches in the next section.

Visualizing feature matches

In OpenCV, we can easily draw matches using cv2.drawMatches. Here, we create our own function for educational purposes as well as for ease of customization of function behavior:

```
def draw_good_matches(img1: np.ndarray,
                      kp1: Sequence[cv2.KeyPoint],
                      img2: np.ndarray,
                      kp2: Sequence[cv2.KeyPoint],
                      matches: Sequence[cv2.DMatch]) -> np.ndarray:
```

The function accepts two images, namely, in our case, the image of the object of interest and the current video frame. It also accepts keypoints from both images as well as the matches. It will draw the images next to each other on a single illustration image, illustrate the matches on the image, and return the image. The latter is achieved with the following steps:

1. Create a new output image of a size that will fit the two images together; make it three-channel in order to draw colored lines on the image:

```
rows1, cols1 = img1.shape[:2]
rows2, cols2 = img2.shape[:2]
out = np.zeros((max([rows1, rows2]), cols1 + cols2, 3),
dtype='uint8')
```

2. Place the first image on the left of the new image and the second image on the right of the first image:

```
out[:rows1, :cols1, :] = img1[..., None]
out[:rows2, cols1:cols1 + cols2, :] = img2[..., None]
```

In these expressions, we used the broadcasting rules of the NumPy arrays, which are rules for operations on arrays when their shapes do not match but meet certain constraints instead. Here, `img[..., None]` assigns one rule to channel (third) dimension of the two-dimensional grayscale image (array). Next, once NumPy meets a dimension that does not match, but instead has the value of one, it broadcasts the array. It means the same value is used for all three channels.

3. For each matching pair of points between both images, we want to draw a small blue circle on each image and connect the two circles with a line. For this purpose, iterate over the list of matching keypoints with a `for` loop, extract the center coordinates from the corresponding keypoints, and shift the coordinate of the second center for drawing:

```
for m in matches:
    c1 = tuple(map(int,kp1[m.queryIdx].pt))
    c2 = tuple(map(int,kp2[m.trainIdx].pt))
    c2 = c2[0]+cols1,c2[1]
```

The keypoints are stored as tuples in Python, with two entries for the x and y coordinates. Each match, m, stores the index in the key point lists, where m.trainIdx points to the index in the first key point list (kp1) and m.queryIdx points to the index in the second key point list (kp2).

4. In the same loop, draw circles with a four-pixel radius, the color blue, and a one-pixel thickness. Then, connect the circles with a line:

```
radius = 4
BLUE = (255, 0, 0)
thickness = 1
# Draw a small circle at both co-ordinates
cv2.circle(out, c1, radius, BLUE, thickness)
cv2.circle(out, c2, radius, BLUE, thickness)

# Draw a line in between the two points
cv2.line(out, c1, c2, BLUE, thickness)
```

5. Finally, `return` the resulting image:

```
return out
```

So, now that we have a convenient function, we can illustrate the matches with the following code:

```
cv2.imshow('imgFlann', draw_good_matches(self.img_train,
    self.key_train, img_query, key_query, good_matches))
```

The blue lines connect the features in the object (left) to the features in the scenery (right), as shown here:

This works fine in a simple example such as this, but what happens when there are other objects in the scene? Since our object contains some lettering that seems highly salient, what happens when there are other words present?

As it turns out, the algorithm works even under such conditions, as you can see in the following screenshot:

Interestingly, the algorithm did not confuse the name of the author as seen on the left with the black-on-white lettering next to the book in the scene, even though they spell out the same name. This is because the algorithm found a description of the object that does not rely purely on the grayscale representation. On the other hand, an algorithm doing a pixel-wise comparison could have easily gotten confused.

Now that we have matched our features, let's move ahead and learn how we can use these results in order to highlight the object of the interest, which we will do with the help of homography estimation in the next section.

Mapping homography estimation

Since we are assuming that the object of our interest is planar (that is, an image) and rigid, we can find the homography transformation between the feature points of the two images.

In the following steps, we will explore how homography can be used to calculate the perspective transformation required to bring matched feature points in the object image (`self.key_train`) into the same plane as corresponding feature points in the current image frame (`key_query`):

1. First, we store the image coordinates of all the keypoints that are good matches in lists for convenience, as shown in the following code snippet:

```
train_points = [self.key_train[good_match.queryIdx].pt
                for good_match in good_matches]
query_points = [key_query[good_match.trainIdx].pt
                for good_match in good_matches]
```

2. Now, let's encapsulate the logic for corner point detections in a separate function:

```
def detect_corner_points(src_points: Sequence[Point],
                         dst_points: Sequence[Point],
                         sh_src: Tuple[int, int]) -> np.ndarray:
```

The previous code shows two sequences of points and the shape of the source image, the function will return the corners of the points, which is accomplished by the following steps:

1. Find the perspective transformation (a homography matrix, `H`) for the given two sequences of coordinates:

```
H, _ = cv2.findHomography(np.array(src_points),
np.array(dst_points), cv2.RANSAC)
```

To find the transformation, the `cv2.findHomography` function will use the **random sample consensus (RANSAC)** method to probe different subsets of input points.

2. If the method fails to find the homography matrix, we `raise` an exception, which we will catch later in our application:

```
if H is None:
    raise Outlier("Homography not found")
```

3. Given the shape of the source image, we store the coordinates of its corners in an array:

```
height, width = sh_src
src_corners = np.array([(0, 0), (width, 0),
                        (width, height),
                        (0, height)], dtype=np.float32)
```

4. A homography matrix can be used to transform any point in the pattern into the scenery, such as transforming a corner point in the training image to a corner point in the query image. In other words, this means that we can draw the outline of the book cover in the query image by transforming the corner points from the training image.

   In order to do this, the list of corner points of the training image (`src_corners`) is taken and projected in the query image by performing a perspective transform:

   ```
   return cv2.perspectiveTransform(src_corners[None, :, :],
   H)[0]
   ```

   Also, the result is returned immediately, that is, an array of image points (two-dimensional NumPY ndarray).

3. Now that we have defined our function, we can call it to detect the corner points:

   ```
   dst_corners = detect_corner_points(
               train_points, query_points, self.sh_train)
   ```

4. All that we need to do is draw a line between each point in `dst_corners` and the very next one, and we will see an outline in the scenery:

   ```
   dst_corners[:, 0] += self.sh_train[1]
   cv2.polylines(
       img_flann,
       [dst_corners.astype(np.int)],
       isClosed=True,
       color=(0,255,0),
       thickness=3)
   ```

Note, in order to draw the image points, first offset the *x* coordinate of the points by the width of the pattern image (because we are showing the two images next to each other). Then, we treat the image points as a closed polyline and draw it with `cv2.polilines`. We also have to change the data type to an integer for drawing.

5. Finally, the outline of the book cover is drawn like this:

This works even when the object is only partially visible, as follows:

Although the book partially lies outside of the frame, the outline of the book is predicted with the boundaries of the outline lying beyond the frame.

In the next section, let's learn how to warp the image in order to make it look closer to the original one.

Warping the image

We can also do the opposite of homography estimation/transformation by going from the probed scenery to the training pattern coordinates. This makes it possible for the book cover to be brought onto the frontal plane as if we were looking at it directly from above. To achieve this, we can simply take the inverse of the homography matrix to get the inverse transformation:

```
Hinv = cv2.linalg.inverse(H)
```

However, this would map the top-left corner of the book cover to the origin of our new image, which would cut off everything to the left of and above the book cover. Instead, we want to roughly center the book cover in the new image. Thus, we need to calculate a new homography matrix.

The book cover should be roughly half of the size of the new image. Hence, instead of using the point coordinates of the train image, the following method demonstrates how to transform the point coordinates such that they appear in the center of the new image:

1. First, find the scaling factor and bias and then, apply the linear scaling and transform the coordinates:

```
@staticmethod
def scale_and_offset(points: Sequence[Point],
                     source_size: Tuple[int, int],
                     dst_size: Tuple[int, int],
                     factor: float = 0.5) -> List[Point]:
    dst_size = np.array(dst_size)
    scale = 1 / np.array(source_size) * dst_size * factor
    bias = dst_size * (1 - factor) / 2
    return [tuple(np.array(pt) * scale + bias) for pt in points]
```

2. As an output, we want an image that has the same shape as the pattern image (`sh_query`):

```
train_points_scaled = self.scale_and_offset(
    train_points, self.sh_train, sh_query)
```

3. Then, we can find the homography matrix between the points in the query image and the transformed points of the train image (make sure that the list is converted to a NumPy array):

```
Hinv, _ = cv2.findHomography(
    np.array(query_points), np.array(train_points_scaled),
cv2.RANSAC)
```

4. After that, we can use the homography matrix to transform every pixel in the image (this is also called warping the image):

```
img_warp = cv2.warpPerspective(img_query, Hinv, (sh_query[1],
sh_query[0]))
```

The result looks like this (with the matching on the left and the warped image on the right):

The image that results from the perspective transformation might not be perfectly aligned with the `frontoparallel` plane, because, after all, the homography matrix just gives an approximation. In most cases, however, our approach works just fine, such as in the example shown in the following screenshot:

Now that we have a pretty good picture about how feature extraction and matching is accomplished with a couple of images, let's move on to the completion of our app and learn how we can track the features in the next section.

Learning feature tracking

Now that our algorithm works for single frames, we want to make sure that the image found in one frame will also be found in the very next frame.

In `FeatureMatching.__init__`, we created some bookkeeping variables that we said we would use for feature tracking. The main idea is to enforce some coherence while going from one frame to the next. Since we are capturing roughly 10 frames per second, it is reasonable to assume that the changes from one frame to the next will not be too radical.

Therefore, we can be sure that the result we get in any given frame has to be similar to the result we got in the previous frame. Otherwise, we discard the result and move on to the next frame.

However, we have to be careful not to get stuck with a result that we think is reasonable but is actually an outlier. To solve this problem, we keep track of the number of frames we have spent without finding a suitable result. We use `self.num_frames_no_success` to hold the value of the number of frames. If this value is smaller than a certain threshold, let's say `self.max_frames_no_success`, we do the comparison between the frames.

If it is greater than the threshold, we assume that too much time has passed since the last result was obtained, in which case it would be unreasonable to compare the results between the frames. Let's learn about early outlier detection and rejection in the next section.

Understanding early outlier detection and rejection

We can extend the idea of outlier rejection to every step in the computation. The goal then becomes minimizing the workload while maximizing the likelihood that the result we obtain is a good one.

The resulting procedure for early outlier detection and rejection is embedded in the `FeatureMatching.match` method. This method first converts the image to grayscale and stores its shape:

```
def match(self, frame):
    # create a working copy (grayscale) of the frame
    # and store its shape for convenience
    img_query = cv2.cvtColor(frame, cv2.COLOR_BGR2GRAY)
    sh_query = img_query.shape # rows,cols
```

Then, if the outlier is detected during any step of the computation, we raise an `Outlier` exception to terminate the computation. The following steps show us the matching procedure:

1. First, we find good matches between the feature descriptors of the pattern and the query image, and then store the corresponding point coordinates from the train and query images:

    ```
    key_query, desc_query = self.f_extractor.detectAndCompute(
        img_query, None)
    good_matches = self.match_features(desc_query)
    train_points = [self.key_train[good_match.queryIdx].pt
                    for good_match in good_matches]
    query_points = [key_query[good_match.trainIdx].pt
                    for good_match in good_matches]
    ```

In order for RANSAC to work in the very next step, we need at least four matches. If fewer matches are found, we admit defeat and raise an `Outlier` exception with a custom message. We wrap the outlier detection in a `try` block:

```
try:
    # early outlier detection and rejection
    if len(good_matches) < 4:
        raise Outlier("Too few matches")
```

2. Then, we find the corner points of the pattern in the query image (`dst_corners`):

```
dst_corners = detect_corner_points(
    train_points, query_points, self.sh_train)
```

If any of these points lie significantly outside the image (by 20 pixels, in our case), it means that either we are not looking at our object of interest, or the object of interest is not entirely in the image. In both cases, we don't have to proceed, and raise or create an instance of `Outlier`:

```
if np.any((dst_corners < -20) | (dst_corners > np.array(sh_query) +
20)):
    raise Outlier("Out of image")
```

3. If the four recovered corner points do not span a reasonable quadrilateral (a polygon with four sides), it means that we are probably not looking at our object of interest. The area of a quadrilateral can be calculated with the following code:

```
for prev, nxt in zip(dst_corners, np.roll(
        dst_corners, -1, axis=0)):
    area += (prev[0] * nxt[1] - prev[1] * nxt[0]) / 2.
```

If the area is either unreasonably small or unreasonably large, we discard the frame and raise an exception:

```
if not np.prod(sh_query) / 16. < area < np.prod(sh_query) / 2.:
    raise Outlier("Area is unreasonably small or large")
```

4. Then, we scale the good points of the train image and find the homography matrix to bring the object to the frontal panel:

```
train_points_scaled = self.scale_and_offset(
    train_points, self.sh_train, sh_query)
Hinv, _ = cv2.findHomography(
    np.array(query_points), np.array(train_points_scaled),
cv2.RANSAC)
```

5. If the recovered homography matrix is too different from the one that we last recovered (self.last_hinv), it means that we are probably looking at a different object. However, we only want to consider self.last_hinv if it is fairly recent, say, from within the last self.max_frames_no_success frames:

```
similar = np.linalg.norm(
Hinv - self.last_hinv) < self.max_error_hinv
recent = self.num_frames_no_success < self.max_frames_no_success
if recent and not similar:
  raise Outlier("Not similar transformation")
```

This will help us to keep track of the same object of interest over time. If, for any reason, we lose track of the pattern image for more than self.max_frames_no_success frames, we skip this condition and accept whatever homography matrix was recovered up to that point. This ensures that we do not get stuck with a self.last_hinv matrix, which is actually an outlier.

If we detect an outlier during the outlier detection process, we increaseself.num_frame_no_success and return False. We might also want to print a message of the outlier in order to see when exactly it appears:

```
except Outlier as e:
    print(f"Outlier:{e}")
    self.num_frames_no_success += 1
    return False, None, None
```

Otherwise, if the outlier was not detected, we can be fairly certain that we have successfully located the object of interest in the current frame. In this case, we first store the homography matrix and reset the counter:

```
else:
    # reset counters and update Hinv
    self.num_frames_no_success = 0
    self.last_h = Hinv
```

The following lines show the warping of the image for illustration:

```
img_warped = cv2.warpPerspective(
    img_query, Hinv, (sh_query[1], sh_query[0]))
```

And finally, we draw good matches and corner points, as we did previously, and return the results:

```
img_flann = draw_good_matches(
    self.img_obj,
    self.key_train,
    img_query,
    key_query,
    good_matches)
# adjust x-coordinate (col) of corner points so that they can be drawn
# next to the train image (add self.sh_train[1])
dst_corners[:, 0] += self.sh_train[1]
cv2.polylines(
    img_flann,
    [dst_corners.astype(np.int)],
    isClosed=True,
    color=(0,255,0),
    thickness=3)
return True, img_warped, img_flann
```

In the preceding code, as explained previously, we shifted the *x* coordinate of the corners by the width of the train image because the query image appears next to the train image, and we changed the data type of the corners to integers because the `polilines` method accepts integers as coordinates.

In the next section, we'll explore how the algorithm works.

Seeing the algorithm in action

The result of the matching procedure in a live stream from a laptop's webcam looks like this:

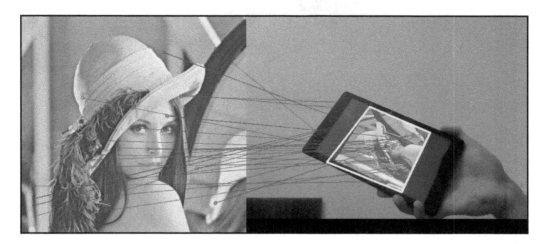

As you can see, most of the keypoints in the pattern image were matched correctly with their counterparts in the query image on the right. The printout of the pattern can now be slowly moved around, tilted, and turned. As long as all the corner points stay in the current frame, the homography matrix is updated accordingly and the outline of the pattern image is drawn correctly.

This works even if the printout is upside down, as shown here:

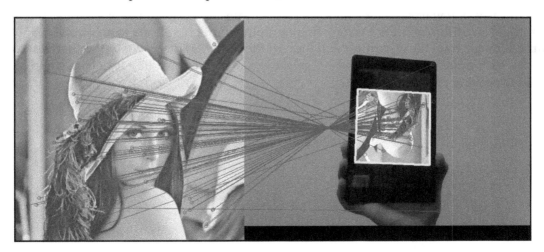

In all cases, the warped image brings the pattern image to an upright, centered position on the `frontoparallel` plane. This creates a cool effect of having the pattern image frozen in place in the center of the screen, while the surroundings twist and turn around it, like this:

In most cases, the warped image looks fairly accurate, as shown in the one earlier. If for any reason the algorithm accepts a wrong homography matrix that leads to an unreasonably warped image, then the algorithm will discard the outlier and recover within half a second (that is, within the `self.max_frames_no_success` frames), leading to accurate and efficient tracking throughout.

Summary

This chapter looked at a robust feature tracking method that is fast enough to run in real time when applied to the live stream of a webcam.

First, the algorithm shows you how to extract and detect important features in an image, which was independent of perspective and size, be it in a template of our object of interest (train image) or a more complex scene in which we expect the object of interest to be embedded (query image).

A match between feature points in the two images is then found by clustering the keypoints using a fast version of the nearest-neighbor algorithm. From there on, it is possible to calculate a perspective transformation that maps one set of feature points to the other. With this information, we can outline the train image as found in the query image and warp the query image so that the object of interest appears upright in the center of the screen.

With this in hand, we now have a good starting point for designing a cutting-edge feature tracking, image stitching, or augmented-reality application.

In the next chapter, we will continue studying the geometrical features of a scene, but, this time, we will be concentrating on the motion. Specifically, we will study how to reconstruct a scene in 3D by inferring its geometrical features from camera motion. For this, we will have to combine our knowledge of feature matching with the optic flow and structure-from-motion techniques.

Attributions

4
3D Scene Reconstruction Using Structure from Motion

In the previous chapter, you learned how to detect and track an object of interest in the video stream of a webcam, even if the object is viewed from different angles or distances, or under partial occlusion. Here, we will take the tracking of interesting features a step further and see what we can learn about the entire visual scene by studying similarities between image frames.

The goal of this chapter is to study how to reconstruct a scene in 3D by inferring the geometrical features of the scene from camera motion. This technique is sometimes referred to as **structure from motion**. By looking at the same scene from different angles, we will be able to infer the real-world 3D coordinates of different features in the scene. This process is known as **triangulation**, which allows us to **reconstruct** the scene as a **3D point cloud**.

If we take two pictures of the same scene from different angles, we can use **feature matching** or **optic flow** to estimate any translational and rotational movement that the camera underwent between taking the two pictures. However, in order for this to work, we will first have to calibrate our camera.

In this chapter, we will cover the following topics:

- Learning about camera calibration
- Setting up the app
- Estimating the camera motion from a pair of images
- Reconstructing the scene
- Understanding 3D point cloud visualization
- Learning about structure from motion

Once you complete the app, you will understand the classical approaches that are used to make a 3D reconstruction of a scene or object given several images taken from different view points. You will be able to apply these approaches in your own apps related to constructing 3D models from camera images or videos.

Getting started

This chapter has been tested with **OpenCV 4.1.0** and **wxPython 4.0.4** (http://www.wxpython.org/download.php). It also requires NumPy (http://www.numpy.org) and Matplotlib (http://www.matplotlib.org/downloads.html).

Note that you may have to obtain the so-called *extra* modules from https://github.com/Itseez/opencv_contrib and install OpenCV with the OPENCV_EXTRA_MODULES_PATH variable set in order to install **scale-invariant feature transform** (**SIFT**). Also, note that you may have to obtain a license to use SIFT in commercial applications.

You can find the code that we present in this chapter in our GitHub repository, https://github.com/PacktPublishing/OpenCV-4-with-Python-Blueprints-Second-Edition/tree/master/chapter4.

Planning the app

The final app will extract and visualize structure from motion on a pair of images. We will assume that these two images have been taken with the same camera, whose internal camera parameters we know. If these parameters are not known, they need to be estimated first in a camera calibration process.

The final app will then consist of the following modules and scripts:

- chapter4.main: This is the main function routine for starting the application.
- scene3D.SceneReconstruction3D: This is a class that contains a range of functionalities for calculating and visualizing structure from motion. It includes the following public methods:
    - __init__: This constructor will accept the intrinsic camera matrix and the distortion coefficients.
    - load_image_pair: This is a method used to load two images that have been taken with the camera described earlier from the file.

- `plot_optic_flow`: This is a method used to visualize the optic flow between the two image frames.
- `draw_epipolar_lines`: This method is used to draw the epipolar lines of the two images.
- `plot_rectified_images`: This method is used to plot a rectified version of the two images.
- `plot_point_cloud`: This is a method used to visualize the recovered real-world coordinates of the scene as a 3D point cloud. In order to arrive at a 3D point cloud, we will need to exploit epipolar geometry. However, epipolar geometry assumes the pinhole camera model, which no real camera follows.

The complete procedure of the app involves the following steps:

1. **Camera calibration**: We will use a chessboard pattern to extract the intrinsic camera matrix as well as the distortion coefficients, which are important for performing the scene reconstruction.
2. **Feature matching**: We will match points in two 2D images of the same visual scene, either via SIFT or via optic flow, as seen in the following screenshot:

3. **Image rectification**: By estimating the camera motion from a pair of images, we will extract the **essential matrix** and rectify the images, as shown in the following screenshot:

4. **Triangulation**: We will reconstruct the 3D real-world coordinates of the image points by making use of constraints from **epipolar geometry**.

5. **3D point cloud visualization**: Finally, we will visualize the recovered 3D structure of the scene using scatterplots in Matplotlib, which is most compelling when studied using the **Pan axes** button from pyplot. This button lets you rotate and scale the point cloud in all three dimensions. In the following screenshot, the color corresponds to the depth of a point in the scene:

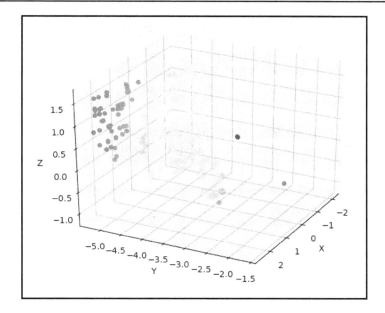

First, we need to rectify our images to make them look as if they have come from a pinhole camera. For that, we need to estimate the parameters of the camera, which leads us to the field of camera calibration.

Learning about camera calibration

So far, we have worked with whatever image came straight out of our webcam, without questioning the way in which it was taken. However, every camera lens has unique parameters, such as focal length, principal point, and lens distortion.

What happens behind the covers when a camera takes a picture is this: light falls through a lens, followed by an aperture, before falling on the surface of a light sensor. This process can be approximated with the pinhole camera model. The process of estimating the parameters of a real-world lens such that it would fit the pinhole camera model is called camera calibration (or **camera resectioning**, and it should not be confused with *photometric* camera calibration). So, let's start by learning about the pinhole camera model in the next section.

Understanding the pinhole camera model

The **pinhole camera model** is a simplification of a real camera in which there is no lens and the camera aperture is approximated by a single point (the pinhole). The formulas described here also hold exactly for a camera with a thin lens as well as describing the main parameters of any usual camera.

When viewing a real-world 3D scene (such as a tree), light rays pass through the point-sized aperture, and fall on a 2D image plane inside the camera, as seen in the following diagram:

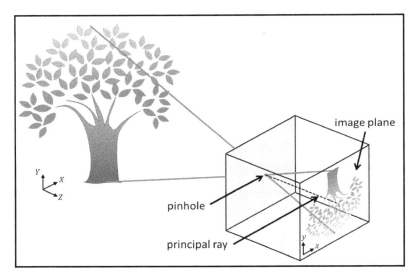

In this model, a 3D point with coordinates (X, Y, Z) is mapped to a 2D point with coordinates (x, y) that lies on the image plane. Note that this leads to the tree appearing upside down on the image plane.

The line that is perpendicular to the image plane and passes through the pinhole is called the **principal ray**, and its length is called the **focal length**. The focal length is a part of the internal camera parameters, as it may vary depending on the camera being used. In a simple camera with a lens, the **pinhole** is replaced with a lens and the focal plane is placed at the focal length of the lens in order to avoid blurring as much as possible.

Hartley and Zisserman found a mathematical formula to describe how a 2D point with coordinates (x, y) can be inferred from a 3D point with coordinates (X, Y, Z) and the camera's intrinsic parameters, as follows:

$$\begin{bmatrix} x \\ y \\ w \end{bmatrix} \begin{bmatrix} f_x & 0 & c_x \\ 0 & f_y & c_y \\ 0 & 0 & 1 \end{bmatrix} = \begin{bmatrix} X \\ Y \\ Z \end{bmatrix}$$

The 3 x 3 matrix in the preceding formula is the **intrinsic camera matrix**—a matrix that compactly describes all internal camera parameters. The matrix comprises focal lengths (f_x and f_y) and optical centers c_x and c_y, which in the case of digital imaging are simply expressed in pixel coordinates. As mentioned earlier, the focal length is the distance between the pinhole and the image plane.

A pinhole camera has only one focal length, in which case, $f_x = f_x = f_x$. However, in real cameras, these two values might differ, for example, due to imperfections of lenses, imperfections of the focal plane (which is represented by a digital camera sensor), or imperfections of assembly. The difference can be also intentional for some purpose, which can be achieved by simply involving a lens that has different curvature in different directions. The point at which the principal ray intersects the image plane is called the **principal point**, and its relative position on the image plane is captured by the optical center (or principal point offset).

In addition, a camera might be subject to radial or tangential distortion, leading to a **fish-eye effect**. This is because of hardware imperfections and lens misalignments. These distortions can be described with a list of the **distortion coefficients**. Sometimes, radial distortions are actually a desired artistic effect. At other times, they need to be corrected.

 For more information on the pinhole camera model, there are many good tutorials out there on the web, such as http://ksimek.github.io/2013/08/13/intrinsic.

Because these parameters are specific to the camera hardware (hence the name *intrinsic*), we need to calculate them only once in the lifetime of a camera. This is called **camera calibration**.

Next, we will cover the parameters of the intrinsic camera.

Estimating the intrinsic camera parameters

In OpenCV, camera calibration is fairly straightforward. The official documentation provides a good overview of the topic and some sample C++ scripts at `http://docs.opencv.org/doc/tutorials/calib3d/camera_calibration/camera_calibration.html`.

For educational purposes, we will develop our own calibration script in Python. We will need to present a special pattern image, with known geometry (chessboard plate or black circles on a white background), to the camera we wish to calibrate.

Because we know the geometry of the pattern image, we can use feature detection to study the properties of the internal camera matrix. For example, if the camera suffers from undesired radial distortion, the different corners of the chessboard pattern will appear distorted in the image and not lie on a rectangular grid. By taking about 10-20 snapshots of the chessboard pattern from different points of view, we can collect enough information to correctly infer the camera matrix and the distortion coefficients.

For this, we will use the `calibrate.py` script, which first imports the following modules:

```
import cv2
import numpy as np
import wx

from wx_gui import BaseLayout
```

Analogous to previous chapters, we will use a simple layout based on `BaseLayout` that embeds processing of the webcam video stream.

The `main` function of the script will generate the GUI and execute the `main` loop of the app:

```
def main():
```

The latter is accomplished with the following steps in the body of the function:

1. First, connect to the camera and set standard VGA resolution:

```
capture = cv2.VideoCapture(0)
assert capture.isOpened(), "Can not connect to camera"
capture.set(cv2.CAP_PROP_FRAME_WIDTH, 640)
capture.set(cv2.CAP_PROP_FRAME_HEIGHT, 480)
```

2. Similarly to the previous chapters, create a `wx` application and the `layout` class, which we will compose later in this section:

```
app = wx.App()
layout = CameraCalibration(capture, title='Camera Calibration',
fps=2)
```

3. Show the GUI and execute the `MainLoop` of the `app`:

```
layout.Show(True)
app.MainLoop()
```

In the next section, we'll prepare the camera calibration GUI, which we used in the `main` function.

Defining the camera calibration GUI

The GUI is a customized version of the generic `BaseLayout`:

```
class CameraCalibration(BaseLayout):
```

The layout consists of only the current camera frame and a single button below it. This button allows us to start the calibration process:

```
def augment_layout(self):
    pnl = wx.Panel(self, -1)
    self.button_calibrate = wx.Button(pnl, label='Calibrate Camera')
    self.Bind(wx.EVT_BUTTON, self._on_button_calibrate)
    hbox = wx.BoxSizer(wx.HORIZONTAL)
    hbox.Add(self.button_calibrate)
    pnl.SetSizer(hbox)
```

For these changes to take effect, `pnl` needs to be added to the list of existing panels:

```
self.panels_vertical.Add(pnl, flag=wx.EXPAND | wx.BOTTOM | wx.TOP,
                         border=1)
```

The rest of the visualization pipeline is handled by the `BaseLayout` class. We only need to make sure that we initialize the required variables and provide `process_frame` methods.

Now that we have defined a GUI for camera calibration, let's initialize a camera calibration algorithm in the next section.

Initializing the algorithm

In order to perform the calibration process, we need to do some bookkeeping. We will do that by following the next steps:

1. For now, let's focus on a single 10 x 7 chessboard. The algorithm will detect all the 9 x 6 inner corners of the chessboard (referred to as *object points*) and store the detected image points of these corners in a list. So, let's first initialize the `chessboard_size` to the number of inner corners:

   ```
   self.chessboard_size = (9, 6)
   ```

2. Next, we need to enumerate all the object points and assign them object point coordinates so that the first point has coordinates (0,0), the second one (top row) has coordinates (1,0), and the last one has coordinates (8,5):

   ```
   # prepare object points
   self.objp = np.zeros((np.prod(self.chessboard_size), 3),
                        dtype=np.float32)
   self.objp[:, :2] = np.mgrid[0:self.chessboard_size[0],
                              0:self.chessboard_size[1]]
                              .T.reshape(-1, 2)
   ```

3. We also need to keep track of whether we are currently recording the object and image points or not. We will initiate this process once the user clicks on the `self.button_calibrate` button. After that, the algorithm will try to detect a chessboard in all subsequent frames until `self.record_min_num_frames` chessboards have been detected:

   ```
   # prepare recording
   self.recording = False
   self.record_min_num_frames = 15
   self._reset_recording()
   ```

4. Whenever the `self.button_calibrate` button is clicked on, we reset all the bookkeeping variables, disable the button, and start recording:

   ```
   def _on_button_calibrate(self, event):
       """Enable recording mode upon pushing the button"""
       self.button_calibrate.Disable()
       self.recording = True
       self._reset_recording()
   ```

Resetting the bookkeeping variables involves clearing the lists of recorded object and image points (`self.obj_points` and `self.img_points`) as well as resetting the number of detected chessboards (`self.recordCnt`) to 0:

```
def _reset_recording(self):
    self.record_cnt = 0
    self.obj_points = []
    self.img_points = []
```

In the next section, we'll collect the image and object points.

Collecting image and object points

The `process_frame` method is responsible for doing the hard work of the calibration technique, and we will collect images and object points by using the following steps:

1. After the `self.button_calibrate` button has been clicked on, this method starts collecting data until a total of `self.record_min_num_frames` chessboards are detected:

```
def process_frame(self, frame):
    """Processes each frame"""
    # if we are not recording, just display the frame
    if not self.recording:
        return frame

    # else we're recording
    img_gray = cv2.cvtColor(frame, cv2.COLOR_BGR2GRAY)
            .astype(np.uint8)
    if self.record_cnt < self.record_min_num_frames:
        ret, corners = cv2.findChessboardCorners(
                        img_gray,
                        self.chessboard_size,
                        None)
```

The `cv2.findChessboardCorners` function will parse a grayscale image (`img_gray`) to find a chessboard of size `self.chessboard_size`. If the image indeed contains a chessboard, the function will return `true` (`ret`) as well as a list of chessboard corners (`corners`).

2. Then, drawing the chessboard is straightforward:

```
if ret:
        print(f"{self.record_min_num_frames -
self.record_cnt} chessboards remain")
        cv2.drawChessboardCorners(frame,
self.chessboard_size, corners, ret)
```

3. The result looks like this (drawing the chessboard corners in color for the effect):

We could now simply store the list of detected corners and move on to the next frame. However, in order to make the calibration as accurate as possible, OpenCV provides a function to refine the corner point measurement:

```
criteria = (cv2.TERM_CRITERIA_EPS + cv2.TERM_CRITERIA_MAX_ITER,
            30, 0.01)
cv2.cornerSubPix(img_gray, corners, (9, 9), (-1, -1), criteria)
```

This will refine the coordinates of the detected corners to subpixel precision. Now we are ready to append the object and image points to the list and advance the frame counter:

```
self.obj_points.append(self.objp)
self.img_points.append(corners)
self.record_cnt += 1
```

In the next section, let's learn how to find the camera matrix, which will be required to accomplish an appropriate 3D reconstruction.

Finding the camera matrix

Once we have collected enough data (that is, once `self.record_cnt` reaches the value of `self.record_min_num_frames`), the algorithm is ready to perform the calibration. This process can be performed with a single call to `cv2.calibrateCamera`:

```
else:
    print("Calibrating...")
    ret, K, dist, rvecs, tvecs = cv2.calibrateCamera(self.obj_points,
                                                     self.img_points,
                                                     (self.imgHeight,
                                                      self.imgWidth),
                                                     None, None)
```

The function returns `true` on success (`ret`), the intrinsic camera matrix (`K`), the distortion coefficients (`dist`), as well as two rotation and translation matrices (`rvecs` and `tvecs`). For now, we are mainly interested in the camera matrix and the distortion coefficients, because these will allow us to compensate for any imperfections of the internal camera hardware.

We will simply `print` them on the console for easy inspection:

```
print("K=", K)
print("dist=", dist)
```

For example, the calibration of my laptop's webcam recovered the following values:

```
K= [[ 3.36696445e+03 0.00000000e+00 2.99109943e+02]
    [ 0.00000000e+00 3.29683922e+03 2.69436829e+02]
    [ 0.00000000e+00 0.00000000e+00 1.00000000e+00]]
dist= [[ 9.87991355e-01 -3.18446968e+02 9.56790602e-02
        -3.42530800e-02 4.87489304e+03]]
```

This tells us that the focal lengths of my webcam are `fx=3366.9644` pixels and `fy=3296.8392` pixels, with the optical center at `cx=299.1099` pixels and `cy=269.4368` pixels.

A good idea might be to double-check the accuracy of the calibration process. This can be done by projecting the object points onto the image using the recovered camera parameters so that we can compare them with the list of image points we collected with the `cv2.findChessboardCorners` function. If the two points are roughly the same, we know that the calibration was successful. Even better, we can calculate the `mean error` of the reconstruction by projecting every object point in the list:

```
mean_error = 0
for obj_point, rvec, tvec, img_point in zip(
        self.obj_points, rvecs, tvecs, self.img_points):
```

```
img_points2, _ = cv2.projectPoints(
    obj_point, rvec, tvec, K, dist)
error = cv2.norm(img_point, img_points2,
                cv2.NORM_L2) / len(img_points2)
mean_error += error

print("mean error=", mean_error)
```

Performing this check on my laptop's webcam resulted in a mean error of 0.95 pixels, which is fairly close to 0.

With the internal camera parameters recovered, we can now set out to take beautiful, undistorted pictures of the world, possibly from different viewpoints so that we can extract some structure from motion. First, let's see how to set up our app.

Setting up the app

Going forward, we will be using a famous open source dataset called `fountain-P11`. It depicts a Swiss fountain viewed from various angles:

The dataset consists of 11 high-resolution images and can be downloaded from `https://icwww.epfl.ch/multiview/denseMVS.html`. Had we taken the pictures ourselves, we would have had to go through the entire camera calibration procedure to recover the intrinsic camera matrix and the distortion coefficients. Luckily, these parameters are known for the camera that took the fountain dataset, so we can go ahead and hardcode these values in our code.

Let's prepare the `main` routine function in the next section.

Understanding the main routine function

Our `main` routine function will consist of creating and interacting with an instance of the `SceneReconstruction3D` class. This code can be found in the `chapter4.py` file. The dependencies of the module are `numpy` and the class itself, which are imported as follows:

```
import numpy as np

from scene3D import SceneReconstruction3D
```

Next, we define the `main` function:

```
def main():
```

The function consists of the following steps:

1. We define the intrinsic camera matrix for the camera that took photos of the fountain dataset (`K`) and set distortion coefficients (`d`):

```
K = np.array([[2759.48 / 4, 0, 1520.69 / 4, 0, 2764.16 / 4,
              1006.81 / 4, 0, 0, 1]]).reshape(3, 3)
d = np.array([0.0, 0.0, 0.0, 0.0, 0.0]).reshape(1, 5)
```

According to the photographer, these images are already distortion-free, so we have set all the distortion coefficients to 0.

Note that if you want to run the code presented in this chapter on a dataset other than `fountain-P11`, you will have to adjust the intrinsic camera matrix and the distortion coefficients.

2. Next, we create an instance of the `SceneReconstruction3D` class and load a pair of images, which we would like to apply to our structure-from-motion techniques. The dataset is downloaded into a subdirectory called `fountain_dense`:

```
scene = SceneReconstruction3D(K, d)
scene.load_image_pair("fountain_dense/0004.png",
    "fountain_dense/0005.png")
```

3. Now we are ready to call methods from the class that perform various computations:

```
scene.plot_rectified_images()
scene.plot_optic_flow()
scene.plot_point_cloud()
```

We will implement these methods throughout the rest of the chapter, and they will be explained in detail in the upcoming sections.

So now that we have prepared the main script of the app, let's start implementing the `SceneReconstruction3D` class, which does all the heavy lifting and incorporates the computations for 3D reconstruction.

Implementing the SceneReconstruction3D class

All of the relevant 3D scene reconstruction code for this chapter can be found as part of the `SceneReconstruction3D` class in the `scene3D` module. Upon instantiation, the class stores the intrinsic camera parameters to be used in all subsequent calculations:

```
import cv2
import numpy as np
import sys

from mpl_toolkits.mplot3d import Axes3D
import matplotlib.pyplot as plt
from matplotlib import cm

class SceneReconstruction3D:
    def __init__(self, K, dist):
        self.K = K
        self.K_inv = np.linalg.inv(K)
        self.d = dist
```

Then, we need to load a pair of images on which to operate.

In order to do it, first, we create a static method that will load an image and convert it to an RGB format if it is grayscale, as other methods expect a three-channel image. In the case of the fountain sequence, all images are of a relatively high resolution. If an optional `downscale` flag is set, the method will downscale the image to a width of roughly 600 pixels:

```
@staticmethod
def load_image(
        img_path: str,
        use_pyr_down: bool,
        target_width: int = 600) -> np.ndarray:

    img = cv2.imread(img_path, cv2.CV_8UC3)
    # make sure image is valid
    assert img is not None, f"Image {img_path} could not be loaded."
    if len(img.shape) == 2:
        img = cv2.cvtColor(img, cv2.COLOR_GRAY2BGR)

    while use_pyr_down and img.shape[1] > 2 * target_width:
        img = cv2.pyrDown(img)
    return img
```

Next, we create a method that loads a pair of images and compensates them for the radial and tangential lens distortions using the distortion coefficients specified earlier (if there are any):

```
def load_image_pair(
        self,
        img_path1: str,
        img_path2: str,
        use_pyr_down: bool = True) -> None:

    self.img1, self.img2 = [cv2.undistort(self.load_image(path,
use_pyr_down),
                                          self.K, self.d)
            for path in (img_path1, img_path2)]
```

Finally, we are ready to move on to the heart of the project—estimating the camera motion and reconstructing the scene!

Estimating the camera motion from a pair of images

Now that we have loaded two images (`self.img1` and `self.img2`) of the same scene, such as two examples from the fountain dataset, we find ourselves in a similar situation as in the previous chapter. We are given two images that supposedly show the same rigid object or static scene but from different viewpoints.

However, this time we want to go a step further—if the only thing that changes between taking the two pictures is the location of the camera, can we infer the relative camera motion by looking at the matching features?

Well, of course we can. Otherwise, this chapter would not make much sense, would it? We will take the location and orientation of the camera in the first image as a given and then find out how much we have to reorient and relocate the camera so that its viewpoint matches that from the second image.

In other words, we need to recover the **essential matrix** of the camera in the second image. An essential matrix is a 4 x 3 matrix that is the concatenation of a 3 x 3 rotation matrix and a 3 x 1 translation matrix. It is often denoted by *[R | t]*. You can think of it as capturing the position and orientation of the camera in the second image relative to the camera in the first image.

The crucial step in recovering the essential matrix (as well as all other transformations in this chapter) is feature matching. We can either apply the SIFT detector to the two images or calculate the optic flow between the two images. The user may choose their favorite method by specifying a feature extraction mode, which will be implemented by the following private method:

```
def _extract_keypoints(self, feat_mode):
    # extract features
    if feat_mode.lower() == "sift":
        # feature matching via sift and BFMatcher
        self._extract_keypoints_sift()
    elif feat_mode.lower() == "flow":
        # feature matching via optic flow
        self._extract_keypoints_flow()
    else:
        sys.exit(f"Unknown feat_mode {feat_mode}. Use 'SIFT' or
                'FLOW'")
```

Let's learn how to perform point matching using rich feature descriptors in the next section.

Applying point matching with rich feature descriptors

A robust way of extracting important features from an image is by using the SIFT detector. In this chapter, we want to use it for two images, `self.img1` and `self.img2`:

```
def _extract_keypoints_sift(self):
    # extract keypoints and descriptors from both images
    detector = cv2.xfeatures2d.SIFT_create()
    first_key_points, first_desc = detector.detectAndCompute(self.img1,
                                                             None)
    second_key_points, second_desc =
detector.detectAndCompute(self.img2,
                                                             None)
```

For feature matching, we will use a `BruteForce` matcher, so that other matchers (such as **FLANN**) can work as well:

```
matcher = cv2.BFMatcher(cv2.NORM_L1, True)
matches = matcher.match(first_desc, second_desc)
```

For each of the `matches`, we need to recover the corresponding image coordinates. These are maintained in the `self.match_pts1` and `self.match_pts2` lists:

```
# generate lists of point correspondences
self.match_pts1 = np.array(
    [first_key_points[match.queryIdx].pt for match in matches])
self.match_pts2 = np.array(
    [second_key_points[match.trainIdx].pt for match in matches])
```

The following screenshot shows an example of the feature matcher applied to two arbitrary frames of the fountain sequence:

In the next section, we'll learn about point matching using optic flow.

Using point matching with optic flow

An alternative to using rich features is using optic flow. Optic flow is the process of estimating motion between two consecutive image frames by calculating a displacement vector. A displacement vector can be calculated for every pixel in the image (dense) or only for selected points (sparse).

One of the most commonly used techniques for calculating dense optic flow is the Lukas-Kanade method. It can be implemented in OpenCV with a single line of code, by using the `cv2.calcOpticalFlowPyrLK` function.

But before that, we need to select some points in the image that are worth tracking. Again, this is a question of feature selection. If we are interested in getting an exact result for only a few highly salient image points, we can use Shi-Tomasi's `cv2.goodFeaturesToTrack` function. This function might recover features like this:

However, in order to infer structure from motion, we might need many more features and not just the most salient Harris corners. An alternative would be to detect the **Features from Accelerated Segment Test (FAST)** features:

```
def _extract_keypoints_flow(self):
    fast = cv2.FastFeatureDetector()
    first_key_points = fast.detect(self.img1, None)
```

We can then calculate the optic flow for these features. In other words, we want to find the points in the second image that most likely correspond to the `first_key_points` from the first image. For this, we need to convert the keypoint list into a NumPy array of (*x*, *y*) coordinates:

```
first_key_list = [i.pt for i in first_key_points]
first_key_arr = np.array(first_key_list).astype(np.float32)
```

Then the optic flow will return a list of corresponding features in the second image (`second_key_arr`):

```
second_key_arr, status, err =
    cv2.calcOpticalFlowPyrLK(self.img1, self.img2,
        first_key_arr)
```

The function also returns a vector of status bits (`status`), which indicate whether the flow for a keypoint has been found or not, and a vector of estimated error values (`err`). If we were to ignore these two additional vectors, the recovered flow field could look something like this:

In this image, an arrow is drawn for each keypoint, starting at the location of the keypoint in the first image and pointing to the location of the same keypoint in the second image. By inspecting the flow image, we can see that the camera moved mostly to the right, but there also seems to be a rotational component.

However, some of these arrows are really large, and some of them make no sense. For example, it is very unlikely that a pixel in the bottom-right image corner actually moved all the way to the top of the image. It is much more likely that the flow calculation for this particular keypoint is wrong. Thus, we want to exclude all the keypoints for which the status bit is 0 or the estimated error is larger than a certain value:

```
condition = (status == 1) * (err < 5.)
concat = np.concatenate((condition, condition), axis=1)
first_match_points = first_key_arr[concat].reshape(-1, 2)
second_match_points = second_key_arr[concat].reshape(-1, 2)

self.match_pts1 = first_match_points
self.match_pts2 = second_match_points
```

If we draw the flow field again with a limited set of keypoints, the image will look like this:

The flow field can be drawn with the following public method, which first extracts the keypoints using the preceding code and then draws the actual arrows on the image:

```
def plot_optic_flow(self):
    self._extract_keypoints_flow()

    img = np.copy(self.img1)
    for pt1, pt2 in zip(self.match_pts1, self.match_pts2):
        cv2.arrowedLine(img, tuple(pt1), tuple(pt2),
                color=(255, 0, 0))

    cv2.imshow("imgFlow", img)
    cv2.waitKey()
```

The advantage of using optic flow instead of rich features is that the process is usually faster and can accommodate the matching of many more points, making the reconstruction denser.

The caveat in working with the optic flow is that it works best for consecutive images taken by the same hardware, whereas rich features are mostly agnostic to this.

Let's learn how to find the camera matrices in the next section.

Finding the camera matrices

Now that we have obtained the matches between keypoints, we can calculate two important camera matrices—the fundamental matrix and the essential matrix. These matrices will specify the camera motion in terms of rotational and translational components. Obtaining the fundamental matrix (self.F) is another OpenCV one-liner:

```
def _find_fundamental_matrix(self):
    self.F, self.Fmask = cv2.findFundamentalMat(self.match_pts1,
            self.match_pts2, cv2.FM_RANSAC, 0.1, 0.99)
```

The only difference between fundamental_matrix and essential_matrix is that the latter operates on rectified images:

```
def _find_essential_matrix(self):
    self.E = self.K.T.dot(self.F).dot(self.K)
```

The essential matrix (`self.E`) can then be decomposed into rotational and translational components, denoted by *[R | t]*, using **singular value decomposition (SVD)**:

```
def _find_camera_matrices(self):
    U, S, Vt = np.linalg.svd(self.E)
    W = np.array([0.0, -1.0, 0.0, 1.0, 0.0, 0.0, 0.0, 0.0,
        1.0]).reshape(3, 3)
```

Using the unitary matrices *U* and *V* in combination with an additional matrix, *W*, we can now reconstruct *[R | t]*. However, it can be shown that this decomposition has four possible solutions and only one of them is the valid second camera matrix. The only thing we can do is check all four possible solutions and find the one that predicts that all the imaged keypoints lie in front of both cameras.

But prior to that, we need to convert the keypoints from 2D image coordinates to homogeneous coordinates. We achieve this by adding a *z* coordinate, which we set to 1:

```
first_inliers = []
second_inliers = []
for pt1,pt2, mask in
zip(self.match_pts1,self.match_pts2,self.Fmask):
    if mask:
        first_inliers.append(self.K_inv.dot([pt1[0], pt1[1], 1.0]))
        second_inliers.append(self.K_inv.dot([pt2[0], pt2[1],
            1.0]))
```

We then iterate over the four possible solutions and choose the one that has `_in_front_of_both_cameras` returning `True`:

```
R = T = None
for r in (U.dot(W).dot(Vt), U.dot(W.T).dot(Vt)):
    for t in (U[:, 2], -U[:, 2]):
        if self._in_front_of_both_cameras(
            first_inliers, second_inliers, r, t):
            R, T = r, t

assert R is not None, "Camera matricies were never found!"
```

Now, we can finally construct the *[R | t]* matrices of the two cameras. The first camera is simply a canonical camera (no translation and no rotation):

```
self.Rt1 = np.hstack((np.eye(3), np.zeros((3, 1))))
```

The second camera matrix consists of *[R | t]*, recovered earlier:

```
self.Rt2 = np.hstack((R, T.reshape(3, 1)))
```

The __InFrontOfBothCameras private method is a helper function that makes sure that every pair of keypoints is mapped to 3D coordinates that make them lie in front of both cameras:

```python
def _in_front_of_both_cameras(self, first_points, second_points, rot,
                              trans):
    """Determines whether point correspondences are in front of both
        images"""
    rot_inv = rot
    for first, second in zip(first_points, second_points):
        first_z = np.dot(rot[0, :] - second[0] * rot[2, :],
                         trans) / np.dot(rot[0, :] - second[0] * rot[2,
                         :],
                                         second)
        first_3d_point = np.array([first[0] * first_z,
                                   second[0] * first_z, first_z])
        second_3d_point = np.dot(rot.T, first_3d_point) - np.dot(rot.T,
                                                                 trans)
```

If the function finds any keypoint that is not in front of both cameras, it will return False:

```python
if first_3d_point[2] < 0 or second_3d_point[2] < 0:
    return False
return True
```

So now that we have found the camera matrices, let's rectify an image in the next section, which is a good means to validating whenever the recovered matrices are correct.

Applying image rectification

Maybe the easiest way to make sure that we have recovered the correct camera matrices is to rectify the images. If they are rectified correctly, then a point in the first image and a point in the second image that corresponds to the same 3D world point will lie on the same vertical coordinate.

In a more concrete example, such as in our case, since we know that the cameras are upright, we can verify that horizontal lines in the rectified image correspond to horizontal lines in the 3D scene. Thus, we follow these steps to rectify our image:

1. First, we perform all the steps described in the previous subsections to obtain the [R | t] matrix of the second camera:

```python
def plot_rectified_images(self, feat_mode="SIFT"):
    self._extract_keypoints(feat_mode)
    self._find_fundamental_matrix()
```

```
self._find_essential_matrix()
self._find_camera_matrices_rt()

R = self.Rt2[:, :3]
T = self.Rt2[:, 3]
```

2. Then, rectification can be performed with two OpenCV one-liners that remap the image coordinates to the rectified coordinates based on the camera matrix (self.K), the distortion coefficients (self.d), the rotational component of the essential matrix (R), and the translational component of the essential matrix (T):

```
R1, R2, P1, P2, Q, roi1, roi2 = cv2.stereoRectify(
    self.K, self.d, self.K, self.d,
    self.img1.shape[:2], R, T, alpha=1.0)
mapx1, mapy1 = cv2.initUndistortRectifyMap(
    self.K, self.d, R1, self.K, self.img1.shape[:2],
    cv2.CV_32F)
mapx2, mapy2 = cv2.initUndistortRectifyMap(
    self.K, self.d, R2, self.K,
    self.img2.shape[:2],
    cv2.CV_32F)
img_rect1 = cv2.remap(self.img1, mapx1, mapy1,
                      cv2.INTER_LINEAR)
img_rect2 = cv2.remap(self.img2, mapx2, mapy2,
                      cv2.INTER_LINEAR)
```

3. To make sure that the rectification is accurate, we plot the two rectified images (img_rect1 and img_rect2) next to each other:

```
total_size = (max(img_rect1.shape[0], img_rect2.shape[0]),
              img_rect1.shape[1] + img_rect2.shape[1], 3)
img = np.zeros(total_size, dtype=np.uint8)
img[:img_rect1.shape[0], :img_rect1.shape[1]] = img_rect1
img[:img_rect2.shape[0], img_rect1.shape[1]:] = img_rect2
```

4. We also draw horizontal blue lines after every 25 pixels, across the side-by-side images, to further help us visually investigate the rectification process:

```
for i in range(20, img.shape[0], 25):
    cv2.line(img, (0, i), (img.shape[1], i), (255, 0, 0))

cv2.imshow('imgRectified', img)
cv2.waitKey()
```

Now we can easily convince ourselves that the rectification was successful, as shown here:

Now that we have rectified our image, let's learn how to reconstruct the 3D scene in the next section.

Reconstructing the scene

Finally, we can reconstruct the 3D scene by making use of a process called **triangulation**. We are able to infer the 3D coordinates of a point because of the way **epipolar geometry** works. By calculating the essential matrix, we get to know more about the geometry of the visual scene than we might think. Because the two cameras depict the same real-world scene, we know that most of the 3D real-world points will be found in both images.

Moreover, we know that the mapping from the 2D image points to the corresponding 3D real-world points will follow the rules of geometry. If we study a sufficiently large number of image points, we can construct, and solve, a (large) system of linear equations to get the ground truth of the real-world coordinates.

Let's return to the Swiss fountain dataset. If we ask two photographers to take a picture of the fountain from different viewpoints at the same time, it is not hard to realize that the first photographer might show up in the picture of the second photographer, and vice versa. The point on the image plane where the other photographer is visible is called the **epipole** or **epipolar point**.

In more technical terms, the epipole is the point on one camera's image plane onto which the center of projection of the other camera projects. It is interesting to note that both the epipoles in their respective image planes, and both the centers of projection, lie on a single 3D line.

By looking at the lines between the epipoles and image points, we can limit the number of possible 3D coordinates of the image points. In fact, if the projection point is known, then the epipolar line (which is the line between the image point and the epipole) is known, and, in turn, the same point projected onto the second image must lie on that particular epipolar line. *Confusing?* I thought so.

Let's just look at these images:

Each line here is the epipolar line of a particular point in the image. Ideally, all the epipolar lines drawn in the left-hand image should intersect at a point, and that point typically lies outside the image. If the calculation is accurate, then that point should coincide with the location of the second camera as seen from the first camera.

In other words, the epipolar lines in the left-hand image tell us that the camera that took the right-hand image is located to our (that is, the first camera's) right-hand side. Analogously, the epipolar lines in the right-hand image tell us that the camera that took the image on the left is located to our (that is, the second camera's) left-hand side.

Moreover, for each point observed in one image, the same point must be observed in the other image on a known epipolar line. This is known as the **epipolar constraint**. We can use this fact to show that if two image points correspond to the same 3D point, then the projection lines of those two image points must intersect precisely at the 3D point. This means that the 3D point can be calculated from two image points, which is what we are going to do next.

Luckily, OpenCV again provides a wrapper to solve an extensive set of linear equations, which is done by following these steps:

1. First, we have to convert our list of matching feature points into a NumPy array:

   ```
   first_inliers = np.array(self.match_inliers1).reshape
       (-1, 3)[:, :2]second_inliers =
   np.array(self.match_inliers2).reshape
       (-1, 3)[:, :2]
   ```

2. **Triangulation** is performed next using the preceding two *[R | t]* matrices (`self.Rt1` for the first camera and `self.Rt2` for the second camera):

   ```
   pts4D = cv2.triangulatePoints(self.Rt1, self.Rt2, first_inliers.T,
       second_inliers.T).T
   ```

3. This will return the triangulated real-world points using 4D homogeneous coordinates. To convert them to 3D coordinates, we need to divide the (*X, Y, Z*) coordinates by the fourth coordinate, usually referred to as *W*:

   ```
   pts3D = pts4D[:, :3]/np.repeat(pts4D[:, 3], 3).reshape(-1, 3)
   ```

So now that we have obtained the points in the 3D space, let's visualize them in the next section to see how they look.

Understanding 3D point cloud visualization

The last step is visualizing the triangulated 3D real-world points. An easy way of creating 3D scatterplots is by using Matplotlib. However, if you are looking for more professional visualization tools, you may be interested in **Mayavi** (`http://docs.enthought.com/mayavi/mayavi`), **VisPy** (`http://vispy.org`), or the **Point Cloud Library** (`http://pointclouds.org`).

Although the last one does not have Python support for point cloud visualization yet, it is an excellent tool for point cloud segmentation, filtering, and sample consensus model fitting. For more information, head over to **Strawlab**'s GitHub repository at `https://github.com/strawlab/python-pcl`.

Before we can plot our 3D point cloud, we obviously have to extract the *[R | t]* matrix and perform the triangulation as explained earlier:

```
def plot_point_cloud(self, feat_mode="SIFT"):
    self._extract_keypoints(feat_mode)
    self._find_fundamental_matrix()
    self._find_essential_matrix()
    self._find_camera_matrices_rt()

    # triangulate points
    first_inliers = np.array(self.match_inliers1)[:, :2]
    second_inliers = np.array(self.match_inliers2)[:, :2]
    pts4D = cv2.triangulatePoints(self.Rt1, self.Rt2, first_inliers.T,
                                  second_inliers.T).T

    # convert from homogeneous coordinates to 3D
    pts3D = pts4D[:, :3] / pts4D[:, 3, None]
```

Then, all we need to do is open a Matplotlib figure and draw each entry of `pts3D` in a 3D scatterplot:

```
Xs, Zs, Ys = [pts3D[:, i] for i in range(3)]

fig = plt.figure()
ax = fig.add_subplot(111, projection='3d')
ax.scatter(Xs, Ys, Zs, c=Ys, cmap=cm.hsv, marker='o')
ax.set_xlabel('X')
ax.set_ylabel('Y')
ax.set_zlabel('Z')
plt.title('3D point cloud: Use pan axes button below to inspect')
plt.show()
```

The result is most compelling when studied using pyplot's `pan axes` button, which lets you rotate and scale the point cloud in all three dimensions. In the following screenshot, two projections are illustrated.

The first one is from the top and the second one is from some vertical angle from the left of the fountain. The color of a point corresponds to the depth of that point (*y* coordinate). Most of the points lie near a plane that makes an angle with the *XZ* plane (points from red to green). These points represent the wall behind the fountain. The other points (from yellow to blue) represent the rest of the structure of the fountain:

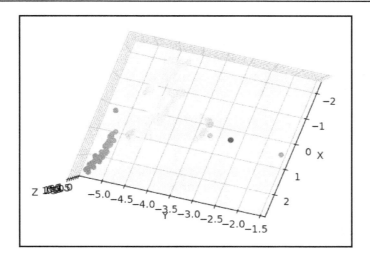

The projection from some vertical angle from the left of the fountain is shown in the following screenshot:

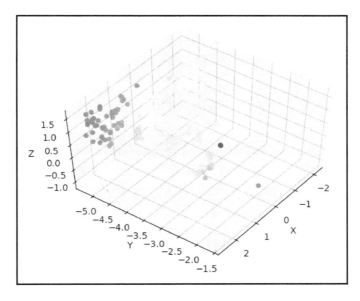

So now that you have completed your first app for 3D reconstruction, you have started to dive into a computer vision field called structure from motion. This is an intensively developing field. Let's understand what this field of research is trying to deal with within the next section.

Learning about structure from motion

So far in this chapter, we have gone through some math and we can reconstruct the depth of a scene based on a couple of images taken from different angles, which is a problem of reconstruction of a 3D structure from camera motion.

In computer vision, the process of reconstruction of 3D structures of the scene based on the sequence of images is usually referred to as **structure from motion**. A similar set of problems is the structure from stereo vision—in reconstruction from stereo vision, there are two cameras, located at a certain distance from each other and in structure from motion, there are different images taken from different angles and positions. *There's not much difference conceptually, right?*

Let's think about human vision. People are good at estimating distance and relative locations of objects. A person doesn't even need two eyes for it—we can look with one eye and estimate distances and relative locations pretty well. Moreover, stereoscopic vision only takes place when the distance between eyes is of a similar order of magnitude as the distance to an object when the projections of the scene on the eye have noticeable differences.

For example, if one object is a football field away, the relative location of the eyes doesn't matter, whereas if you look at your nose, the view changes a lot. To illustrate further that stereoscopy is not the essence of our vision, we could look at a photograph where we can describe the relative location of the objects pretty well, but what we are actually looking at is a flat surface.

People do not have such skills at infancy; observations show that infants are bad at locating the placements of the objects. So, probably, a person learns this skill during their conscious life by looking at the world and playing with objects. Next, a question arises—*if a person learns the 3D structure of the world, can't we make a computer to do so?*

There are already interesting models that try to do so. For example, **Vid2Depth** (https://arxiv.org/pdf/1802.05522.pdf) is a deep learning model where the authors train a model that predicts depth in a single image; meanwhile, the model is trained on a sequence of video frames without any depth annotation. Similar problems are active topics for research nowadays.

Summary

In this chapter, we explored a way of reconstructing a scene in 3D by inferring the geometrical features of 2D images taken by the same camera. We wrote a script to calibrate a camera, and you learned about fundamental and essential matrices. We used this knowledge to perform triangulation. We then went on to visualize the real-world geometry of a scene in a 3D point cloud using simple 3D scatterplots in Matplotlib.

Going forward from here, it will be possible to store the triangulated 3D points in a file that can be parsed by the Point Cloud Library or to repeat the procedure for different image pairs so that we can generate a denser and more accurate reconstruction. Although we have covered a lot in this chapter, there is a lot more left to do.

Typically, when talking about a structure-from-motion pipeline, we include two additional steps that we have not talked about so far—**bundle adjustment** and **geometry fitting**. One of the most important steps in such a pipeline is to refine the 3D estimate in order to minimize reconstruction errors. Typically, we would also want to get all points that do not belong to our object of interest out of the cloud. But with the basic code in hand, you can now go ahead and write your own advanced structure-from-motion pipeline!

In the next chapter, we will use the concepts we learned in 3D Scene reconstruction. We will use the key points and features that we learned to extract in this chapter, and we'll apply other alignment algorithms to create panoramas. We will also dive deep into other topics in computational photography, understand the core concepts, and create **High Dynamic Range (HDR)** images.

5
Using Computational Photography with OpenCV

0The goal of this chapter is to build on what we have covered in the previous chapters about photography and image processing and investigate some algorithms that OpenCV gives you access in a lot more detail. We'll focus on working with digital photography and building tools that will allow you to harness the power of OpenCV, and even think about using it as your go-to tool for editing your photos.

In this chapter, we will cover the following concepts:

- Planning the app
- Understanding the 8-bit problem
- Using **gamma correction**
- Understanding **high-dynamic-range imaging** (**HDRI**)
- Understanding panorama stitching
- Improving panorama stitching

Learning the basics of digital photography and the concepts of high dynamic imaging will not only allow you to understand computational photography better, but it will make you a better photographer. Since we will explore these topics in detail, you will also understand how much work it takes to write a new algorithm.

Through this chapter, you will learn how to work with unprocessed (RAW) images directly from digital cameras, how to use OpenCV's computational photography tools, and how to use low-level OpenCV APIs to build a panorama stitching algorithm.

We have quite a few topics to cover, so let's roll up our sleeves and get started.

Getting started

You can find the code that we present in this chapter at our GitHub repository at `https://github.com/PacktPublishing/OpenCV-4-with-Python-Blueprints-Second-Edition/tree/master/chapter5`.

We will also use the `rawpy` and `exifread` Python packages for reading RAW images and reading image metadata. For the full list of requirements, you can refer to the `requirements.txt` file in the book's Git repository.

Planning the app

We have multiple concepts to familiarize ourselves with. With a view to building your toolbox for image processing, we are going to develop the algorithms that we are going to familiarize ourselves with into Python scripts that use OpenCV to accomplish real-life problems.

We will use OpenCV to implement the following scripts so that you will be able to use them whenever you need to do photo processing:

- `gamma_correct.py`: This is a script that applies gamma correction to the input image and shows the resulting image.
- `hdr.py`: This is a script that takes images as input and produces a **high dynamic range (HDR)** image as an output.
- `panorama.py`: This is a script that takes multiple images as input and produces a single stitched image that is larger than the individual images.

We'll first start with a discussion of how digital photography works and the reason we can't take perfect pictures without needing to do post-processing. Let's start with the 8-bit problem for images.

Understanding the 8-bit problem

Typical **Joint Photographic Experts Group (JPEG)** images that we are used to seeing, work by encoding each pixel into 24 bits—one 8-bit number per **RGB (red, green, blue)** color component, which gives us an integer within the 0-255 range. This is just a number, 255, *but is it enough information or not?* To understand this, let's try to understand how these numbers are recorded and what these numbers mean.

Most current digital cameras use a **Bayer filter,** or equivalent, that works using the same principles. A Bayer filter is an array of sensors of different colors placed on a grid similar to the following diagram:

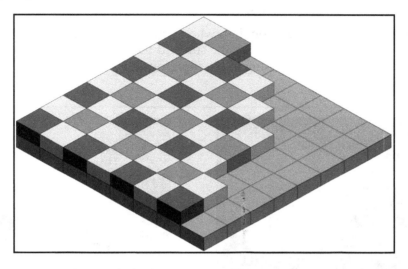

Image source—https://en.wikipedia.org/wiki/Bayer_filter#/media/File:Bayer_pattern_on_sensor.svg (CC SA 3.0)

In the previous diagram, each of these sensors measures the intensity of the light that gets into it, and a group of four sensors represents a single pixel. The data from these four sensors are combined to provide us with the three values for R, G, and B.

Different cameras might have a slightly different layout of red, green, and blue pixels, but at the end of the day, they are using small sensors that discretize the amount of radiation they get into a single value within the 0-255 range, where 0 means no radiation at all and 255 means the brightest radiation that the sensor can record.

The range of brightness that is detectable is called the **dynamic range** or the **luminance range**. The ratio between the smallest amount of radiation that could be registered (that is, 1) and the highest (that is, 255) is called the **contrast ratio.**

As we said, JPEG files have a contrast ratio of *255:1*. Most current LCD monitors have already surpassed that and have a contrast ratio of up to *1,000:1*. I bet you are waiting for your eye's ratio. I'm not sure about you, but most humans can see up to *15,000:1*.

So, we can see quite a lot more than even our best monitor can show, and a lot more than a simple JPEG file stores. Don't despair too much, because the latest digital cameras have been catching up and can now capture intensity ratios of up to *28,000:1* (the really expensive ones).

The small dynamic range is the reason that, when you are shooting a picture and you have the sun in the background, you either see the sun and the surroundings are all white without any detail, or everything in the foreground is extremely dark. Here is an example screenshot:

Image source—https://github.com/mamikonyana/winter-hills (CC SA 4.0)

So, the problem is that we either display things that are too bright, or we display things that are too dark. Before we move forward, let's take a look at how to read files that have more than 8 bits and import the data into OpenCV.

Learning about RAW images

Since this chapter is about computational photography, some of you reading it are probably photography enthusiasts and love taking pictures using the RAW formats that your camera supports—be it **Nikon Electronic Format** (**NEF**) or **Canon Raw Version 2** (**CR2**).

Raw files usually capture a lot more information (usually more bits per pixel) than JPEG files, and if you are going to do a lot of post-processing, these files are a lot more convenient to work with, since they will produce higher-quality final images.

So let's take a look at how to open a CR2 file using Python and load it into OpenCV. For that, we will use a Python library called `rawpy`. For convenience, we will write a function called `load_image` that can handle both RAW images and regular JPEG files so we can abstract this part away and concentrate on more fun things in the rest of the chapter:

1. First, we take care of the imports (as promised, just one small extra library):

```
import rawpy
import cv2
```

2. We define the function, adding an optional `bps` argument, which will let us control how much precision we want the images to have, that is, we want to check if we want the full 16 bits or are just 8 bits good enough:

```
def load_image(path, bps=16):
```

3. Then, if the file has a `.CR2` extension, we open the file with `rawpy` and extract the image without trying to do any post-processing, since we want to do that with OpenCV:

```
if path.suffix == '.CR2':
    with rawpy.imread(str(path)) as raw:
        data = raw.postprocess(no_auto_bright=True,
                               gamma=(1, 1),
                               output_bps=bps)
```

4. As Canon (Canon Inc.—an optical products company) and OpenCV use a different ordering of colors, we switch from RGB to **BGR** (**blue**, **green**, and **red**), which is the default ordering in OpenCV and we `return` the resulting image:

```
return cv2.cvtColor(data, cv2.COLOR_RGB2BGR)
```

For anything that is not `.CR2`, we use OpenCV:

```
else:
    return cv2.imread(str(path))
```

Now we know how to get all our images into OpenCV, it's time to get started with one of the brightest algorithms we have.

Since my camera has a 14-bit dynamic range, we are going to use images captured with my camera:

```
def load_14bit_gray(path):
    img = load_image(path, bps=16)
    return (cv2.cvtColor(img, cv2.COLOR_BGR2GRAY) / 4).astype(np.uint16)
```

Once we know how to load our pictures, let's try to see how we can best display them on the screen.

Using gamma correction

Why is everybody still using JPEG files if they can only distinguish between 255 different levels? Does it mean it can only capture a dynamic range of 1:255? It turns out there are clever tricks that people use.

As we mentioned before, the camera sensors capture values that are linear, that is, 4 means that it has 4 times more light than 1, and 80 has 8 times more light than 10. But does the JPEG file format have to use a linear scale? It turns out that it doesn't. So, if we are willing to sacrifice the difference between two values, for example, 100 and 101, we can fit another value there.

To understand this better, let's look at the histogram of gray pixel values of a RAW image. Here is the code to generate that—just load the image, convert it to grayscale, and show the histogram using `pyplot`:

```
images = [load_14bit_gray(p) for p in args.images]
fig, axes = plt.subplots(2, len(images), sharey=False)
for i, gray in enumerate(images):
    axes[0, i].imshow(gray, cmap='gray', vmax=2**14)
    axes[1, i].hist(gray.flatten(), bins=256)
```

Here is the result of the histogram:

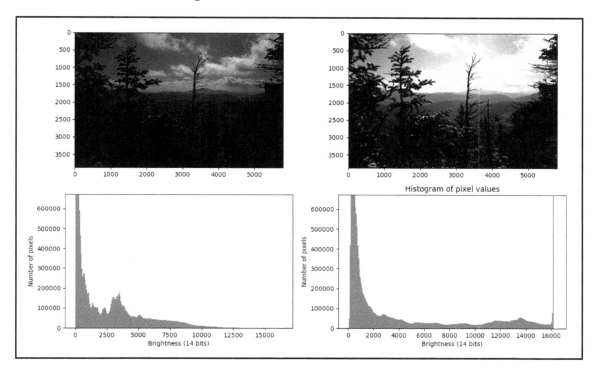

We have two pictures: the left one is a *normal* picture, where you can see some clouds, but it's almost impossible to see anything in the foreground, and the right one has tried to capture some detail in the trees, and because of that has burned all the clouds. *Is there a way to combine these?*

If we take a closer look at the histograms, we see that the burned-out part is visible on the right-hand histogram because there are values that are 16,000 that get encoded as 255, that is, white pixels. But on the left-hand picture, there are no white pixels. The way we encode 14-bit values into 8-bit values is very rudimentary: we just divide the values by *64 (=2^6)*, so we lose the distinction between 2,500 and 2,501 and 2,502; instead, we only have 39 (out of 255) because the values in the 8-bit format have to be integers.

This is where gamma corrections come in. Instead of simply showing the recorded value as the intensity, we are going to make some corrections, to make the image more visually appealing.

We are going to use a non-linear function to try to emphasize the parts that we think are more important:

$$O = (\frac{I}{255})^\gamma \times 255$$

Let's try to visualize this formula for two different values—$\gamma = 0.3$ and $\gamma = 3$:

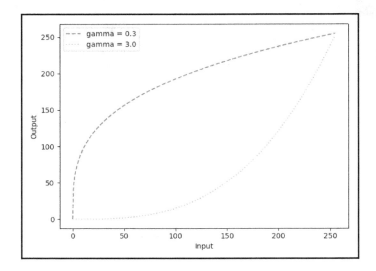

As you can see, small gammas put an emphasis on lower values; the pixel values from **0-50** are mapped to pixel values from **0-150** (more than half of the available values). The reverse is true of the higher gammas—the values from **200-250** are mapped to the values **100-250** (more than half of the available values). So, if you want to make your photo brighter, you should pick a gamma value of $\gamma < 1$, which is often called **gamma compression**. And if you want to make your photos dimmer to show more detail, you should pick a gamma value of $\gamma > 1$, which is called **gamma expansion.**

Instead of using integers for I, we can start with a float number and get to O, then convert that number to an integer to lose even less of information. Let's write some Python code to implement gamma correction:

1. First, let's write a function to apply our formula. Because we are using 14-bit numbers, we will have to change it to the following:

$$O = (\frac{I}{2^{14}})^\gamma \times 255$$

Thus, the relevant code will be as follows:

```
@functools.lru_cache(maxsize=None)
def gamma_transform(x, gamma, bps=14):
    return np.clip(pow(x / 2**bps, gamma) * 255.0, 0, 255)
```

Here, we have used the `@functools.lru_cache` decorator to make sure we don't compute anything twice.

2. Then, we just iterate over all the pixels and apply our transformation function:

```
def apply_gamma(img, gamma, bps=14):
    corrected = img.copy()
    for i, j in itertools.product(range(corrected.shape[0]),
                                  range(corrected.shape[1])):
        corrected[i, j] = gamma_transform(corrected[i, j], gamma,
bps=bps)
    return corrected
```

Now let's take a look at how to use this to show the new image alongside the regularly transformed 8-bit image. We will write a script for this:

1. First, let's configure a `parser` to load an image and allow setting the `gamma` value:

```
if __name__ == '__main__':
    parser = argparse.ArgumentParser()
    parser.add_argument('raw_image', type=Path,
                        help='Location of a .CR2 file.')
    parser.add_argument('--gamma', type=float, default=0.3)
    args = parser.parse_args()
```

2. Load the `gray` image as a `14bit` image:

```
gray = load_14bit_gray(args.raw_image)
```

3. Use linear transformation to get output values as an integer in the range [0-255]:

```
normal = np.clip(gray / 64, 0, 255).astype(np.uint8)
```

4. Use our `apply_gamma` function we wrote previously to get a gamma-corrected image:

```
corrected = apply_gamma(gray, args.gamma)
```

5. Then, plot both of the images together with their histogram:

```
fig, axes = plt.subplots(2, 2, sharey=False)
for i, img in enumerate([normal, corrected]):
    axes[0, i].imshow(img, cmap='gray', vmax=255)
    axes[1, i].hist(img.flatten(), bins=256)
```

6. Finally, `show` the image:

```
plt.show()
```

We have now plotted the histogram and will look at the magic that is elaborated in the following two images with their histograms:

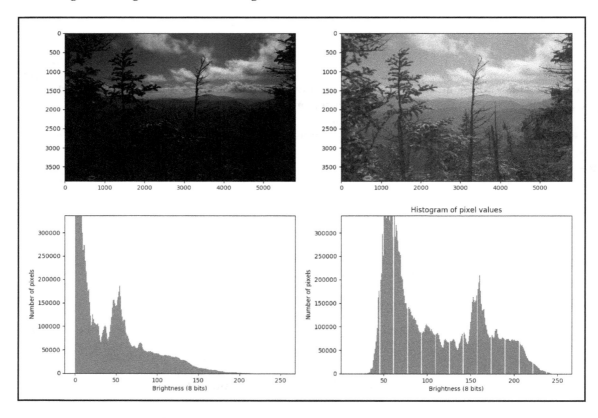

Look at the picture at the top right—you can see almost everything! And we are only getting started.

It turns out gamma compensation works great on black and white images, but it can't do everything! It can either correct brightness and we lose most of the color information, or it can correct color information and we lose the brightness information. So, we have to find a new best friend—that is, HDRI.

Understanding high-dynamic-range imaging

High-dynamic-range imaging (**HDR**) is a technique to produce images that have a greater dynamic range of luminosity (that is, contrast ratio) than could be displayed through the display medium, or captured with the camera using a single shot. There are two main ways to create such images—using special image sensors, such as an oversampled binary image sensor, or the way we will focus on here, by combining multiple **Standard Dynamic Range** (**SDR**) images to produce a combined HDR image.

HDR imaging works with images that use more than 8 bits per channel (usually 32-bit float values), allowing a much wider dynamic range. As we know, the *dynamic range* of a scene is the contrast ratio between its brightest and darkest parts.

Let's take a closer look at what the luminance values are of certain things that we can see. The following diagram shows values that we can easily see, from the dark sky (around 10^{-4} cd/m^2) to the sun during sunset (10^5 cd/m^2):

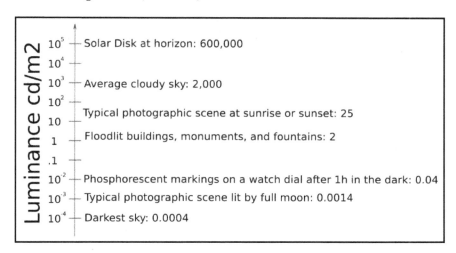

We can see more than these values. Because some people can adjust their eyes to even darker places, we can definitely see the sun when it's not on the horizon but is higher up in the sky, probably up to 10^8 cd/m², but this range is already quite a big range, so let's stick to it for now. For comparison, a usual 8-bit image has a contrast ratio of *256:1*, the human eye can see at one time around million to 1, and the 14-bit RAW format shows $2^{14}:1$.

Display media also have limitations; for example, a typical IPS monitor has a contrast ratio of around *1,000:1*, and a VA monitor could have a contrast ratio of up to *6,000:1*. So, let's place these values on this spectrum and see how they compare:

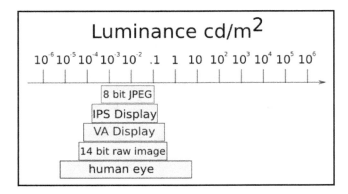

Now, this doesn't look like we can see much, which is true since it takes time for us to adjust to different lighting conditions. The same is true about a camera. But in just one glance, our naked eye can see quite a lot more than even the best camera can. *So how can we remedy this?*

As we said, the trick is to take multiple pictures in quick succession, which most cameras allow with ease. If we were to take pictures in quick succession that complement each other, we could cover quite a big part of the spectrum with just five JPEGs:

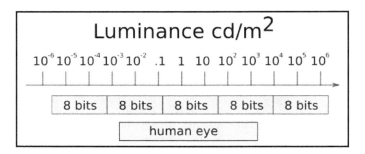

This seems a little too easy, but remember, taking five pictures is quite easy. But, we are talking about one picture that has all the dynamic range, not five separate pictures. There are two big problems with HDR images:

- *How can we combine multiple images into a single image?*
- *How can we display an image that has a higher dynamic range than our display media?*

However, even before we can combine those images, let's take a closer look at how can we vary the exposure of the camera, that is, its sensitivity to light.

Exploring ways to vary exposure

As we discussed earlier in this chapter, modern **Digital Single Lens Reflector** cameras (**DSLRs**), and other digital cameras as well, have a fixed sensor grid (usually placed as a Bayer filter), which just measures the light intensity of the camera.

I bet you have seen the same camera used to capture beautiful night pictures where the water looks like a silky cloud and stills that sports photographers have taken of a player at full stretch. *So how can they use the same camera for such different settings and get results that we see on the screen?*

When measuring the exposure, it's really hard to measure the luminance that is being captured. It's a lot easier to measure relative speed instead of measuring luminance in the power of 10, which could be quite difficult to adjust. We measure the speed in the power of 2; we call that a **stop**.

The trick is that, even though the camera is restricted, it has to be able to capture a limited luminance range per picture. The range itself could be moved along the luminance spectrum. To overcome this, let's study the shutter speed, aperture, and ISO speed parameters of the camera.

Shutter speed

Shutter speed is not really the speed of the shutter, but it's the length of time for which a camera's shutter is open when taking a photograph. Thus, it's the amount of time for which the digital sensor inside the camera is exposed to light for collecting information. It's the most intuitive control out of all the camera controls because we can feel it happening.

Shutter speeds are usually measured in fractions of a second. For example, *1/60* is the fastest speed for which, if we shake the camera while clicking photos while it is held in our hands, it doesn't introduce a blur in the photograph. So if you are going to use your own pictures, make sure to not do this, or get yourself a tripod.

Aperture

Aperture is the diameter of the hole in the optical lens through which the light passes into the camera. The following picture shows examples of the opening set to different aperture values:

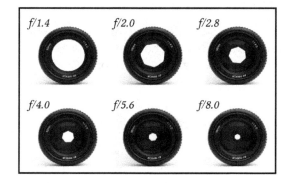

Image source—https://en.wikipedia.org/wiki/Aperture#/media/File:Lenses_with_different_apertures.jpg (CC SA 4.0)

Aperture is usually measured using an *f-number*. The f-number is the ratio of the system's focal length to the diameter of the opening (the entrance pupil). We won't concern ourselves with the focal length of the lens; the only thing we need to know is that only zoom lenses have variable focal lengths, thus if we don't change the magnification on the lens, the focal length will stay the same. So we can measure the **area** of the entrance pupil by squaring the inverse of the **f-number**:

$$\text{area} \propto \frac{1}{\text{f-number}^2}$$

And, we know that the bigger the area, the more light we will get in our pictures. Thus, if we were to increase the f-number, that would correspond to a decrease in the size of the entrance pupil and our pictures would become darker, enabling us to take pictures during the afternoon.

ISO speed

ISO speed is the sensitivity of the sensors used in cameras. It is measured using numbers that map the sensitivity of the digital sensor to the chemical films that were used when computers were not around yet.

ISO speed is measured in two numbers; for example, *100/21°*, where the first number is the speed on the arithmetic scale and the second number is the number on the logarithmic scale. Since these numbers have a one-to-one mapping, usually the second one is omitted, and we simply write *ISO 100*. ISO 100 is two times less sensitive to light than ISO 200 and it is said that the difference is **1 stop**.

It is easier to talk in powers of 2 rather than powers of 10, so photographers came up with the notion of **stops**. One stop is two times different, 2 stops are 4 times different, and so on. Thus, n stops are 2^n times different. This analogy has become so widespread that people have started using fractional and real numbers for stops.

Now that we understand how to control the exposure, let's try to look at the algorithms that can combine multiple pictures with different exposures into a single image.

Generating HDR images using multiple exposure images

Now, once we know how it's possible to get more pictures, we can take multiple photos that have very little or no overlapping dynamic range. Let's have a look at the most popular algorithm for HDR, first published by Paul E Debevec and Jitendra Malik in 2008.

It turns out that if you want to have good results, you have to have pictures that are overlapping, to make sure you have good accuracy and since there is noise in the photos. It's usually common to have 1, 2, or at most 3 stops difference from picture to picture. If we were to shoot five 8-bit photos with a difference of 3 stops, we would cover the human eye's one million to one sensitivity ratio:

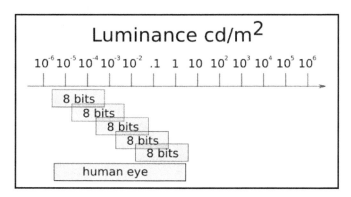

Now let's take a closer look at how the Debevec HDR algorithm works.

First, let's assume that the recorded values the camera sees are some function of the scene's irradiance. We talked about this being linear before, but nothing is truly linear in real life. Let the recorded value matrix be **Z** and the irradiance matrix be **X**; we have the following:

$$Z = f(E\Delta t)$$

Here, we have also used **Δt** as the measure of exposure time, and the function f is called the **response function** of our camera. Also, we assume that if we double the exposure and half the irradiance, we will have the same output and vice versa. This should be true across all images, and the value of E should not change from picture to picture; only the recorded values of **Z** and the exposure time **Δt** can change. If we apply the **inverse response function**(f^{-1}) and take the logarithm of both sides, then we get that for all of the pictures(i) that we have:

$$\ln f^{-1}(Z_i) = \ln E + \ln \Delta t_i$$

Now the trick is to come up with an algorithm that can calculate the f^{-1}, and that's what Debevec et al. have done.

Of course, our pixel values are not going to follow this rule exactly, and we will have to fit an approximate solution, but, let's take a more detailed look at what these values are.

Before we move forward, let's take a look at how we can recover Δt_i values from the picture files in the next section.

Extracting exposure strength from images

Assuming the **principle of reciprocity** for all the camera parameters that we discussed previously, let's try to come up with a function—exposure_strength—that returns a time equivalent to the exposure:

1. First, let's set a reference for ISO speed and f-stop:

```
def exposure_strength(path, iso_ref=100, f_stop_ref=6.375):
```

2. Then, let's use the exifread Python package, which makes it easy to read the metadata associated with the images. Most modern cameras record the metadata in this standard format:

```
with open(path, 'rb') as infile:
    tags = exifread.process_file(infile)
```

3. Then, let's extract the f_stop value and see how much bigger the entrance pupil area to the reference was:

```
[f_stop] = tags['EXIF ApertureValue'].values
rel_aperture_area = 1 / (f_stop.num / f_stop.den / f_stop_ref)
** 2
```

4. Then, let's see how much more sensitive the ISO setting was:

```
[iso_speed] = tags['EXIF ISOSpeedRatings'].values
iso_multiplier = iso_speed / iso_ref
```

5. Finally, let's combine all the values with the shutter speed and return exposure_time:

```
[exposure_time] = tags['EXIF ExposureTime'].values
exposure_time_float = exposure_time.num / exposure_time.den
return rel_aperture_area * exposure_time_float * iso_multipli
```

Here is an example of the values of the photographs that I am using for this demo, taken from the **Frozen River** photo collection:

Photograph	Aperture	ISO Speed	Shutter Speed
AM5D5669.CR2	6 3/8	100	1/60
AM5D5670.CR2	6 3/8	100	1/250
AM5D5671.CR2	6 3/8	100	1/160
AM5D5672.CR2	6 3/8	100	1/100
AM5D5673.CR2	6 3/8	100	1/40
AM5D5674.CR2	6 3/8	160	1/40
AM5D5676.CR2	6 3/8	250	1/40

This is the output of the time estimates for these pictures using the `exposure_strength` function:

```
[0.016666666666666666, 0.004, 0.00625, 0.01, 0.025, 0.04, 0.0625
```

Now, once we have the exposure times, let's see how this can be used to get the camera response function.

Estimating the camera response function

Let's plot $\ln \Delta t_i$ on the y axis, and Z_i on the x axis:

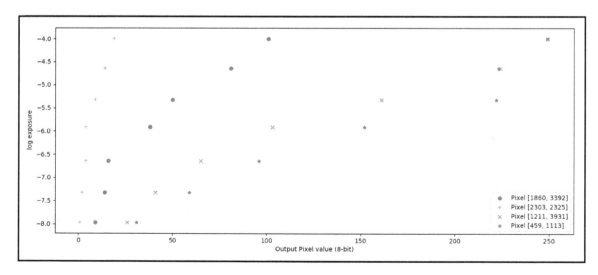

What we are trying to do is to find an f^1 and, more importantly, the $\ln E$ of all the pictures, such that when we add **log(E)** to the log exposure, we will have all the pixels on the same function. You can see the results of the Debevec algorithm in the following screenshot:

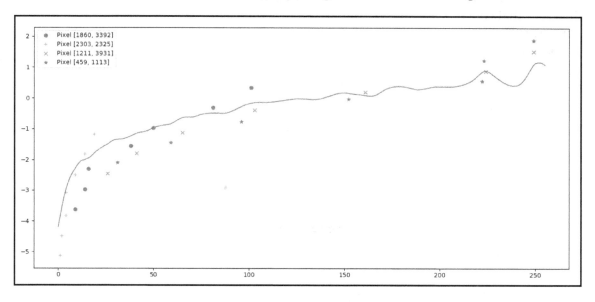

The Debevec algorithm estimates both the f^1, which passes approximately through all the pixels, and the $\ln E$. The E matrix is the resulting HDR image matrix that we recover.

Now let's take a look at how to implement this using OpenCV.

Writing an HDR script using OpenCV

The first step of the script is going to be setting up the script arguments using Python's built-in `argparse` module:

```
import argparse

if __name__ == '__main__':
    parser = argparse.ArgumentParser()
    img_group = parser.add_mutually_exclusive_group(required=True)
    img_group.add_argument('--image-dir', type=Path)
    img_group.add_argument('--images', type=Path, nargs='+')
    args = parser.parse_args()
```

```
if args.image_dir:
    args.images = sorted(args.image_dir.iterdir())
```

As you can see, we have set up two mutually exclusive arguments—`--image-dir`, a directory that contains the images, and `--images`, a list of images that we are going to use. And we make sure that we populate `args.images` with the list of all the images, so the rest of the script shouldn't worry about which of the options the user has chosen.

After we have all the command-line arguments, the rest of the procedure is as follows:

1. Read all `images` into the memory:

   ```
   images = [load_image(p, bps=8) for p in args.images]
   ```

2. Read the metadata and estimate exposure times using `exposure_strength`:

   ```
   times = [exposure_strength(p)[0] for p in args.images]
   times_array = np.array(times, dtype=np.float32)
   ```

3. Calculate the **camera response function**—`crf_debevec`:

   ```
   cal_debevec = cv2.createCalibrateDebevec(int samples=200)
   crf_debevec = cal_debevec.process(images, times=times_array)
   ```

4. Use the camera response function to calculate the HDR image:

   ```
   merge_debevec = cv2.createMergeDebevec()
   hdr_debevec = merge_debevec.process(images,
   times=times_array.copy(),
                                       response=crf_debevec)
   ```

Notice that the HDR image is of type `float32` and not `uint8`, as it contains the full dynamic range of all exposure images.

Now we have the HDR image and we've come to the next important part. Let's see how we can show the HDR image using our 8-bit image representation.

Displaying HDR images

Displaying HDR images is tricky. As we said, HDR has more values than the camera, so we need to figure out a way to display that. Luckily, OpenCV is here to help us again, and, as you've probably guessed by now, we can use gamma correction to map all the different values we have into a smaller spectrum of values in the range 0 to 255. This process is called **Tone Mapping**.

OpenCV has a method for it that takes gamma as an argument:

```
tonemap = cv2.createTonemap(gamma=2.2)
res_debevec = tonemap.process(hdr_debevec)
```

Now we have to clip all the values to become integers:

```
res_8bit = np.clip(res_debevec * 255, 0, 255).astype('uint8')
```

After that, we can show our resulting HDR image using pyplot:

```
plt.imshow(res_8bit)
plt.show()
```

This results in the following gorgeous image:

Now, let's see how can we extend the camera's field of view—potentially to 360 degrees!

Understanding panorama stitching

Another very interesting topic in computational photography is **panorama stitching**. I'm sure most of you have a panorama function on your phone. This section will focus on the ideas behind panorama stitching and, instead of just calling a single function, we will go through all the steps involved in creating a panorama from a bunch of separate photos.

Writing script arguments and filtering images

We want to write a script that will take a list of images and will produce a single panorama picture. So, let's set up the `ArgumentParser` for our script:

```
def parse_args():
    parser = argparse.ArgumentParser()
    img_group = parser.add_mutually_exclusive_group(required=True)
    img_group.add_argument('--image-dir', type=Path)
    img_group.add_argument('--images', type=Path, nargs='+')
    args = parser.parse_args()

    if args.image_dir:
        args.images = sorted(args.image_dir.iterdir())
    return args
```

Here, we created an instance of `ArgumentParser` and added arguments to pass either an image directory of a list of images. Then, we make sure we get all the images from the image directory if it is passed, instead of passing a list of images.

Now, as you can imagine, the next step is to use a feature extractor and see what the common features that images share are. This is very much like the previous two chapters, that is, Chapter 3, *Finding Objects via Feature Matching and Perspective Transforms,* and Chapter 4, *3D Scene Reconstruction Using Structure from Motion.* We will also write a function to filter those images that have common features, so the script is even more versatile. Let's go through the function step by step:

1. Create the SURF feature extractor and compute all of the features of all images:

```
def largest_connected_subset(images):
    finder = cv2.xfeatures2d_SURF.create()
    all_img_features = [cv2.detail.computeImageFeatures2(finder,
img)
                        for img in images]
```

2. Create a `matcher` class that matches an image to its closest neighbors that share the most features:

```
matcher = cv2.detail.BestOf2NearestMatcher_create(False, 0.6)
pair_matches = matcher.apply2(all_img_features)
matcher.collectGarbage()
```

3. Filter the images and make sure that we have at least two images that share features so we can proceed with the algorithm:

```
_conn_indices =
cv2.detail.leaveBiggestComponent(all_img_features, pair_matches,
0.4)
    conn_indices = [i for [i] in _conn_indices]
    if len(conn_indices) < 2:
        raise RuntimeError("Need 2 or more connected images.")

    conn_features = np.array([all_img_features[i] for i in
conn_indices])
    conn_images = [images[i] for i in conn_indices]
```

4. Run the `matcher` again to check whether we have removed any of the images and `return` the variables we will need in the future:

```
if len(conn_images) < len(images):
    pair_matches = matcher.apply2(conn_features)
    matcher.collectGarbage()

return conn_images, conn_features, pair_matches
```

After we have filtered the images and have all the features, we move on to the next step, which is setting up a blank canvas for the panorama stitching.

Figuring out relative positions and the final picture size

Once we have separated all the connected pictures and know all the features, it's time to figure out how big the merged panorama is going to be and create the blank canvas to start adding pictures to it. First, we need to find the parameters of the pictures.

Finding camera parameters

In order to be able to merge images, we need to compute homography matrices of all the images and then use those to adjust the images so they can be merged together. We will write a function to do that:

1. First, we are going to create the `HomographyBasedEstimator()` function:

```
def find_camera_parameters(features, pair_matches):
    estimator = cv2.detail_HomographyBasedEstimator()
```

2. Once we have the `estimator`, for extracting all the camera parameters, we use the matched `features` from different images:

```
success, cameras = estimator.apply(features, pair_matches,
None)
    if not success:
        raise RuntimeError("Homography estimation failed.")
```

3. We make sure the `R` matrices have the correct type:

```
for cam in cameras:
    cam.R = cam.R.astype(np.float32)
```

4. Then, we `return` all the parameters:

```
return cameras
```

It is possible to make these parameters better using a refiner, for example, `cv2.detail_BundleAdjusterRay`, but we'll keep things simple for now.

Creating the canvas for the panorama

Now it's time to create the canvas. For that, we create a `warper` object based on our desired rotation schema. For simplicity, let's assume a planar model:

```
warper = cv2.PyRotationWarper('plane', 1)
```

Then, we `enumerate` over all the connected images and get all the regions of interest in each of the images:

```
stitch_sizes, stitch_corners = [], []
for i, img in enumerate(conn_images):
    sz = img.shape[1], img.shape[0]
    K = cameras[i].K().astype(np.float32)
    roi = warper.warpRoi(sz, K, cameras[i].R)
```

```
stitch_corners.append(roi[0:2])
stitch_sizes.append(roi[2:4])
```

Finally, we estimate the final `canvas_size` based on all regions of interest:

```
canvas_size = cv2.detail.resultRoi(corners=stitch_corners,
sizes=stitch_sizes)
```

Now, let's see how to use the canvas size to blend all the images together.

Blending the images together

First, we create a `MultiBandBlender` object, which will help us merge images together. Instead of just picking values from one or the other image, `blender` will do interpolation between the available values:

```
blender = cv2.detail_MultiBandBlender()
blend_width = np.sqrt(canvas_size[2] * canvas_size[3]) * 5 / 100
blender.setNumBands((np.log(blend_width) / np.log(2.) -
1.).astype(np.int))
blender.prepare(canvas_size)
```

Then, for each of the connected images, we do the following:

1. We `warp` the image and get the `corner` locations:

```
for i, img in enumerate(conn_images):
    K = cameras[i].K().astype(np.float32)
    corner, image_wp = warper.warp(img, K, cameras[i].R,
                                   cv2.INTER_LINEAR,
cv2.BORDER_REFLECT)
```

2. Then, calculate the `mask` of the image on the canvas:

```
mask = 255 * np.ones((img.shape[0], img.shape[1]),
np.uint8)
    _, mask_wp = warper.warp(mask, K, cameras[i].R,
                             cv2.INTER_NEAREST,
cv2.BORDER_CONSTANT)
```

3. After that, convert the values into `np.int16` and `feed` it into `blender`:

```
image_warped_s = image_wp.astype(np.int16)
    blender.feed(cv2.UMat(image_warped_s), mask_wp,
stitch_corners[i])
```

4. After that, we use the `blend` function on `blender`, to get the final `result`, and save it:

```
result, result_mask = blender.blend(None, None)
cv2.imwrite('result.jpg', result)
```

We can also scale the image down to 600 pixels wide and display it:

```
zoomx = 600.0 / result.shape[1]
dst = cv2.normalize(src=result, dst=None, alpha=255.,
                    norm_type=cv2.NORM_MINMAX, dtype=cv2.CV_8U)
dst = cv2.resize(dst, dsize=None, fx=zoomx, fy=zoomx)
cv2.imshow('panorama', dst)
cv2.waitKey()
```

When we use the images from https://github.com/mamikonyana/yosemite-panorama, we have this wonderful panorama picture in the end:

You can see that it's not perfect and the white balance requires correcting from picture to picture, but this is a great start. In the next section, we will work on refining the stitching output.

Improving panorama stitching

You can either play with the script that we already have and add or remove certain features (for example, you can add a white balance compensator, to make sure you have a smoother transition from one picture to another), or you can tweak other parameters to learn.

But know this—when you need a quick panorama, OpenCV also has a handy `Stitcher` class that does most of what we have discussed already:

```
images = [load_image(p, bps=8) for p in args.images]

stitcher = cv2.Stitcher_create()
(status, stitched) = stitcher.stitch(images)
```

This code snippet is probably a lot faster than uploading your photos to a panorama service to get a good picture—so enjoy creating panoramas!

Don't forget to add some code to crop the panorama so it doesn't have black pixels!

Summary

In this chapter, we learned how to take simple images that we can take from our cameras with limited abilities—either with limited dynamic range or limited field of view and use OpenCV to merge multiple images into a single one that is better than the original one.

We left you with three scripts that you could build upon. Most importantly, there are still a lot of features missing from `panorama.py`, and there are a lot of other HDR techniques. Best of all, it's possible to do HDR and panorama stitching at the same time. *Wouldn't it be splendid to just look around from the mountain top at sunset? Imagine that!*

This was the last chapter about camera photography. The rest of this book will focus on video monitoring and applying machine learning techniques to image processing tasks.

In the next chapter, we will focus on tracking visually salient and moving objects in a scene. This will give you an understanding of how to deal with non-static scenes. We will also explore how we can make an algorithm focus on what's important in a scene quickly, which is a technique known to speed up object detection, object recognition, object tracking, and content-aware image editing.

Further reading

There are a lot of other topics to explore in computational photography:

- It's especially worth taking a look at the **Exposure Fusion** technique developed by Tom Mertens, et al. The *Exposure fusion* article by Tom Mertens, Jan Kautz, and Frank Van Reeth, in Computer Graphics and Applications, 2007, Pacific Graphics 2007, proceedings at 15th Pacific Conference on, pages 382–390, IEEE, 2007.
- The *Recovering High Dynamic Range Radiance Maps from Photographs* article by Paul E Debevec and Jitendra Malik, in ACM SIGGRAPH 2008 classes, 2008, page 31, ACM, 2008.

Attributions

The **Frozen River** photo collection can be found at `https://github.com/mamikonyana/frozen-river` and is verified with a CC-BY-SA-4.0 license.

6
Tracking Visually Salient Objects

The goal of this chapter is to track multiple visually salient objects in a video sequence at once. Instead of labeling the objects of interest in the video ourselves, we will let the algorithm decide which regions of a video frame are worth tracking.

We have previously learned how to detect simple objects of interest (such as a human hand) in tightly controlled scenarios and how to infer geometrical features of a visual scene from camera motion. In this chapter, we ask what we can learn about a visual scene by looking at the *image statistics* of a large number of frames.

In this chapter, we will cover the following topics:

- Planning the app
- Setting up the app
- Mapping visual saliency
- Understanding mean-shift tracking
- Learning about the OpenCV Tracking API
- Putting it all together

By analyzing the **Fourier spectrum** of natural images, we will build a **saliency map**, which allows us to label certain statistically interesting patches of the image as (potential or actual) *proto-objects*. We will then feed the location of all the proto-objects to a **mean-shift tracker**, which will allow us to keep track of where the objects move from one frame to the next.

Getting started

This chapter uses **OpenCV 4.1.0**, as well as the additional packages **NumPy** (http://www.numpy.org), **wxPython 2.8** (http://www.wxpython.org/download.php), and **matplotlib** (http://www.matplotlib.org/downloads.html). Although parts of the algorithms presented in this chapter have been added to an optional Saliency module of the **OpenCV 3.0.0** release, there is currently no Python API for it, so we will write our own code.

The code for this chapter can be found in the book's GitHub repository, available at https:/ /github.com/PacktPublishing/OpenCV-4-with-Python-Blueprints-Second-Edition/ tree/master/chapter6.

Understanding visual saliency

Visual saliency is a technical term from *cognitive psychology* that tries to describe the visual quality of certain objects or items that allows them to grab our immediate attention. Our brains constantly drive our gaze toward the *important* regions of the visual scene and keep track of them over time, allowing us to quickly scan our surroundings for interesting objects and events while neglecting the less important parts.

An example of a regular RGB image and its conversion to a **saliency map**, where the statistically interesting *pop-out* regions appear bright and the others dark, is shown in the following screenshot:

Fourier analysis will enable us to get a general understanding of natural image statistics, which will help us build a model of what general image backgrounds look like. By comparing and contrasting the background model to a specific image frame, we can locate subregions of the image that *pop out* of their surroundings (as shown in the previous screenshot). Ideally, these subregions correspond to the image patches that tend to grab our immediate attention when looking at the image.

Traditional models might try to associate particular features with each target (much like our feature-matching approach in Chapter 3, *Finding Objects via Feature Matching and Perspective Transforms*), which would convert the problem to the detection of specific categories of objects. However, these models require manual labeling and training. But what if the features or the number of the objects to track is not known?

Instead, we will try to mimic what the brain does, that is, tune our algorithm to the statistics of the natural images, so that we can immediately locate the patterns or subregions that *"grab our attention"* in the visual scene (that is, patterns that deviate from these statistical regularities) and flag them for further inspection. The result is an algorithm that works for any number of proto-objects in the scene, such as tracking all the players on a soccer field. Refer to the following set of screenshots to see it in action:

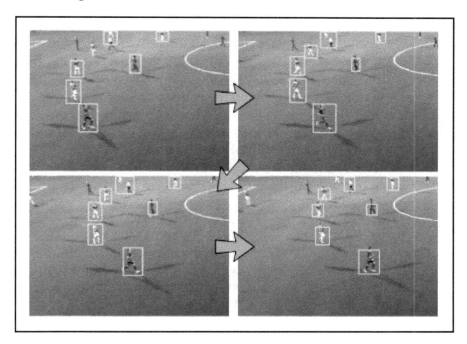

As we can see in these four screenshots, once all the potentially *interesting* patches of an image have been located, we can track their movement over many frames using a simple yet effective method called **object mean-shift tracking**. Because it is possible to have multiple proto-objects in the scene that might change appearance over time, we need to be able to distinguish between them and keep track of all of them.

Planning the app

To build the app, we need to combine the two main features discussed previously—a saliency map and object tracking. The final app will convert each RGB frame of a video sequence into a saliency map, extract all the interesting proto-objects, and feed them to a mean-shift tracking algorithm. To do this, we need the following components:

- `main`: This is the main function routine (in `chapter6.py`) to start the application.
- `saliency.py`: This is a module to generate a saliency map and proto-object map from an RGB color image. It includes the following functions:
    - `get_saliency_map`: This is a function to convert an RGB color image to a saliency map.
    - `get_proto_objects_map`: This is a function to convert a saliency map into a binary mask containing all the proto-objects.
    - `plot_power_density`: This is a function to display the two-dimensional power density of an RGB color image, which is helpful to understand the Fourier transform.
    - `plot_power_spectrum`: This is a function to display the radially averaged power spectrum of an RGB color image, which is helpful to understand natural image statistics.
    - `MultiObjectTracker`: This is a class that tracks multiple objects in a video using mean-shift tracking. It includes the following public methods:
        - `MultiObjectTracker.advance_frame`: This is a method to update the tracking information for a new frame, using the mean-shift algorithm on the saliency map of the current frame to update the positions of boxes from the previous frame to the current frame.

- `MultiObjectTracker.draw_good_boxes`: This is a method to illustrate tracking results in the current frame.

In the following sections, we will discuss these steps in detail.

Setting up the app

In order to run our app, we will need to execute the `main` function ,which reads a frame of a video stream, generates a saliency map, extracts the location of the proto-objects, and tracks these locations from one frame to the next.

Let's learn about the `main` function routine in the next section.

Implementing the main function

The main process flow is handled by the `main` function in `chapter6.py`, which instantiates the tracker (`MultipleObjectTracker`) and opens a video file showing the number of soccer players on the field:

```
import cv2
from os import path

from saliency import get_saliency_map, get_proto_objects_map
from tracking import MultipleObjectsTracker


def main(video_file='soccer.avi', roi=((140, 100), (500, 600))):
    if not path.isfile(video_file):
        print(f'File "{video_file}" does not exist.')
        raise SystemExit

    # open video file
    video = cv2.VideoCapture(video_file)

    # initialize tracker
    mot = MultipleObjectsTracker()
```

The function will then read the video frame by frame and extract some meaningful region of interest (for illustration purposes):

```
while True:
    success, img = video.read()
    if success:
        if roi:
            # grab some meaningful ROI
            img = img[roi[0][0]:roi[1][0],
                roi[0][1]:roi[1][1]]
```

After that, the region of interest will be passed to a function that will generate a saliency map of the region. Then, *interesting* proto-objects will be generated based on the saliency map, which finally will be fed into the tracker together with the region of interest. The output of the tracker is the input region annotated with bounding boxes as shown in the preceding set of screenshots:

```
saliency = get_saliency_map(img, use_numpy_fft=False,
                            gauss_kernel=(3, 3))
objects = get_proto_objects_map(saliency, use_otsu=False)
cv2.imshow('tracker', mot.advance_frame(img, objects))
```

The app will run through all the frames of the video until the end of the file is reached or the user presses the q key:

```
if cv2.waitKey(100) & 0xFF == ord('q'):
    break
```

In the next section, we'll learn about the `MultiObjectTracker` class.

Understanding the MultiObjectTracker class

The constructor of the tracker class is straightforward. All it does is set up the termination criteria for mean-shift tracking and store the conditions for the minimum contour area (`min_area`) and the minimum average speed normalized by object size (`min_speed_per_pix`) to be considered in the subsequent computation steps:

```
def __init__(self, min_object_area: int = 400,
            min_speed_per_pix: float = 0.02):
    self.object_boxes = []
    self.min_object_area = min_object_area
    self.min_speed_per_pix = min_speed_per_pix
    self.num_frame_tracked = 0
    # Setup the termination criteria, either 100 iteration or move by
at
```

```
# least 1 pt
self.term_crit = (cv2.TERM_CRITERIA_EPS | cv2.TERM_CRITERIA_COUNT,
                  5, 1)
```

From then on, the user may call the `advance_frame` method to feed a new frame to the tracker.

However, before we make use of all this functionality, we need to learn about image statistics and how to generate a saliency map.

Mapping visual saliency

As already mentioned earlier in the chapter, visual saliency tries to describe the visual quality of certain objects or items that allows them to grab our immediate attention. Our brains constantly drive our gaze toward the important regions of the visual scene, as if it were shining a flashlight on different subregions of the visual world, allowing us to quickly scan our surroundings for interesting objects and events while neglecting the less important parts.

It is thought that this is an evolutionary strategy to deal with the constant **information overflow** that comes with living in a visually rich environment. For example, if you take a casual walk through a jungle, you want to be able to notice the attacking tiger in the bush to your left before admiring the intricate color pattern on the butterfly's wings in front of you. As a result, the visually salient objects have the remarkable quality of *popping out* of their surroundings, much like the target bars in the following screenshot:

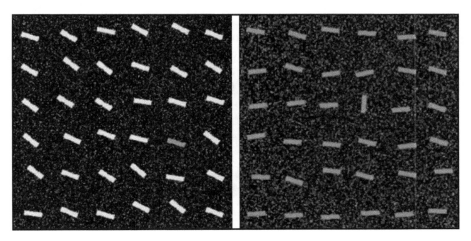

Identifying the visual quality that makes these targets pop out may not always be trivial though. If you are viewing the image on the left in color, you may immediately notice the only red bar in the image. However, if you are looking at this image in grayscale, the target bar may be a little difficult to find (it is the fourth bar from the top, fifth bar from the left).

Similar to color saliency, there is a visually salient bar in the image on the right. Although the target bar is of unique color in the left-hand image and of unique orientation in the right-hand image, we put the two characteristics together and suddenly the unique target bar does not pop out anymore:

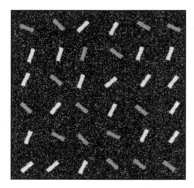

In the preceding display, there is again one bar that is unique and different from all the other ones. However, because of the way the distracting items were designed, there is little salience to guide you toward the target bar. Instead, you find yourself scanning the image, seemingly at random, looking for something interesting. (*Hint*: the target is the only red and almost vertical bar in the image, second row from the top, third column from the left.)

What does this have to do with computer vision, you ask? Quite a lot, actually. Artificial vision systems suffer from information overload much like you and me, except that they know even less about the world than we do. *What if we could extract some insights from biology and use them to teach our algorithms something about the world?*

Imagine a dashboard camera in your car that automatically focuses on the most relevant traffic sign. Imagine a surveillance camera that is part of a wildlife observation station that will automatically detect and track the sighting of the *notoriously shy platypus* but will ignore everything else. *How can we teach the algorithm what is important and what is not? How can we make that platypus "pop out"?*

Thus, we enter the Fourier analysis domain.

Learning about Fourier analysis

To find the visually salient subregions of an image, we need to look at its **frequency spectrum**. So far we have treated all our images and video frames in the **spatial domain**, that is, by analyzing the pixels or studying how the image intensity changes in different subregions of the image. However, the images can also be represented in the **frequency domain**, that is, by analyzing the pixel frequencies or studying how often and with what periodicity the pixels show up in the image.

An image can be transformed from the space domain into the frequency domain by applying the **Fourier transform**. In the frequency domain, we no longer think in terms of image coordinates (x,y). Instead, we aim to find the spectrum of an image. Fourier's radical idea basically boils down to the following question—*what if any signal or image could be transformed into a series of circular paths (also called **harmonics**)?*

For example, think of a rainbow. *Beautiful, isn't it?* In a rainbow, white sunlight (composed of many different colors or parts of the spectrum) is spread into its spectrum. Here, the color spectrum of the sunlight is exposed when the rays of light pass through raindrops (much like white light passing through a glass prism). The Fourier transform aims to do the same thing—to recover all the different parts of the spectrum that are contained in the sunlight.

A similar thing can be achieved for arbitrary images. In contrast to rainbows, where frequency corresponds to electromagnetic frequency, with images we consider spatial frequency, that is, the spatial periodicity of the pixel values. In an image of a prison cell, you can think of spatial frequency as (the inverse of) the distance between two adjacent prison bars.

The insights that can be gained from this change of perspective are very powerful. Without going into too much detail, let's just remark that a Fourier spectrum comes with both a magnitude and a phase. While the magnitude describes the number/amount of different frequencies in the image, the phase talks about the spatial location of these frequencies. The following screenshot shows a natural image on the left and the corresponding Fourier magnitude spectrum (of the grayscale version) on the right:

The magnitude spectrum on the right tells us which frequency components are the most prominent (bright) in the grayscale version of the image on the left. The spectrum is adjusted so that the center of the image corresponds to zero frequency in x and y. The further you move to the border of the image, the higher the frequency gets. This particular spectrum is telling us that there are a lot of low-frequency components in the image on the left (clustered around the center of the image).

In OpenCV, this transformation can be achieved with the help of the **Discrete Fourier Transform (DFT)**. Let's construct a function that does the job. It consists of the following steps:

1. First, convert the image to grayscale if necessary. The function accepts both grayscale and RGB color images, so we need to make sure that we operate on a single-channel image:

```
def calc_magnitude_spectrum(img: np.ndarray):
    if len(img.shape) > 2:
        img = cv2.cvtColor(img, cv2.COLOR_BGR2GRAY)
```

2. We resize the image to an optimal size. It turns out that the performance of a DFT depends on the image size. It tends to be fastest for the image sizes that are multiples of the number 2. It is therefore generally a good idea to pad the image with 0:

```
rows, cols = img.shape
nrows = cv2.getOptimalDFTSize(rows)
ncols = cv2.getOptimalDFTSize(cols)
frame = cv2.copyMakeBorder(img, 0, ncols-cols, 0, nrows-rows,
                           cv2.BORDER_CONSTANT, value=0)
```

3. Then we apply the DFT. This is a single function call in NumPy. The result is a two-dimensional matrix of complex numbers:

```
img_dft = np.fft.fft2(img)
```

4. Then, transform the real and complex values to magnitude. A complex number has a real and complex (imaginary) part. To extract the magnitude, we take the absolute value:

```
magn = np.abs(img_dft)
```

5. Then we switch to a logarithmic scale. It turns out that the dynamic range of the Fourier coefficients is usually too large to be displayed on the screen. We have some low and some high changing values that we can't observe like this. Therefore, the high values will all turn out as white points, and the low ones as black points.

   To use the grayscale values for visualization, we can transform our linear scale to a logarithmic one:

```
log_magn = np.log10(magn)
```

6. We then shift quadrants, to center the spectrum on the image. This makes it easier to visually inspect the magnitude spectrum:

```
spectrum = np.fft.fftshift(log_magn)
```

7. We `return` the result for plotting:

```
return spectrum/np.max(spectrum)*255
```

The result can be plotted with `pyplot`.

Now that we understand what the Fourier spectrum of an image is and how to calculate it, let's analyze natural scene statistics in the next section.

Understanding the natural scene statistics

The human brain figured out how to focus on visually salient objects a long time ago. The natural world in which we live has some statistical regularities that make it uniquely *natural*, as opposed to a chessboard pattern or a random company logo. Probably, the most commonly known statistical regularity is the *1/f* law. It states that the amplitude of the ensemble of natural images obeys a *1/f* distribution (as shown in the following screenshot). This is sometimes also referred to as **scale invariance**.

A one-dimensional power spectrum (as a function of frequency) of a two-dimensional image can be visualized with the following `plot_power_spectrum` function. We can use a similar recipe as for the magnitude spectrum used previously, but we will have to make sure that we correctly collapse the two-dimensional spectrum onto a single axis:

1. Define the function and convert the image to grayscale if necessary (this is the same as earlier):

```
def plot_power_spectrum(frame: np.ndarray, use_numpy_fft=True) ->
None:
    if len(frame.shape) > 2:
        frame = cv2.cvtColor(frame, cv2.COLOR_BGR2GRAY)
```

2. Expand the image to its optimal size (this is the same as earlier):

```
rows, cols = frame.shape
nrows = cv2.getOptimalDFTSize(rows)
ncols = cv2.getOptimalDFTSize(cols)
frame = cv2.copyMakeBorder(frame, 0, ncols-cols, 0,
    nrows-rows, cv2.BORDER_CONSTANT, value = 0)
```

3. We then apply the DFT and get the log spectrum. Here we give the user an option (via the `use_numpy_fft` flag) to use either NumPy's or OpenCV's Fourier tools:

```
if use_numpy_fft:
    img_dft = np.fft.fft2(frame)
    spectrum = np.log10(np.real(np.abs(img_dft))**2)
else:
    img_dft = cv2.dft(np.float32(frame),
flags=cv2.DFT_COMPLEX_OUTPUT)
    spectrum = np.log10(img_dft[:, :, 0]**2 + img_dft[:, :,
1]**2)
```

4. We then perform radial averaging. This is the tricky part. It would be wrong to simply average the two-dimensional spectrum in the direction of *x* or *y*. What we are interested in is a spectrum as a function of frequency, independent of the exact orientation. This is sometimes also called the **Radially Averaged Power Spectrum** (**RAPS**).

It can be achieved by summing up all the frequency magnitudes, starting at the center of the image, looking into all possible (radial) directions, from some frequency r to r+dr. We use the binning function of NumPy's histogram to sum up the numbers, and accumulate them in the `histo` variable:

```
L = max(frame.shape)
freqs = np.fft.fftfreq(L)[:L/2]
dists = np.sqrt(np.fft.fftfreq(frame.shape[0])
    [:,np.newaxis]**2 + np.fft.fftfreq
        (frame.shape[1])**2)
dcount = np.histogram(dists.ravel(), bins=freqs)[0]
histo, bins = np.histogram(dists.ravel(), bins=freqs,
    weights=spectrum.ravel())
```

5. We then plot the result and, finally, we can plot the accumulated numbers in `histo`, but must not forget to normalize these by the bin size (`dcount`):

```
centers = (bins[:-1] + bins[1:]) / 2
plt.plot(centers, histo/dcount)
plt.xlabel('frequency')
plt.ylabel('log-spectrum')
plt.show()
```

The result is a function that is inversely proportional to the frequency. If you want to be absolutely certain of the *1/f* property, you could take `np.log10` of all the *x* values and make sure the curve is decreasing in a roughly linear fashion. On a linear *x* axis and logarithmic *y* axis, the plot looks like the following screenshot:

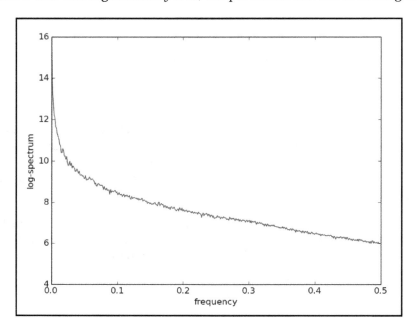

This property is quite remarkable. It states that if we were to average all the spectra of all the images ever taken of natural scenes (neglecting all the ones taken with fancy image filters, of course), we would get a curve that would look remarkably like the one shown in the preceding image.

But, going back to the image of a peaceful little boat on the **Limmat** river, *what about single images?* We have just looked at the power spectrum of this image and witnessed the *1/f* property. *How can we use our knowledge of natural image statistics to tell an algorithm not to stare at the tree on the left, but instead focus on the boat that is chugging in the water?* The following photo depicts a scene at the Limmat river:

This is where we realize what saliency really means.

Let's see how to generate a saliency map with the spectral residual approach in the next section.

Generating a saliency map with the spectral residual approach

The things that deserve our attention in an image are not the image patches that follow the $1/f$ law, but the patches that stick out of the smooth curves, in other words, statistical anomalies. These anomalies are termed the **spectral residual** of an image and correspond to the potentially *interesting* patches of an image (or proto-objects). A map that shows these statistical anomalies as bright spots is called a **saliency map**.

The spectral residual approach described here is based on the original scientific publication article *Saliency Detection: A Spectral Residual Approach* by Xiaodi Hou and Liqing Zhang (2007), IEEE Transactions on Computer Vision and Pattern Recognition (CVPR), p.1-8, DOI: 10.1109/CVPR.2007.383267.

The saliency map of a single channel can be generated with
the _get_channel_sal_magn function using the following process. In order to generate a
saliency map based on the spectral residual approach, we need to process each channel of
an input image separately (a single channel in the case of a grayscale input image, and three
separate channels in the case of an RGB input image):

1. Calculate the (magnitude and phase of the) Fourier spectrum of an image, by
   again using either the fft module of NumPy or the OpenCV functionality:

```
def _calc_channel_sal_magn(channel: np.ndarray,
                           use_numpy_fft: bool = True) ->
np.ndarray:
    if use_numpy_fft:
        img_dft = np.fft.fft2(channel)
        magnitude, angle = cv2.cartToPolar(np.real(img_dft),
                                           np.imag(img_dft))
    else:
        img_dft = cv2.dft(np.float32(channel),
                          flags=cv2.DFT_COMPLEX_OUTPUT)
        magnitude, angle = cv2.cartToPolar(img_dft[:, :, 0],
                                           img_dft[:, :, 1])
```

2. Calculate the log amplitude of the Fourier spectrum. We will clip the lower
   bound of magnitudes to 1e-9 in order to prevent a division by 0 while
   calculating the log:

```
log_ampl = np.log10(magnitude.clip(min=1e-9))
```

3. Approximate the averaged spectrum of a typical natural image by convolving the
   image with a local averaging filter:

```
log_ampl_blur = cv2.blur(log_amlp, (3, 3))
```

4. Calculate the spectral residual. The spectral residual primarily contains the
   non-trivial (or unexpected) parts of a scene:

```
residual = np.exp(log_ampl - log_ampl_blur)
```

5. Calculate the saliency map by using the inverse Fourier transform, again either
   via the fft module in NumPy or with OpenCV:

```
    if use_numpy_fft:
        real_part, imag_part = cv2.polarToCart(residual, angle)
        img_combined = np.fft.ifft2(real_part + 1j * imag_part)
        magnitude, _ = cv2.cartToPolar(np.real(img_combined),
                                       np.imag(img_combined))
```

```
        else:
            img_dft[:, :, 0], img_dft[:, :, 1] =%MCEPASTEBIN%
        cv2.polarToCart(residual,
                                                            angle)
            img_combined = cv2.idft(img_dft)
            magnitude, _ = cv2.cartToPolar(img_combined[:, :, 0],
                                            img_combined[:, :, 1])

        return magnitude
```

A single-channel saliency map (`magnitude`) is used by `get_saliency_map`, where the procedure is repeated for all channels of the input image. If the input image is grayscale, we are pretty much done:

```
def get_saliency_map(frame: np.ndarray,
                     small_shape: Tuple[int] = (64, 64),
                     gauss_kernel: Tuple[int] = (5, 5),
                     use_numpy_fft: bool = True) -> np.ndarray:
    frame_small = cv2.resize(frame, small_shape)
    if len(frame.shape) == 2:
        # single channelsmall_shape[1::-1]
        sal = _calc_channel_sal_magn(frame, use_numpy_fft)
```

However, if the input image has multiple channels, as is the case for an RGB color image, we need to consider each channel separately:

```
    else:
        sal = np.zeros_like(frame_small).astype(np.float32)
        for c in range(frame_small.shape[2]):
            small = frame_small[:, :, c]
            sal[:, :, c] = _calc_channel_sal_magn(small, use_numpy_fft)
```

The overall salience of a multichannel image is then determined by the average overall channels:

```
        sal = np.mean(sal, 2)
```

Finally, we need to apply some post-processing, such as an optional blurring stage to make the result appear smoother:

```
    if gauss_kernel is not None:
        sal = cv2.GaussianBlur(sal, gauss_kernel, sigmaX=8, sigmaY=0)
```

Also, we need to square the values in `sal` in order to highlight the regions of high salience, as outlined by the authors of the original paper. In order to display the image, we scale it back up to its original resolution and normalize the values, so that the largest value is 1.

Next, normalize the values in `sal` so that the largest value is 1, then square them in order to highlight the regions of high salience as outlined by the authors of the original paper, and, lastly, scale back to its original resolution in order to display the image:

```
sal = sal**2
sal = np.float32(sal)/np.max(sal)
sal = cv2.resize(sal, self.frame_orig.shape[1::-1])
sal /= np.max(sal)
return cv2.resize(sal ** 2, frame.shape[1::-1])
```

The resulting saliency map then looks like the following:

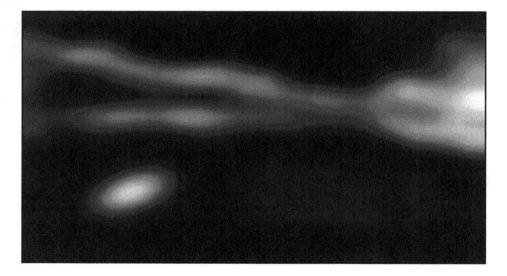

Now we can clearly spot the boat in the water (in the lower-left corner), which appears as one of the most salient subregions of the image. There are other salient regions, too, such as the **Grossmünster** on the right (*have you guessed the city yet?*).

 By the way, the fact that these two areas are the most salient ones in the image seems to be clear and indisputable evidence that the algorithm is aware of the ridiculous number of church towers in the city center of **Zurich**, effectively prohibiting any chance of them being labeled as *"salient"*.

In the next section, we'll see how to detect proto-objects in a scene.

Detecting proto-objects in a scene

In a sense, the saliency map is already an explicit representation of proto-objects, as it contains only the *interesting* parts of an image. So now that we have done all the hard work, all that is left to do in order to obtain a proto-object map is to threshold the saliency map.

The only open parameter to consider here is the threshold. Setting the threshold too low will result in labeling a lot of regions as proto-objects, including some that might not contain anything of interest (false alarm). On the other hand, setting the threshold too high will ignore most of the salient regions in the image and might leave us with no proto-objects at all.

The authors of the original spectral residual paper chose to label only those regions of the image as proto-objects whose saliency was larger than three times the mean saliency of the image. We give the user the choice either to implement this threshold or to go with the **Otsu threshold** by setting the input flag use_otsu to True:

```
def get_proto_objects_map(saliency: np.ndarray, use_otsu=True) ->
np.ndarray:
```

We then convert saliency to uint8 precision so that it can be passed to cv2.threshold, set parameters for thresholding, and, finally, we apply thresholding and return the proto-objects:

```
saliency = np.uint8(saliency * 255)
if use_otsu:
    thresh_type = cv2.THRESH_OTSU
    # For threshold value, simply pass zero.
    thresh_value = 0
else:
    thresh_type = cv2.THRESH_BINARY
    thresh_value = np.mean(saliency) * 3

_, img_objects = cv2.threshold(saliency,
                               thresh_value, 255, thresh_type)
return img_objects
```

The resulting proto-objects mask looks as follows:

The proto-objects mask then serves as an input to the tracking algorithm, which we will see in the next section.

Understanding mean-shift tracking

So far we used the salience detector discussed previously to find bounding boxes of proto-objects. We could simply apply the algorithm to every frame of a video sequence and get a good idea of the location of the objects. However, what is getting lost is correspondence information.

Imagine a video sequence of a busy scene, such as from a city center or a sports stadium. Although a saliency map could highlight all the proto-objects in every frame of a recorded video, the algorithm would have no way to establish a correspondence between proto-objects from the previous frame and proto-objects in the current frame.

Also, the proto-objects map might contain some *false positives*, and we need an approach to select the most probable boxes that correspond to real-world objects. Such *false positives* can be noticed in the following example:

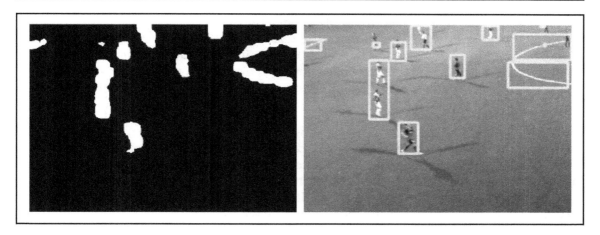

Note that the bounding boxes extracted from the proto-objects map made (at least) three mistakes in the preceding example—it missed highlighting a player (upper-left), merged two players into the same bounding box, and highlighted some additional arguably non-interesting (although visually salient) objects. In order to improve these results and maintain correspondence, we want to take advantage of a tracking algorithm.

To solve the correspondence problem, we could use the methods we have learned about previously, such as feature matching and optical flow, but in this case, we will use the mean-shift algorithm for tracking.

Mean-shift is a simple yet very effective technique for tracking arbitrary objects. The intuition behind the mean-shift is to consider the pixels in a small region of interest (say, the bounding box of an object we want to track) as sampled from an underlying probability density function that best describes a target.

Consider, for example, the following image:

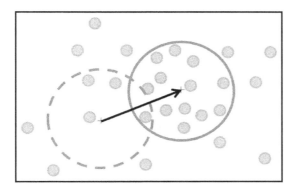

Here, the small gray dots represent samples from a probability distribution. Assume that the closer the dots, the more similar they are to each other. Intuitively speaking, what mean-shift is trying to do is to find the densest region in this landscape and draw a circle around it. The algorithm might start out centering a circle over a region of the landscape that is not dense at all (the dashed circle). Over time, it will slowly move toward the densest region (the solid circle) and anchor on it.

If we design the landscape to be more meaningful than dots, we can use mean-shift tracking to find the objects of interest in the scene. For example, if we assign to each dot some value for correspondence between the color histogram of an object and the color histogram of a neighborhood of an image of the same size as the object, we can use mean-shift on the resulting dots to track the object. It is the latter approach that is usually associated with mean-shift tracking. In our case, we will simply use the saliency map itself.

Mean-shift has many applications (such as clustering, or finding the mode of probability density functions), but it is also particularly well suited to target tracking. In OpenCV, the algorithm is implemented in `cv2.meanShift` and accepts a two-dimensional array (for example, a grayscale image such as a saliency map) and window (in our case, we use the bounding box of an object) as input. It returns new positions of the window in accordance with the mean-shift algorithm as follows:

1. It fixes a window position.
2. It computes the mean of the data within the window.
3. It shifts the window to the mean and repeats until convergence. We can control the length and accuracy of the iterative method by specifying the termination criteria.

Next, let's see how the algorithm tracks and visually maps (with bounding boxes) a player on the field.

Automatically tracking all players on a soccer field

Our goal is to combine the saliency detector with mean-shift tracking to automatically track all the players on a soccer field. The proto-objects identified by the saliency detector will serve as input to the mean-shift tracker. Specifically, we will focus on a video sequence from the Alfheim dataset, which can be freely obtained from `http://home.ifi.uio.no/paalh/dataset/alfheim/`.

The reason for combining the two algorithms (saliency map and mean-shift tracking), is to maintain correspondence information between objects in different frames as well as to remove some false positives and improve the accuracy of detected objects.

The hard work is done by the previously introduced `MultiObjectTracker` class and its `advance_frame` method. The `advance_frame` method is called whenever a new frame arrives, and accepts proto-objects and saliency as input:

```
def advance_frame(self,
                  frame: np.ndarray,
                  proto_objects_map: np.ndarray,
                  saliency: np.ndarray) -> np.ndarray:
```

The following steps are covered in this method:

1. Create contours from `proto_objects_map` and find bounding rectangles for all contours that have an area greater than `min_object_area`. The latter is the candidate bounding boxes for tracking with the mean shift algorithm:

```
object_contours, _ = cv2.findContours(proto_objects_map, 1, 2)
object_boxes = [cv2.boundingRect(contour)
                for contour in object_contours
                if cv2.contourArea(contour) >
self.min_object_area]
```

2. The candidate boxes might be not the best ones for tracking them throughout the frames. For example, in this case, if two players are close to each other, they result in a single object box. We need some approach to select the best boxes. We could think about some algorithm that will analyze boxes tracked from previous frames in combination with boxes obtained from saliency, and deduce the most probable boxes.

   But we will do it in a simple manner here—if the number of boxes from the saliency map doesn't increase, boxes from the previous frame to the current frame using the saliency map of the current frame are tracked, which are saved as `objcect_boxes`:

```
if len(self.object_boxes) >= len(object_boxes):
    # Continue tracking with meanshift if number of salient
objects
    # didn't increase
    object_boxes = [cv2.meanShift(saliency, box,
self.term_crit)[1]
                    for box in self.object_boxes]
    self.num_frame_tracked += 1
```

3. If it did increase, we reset the tracking information, which is the number of frames through which the objects were tracked and the initial centers of the objects were calculated:

```
else:
    # Otherwise restart tracking
    self.num_frame_tracked = 0
    self.object_initial_centers = [
        (x + w / 2, y + h / 2) for (x, y, w, h) in
object_boxes]
```

4. Finally, save the boxes and make an illustration of the tracking information on the frame:

```
self.object_boxes = object_boxes
return self.draw_good_boxes(copy.deepcopy(frame))
```

We are interested in boxes that move. For that purpose, we calculate the displacements of each box from their initial location at the start of tracking. We suppose that objects that appear larger on a frame should move faster, hence we normalize the displacements on box width:

```
def draw_good_boxes(self, frame: np.ndarray) -> np.ndarray:
    # Find total displacement length for each object
    # and normalize by object size
    displacements = [((x + w / 2 - cx)**2 + (y + w / 2 - cy)**2)**0.5 /
w
                     for (x, y, w, h), (cx, cy)
                     in zip(self.object_boxes,
self.object_initial_centers)]
```

Next, we draw boxes and their number, which have average displacement per frame (or speed) greater than the value that we specified on the initialization of the tracker. A small number is added in order not to divide by 0 on the first frame of tracking:

```
for (x, y, w, h), displacement, i in zip(
        self.object_boxes, displacements, itertools.count()):
    # Draw only those which have some avarage speed
    if displacement / (self.num_frame_tracked + 0.01) >
self.min_speed_per_pix:
        cv2.rectangle(frame, (x, y), (x + w, y + h),
                      (0, 255, 0), 2)
        cv2.putText(frame, str(i), (x, y),
                    cv2.FONT_HERSHEY_SIMPLEX, 0.5, (255, 255, 255))
    return frame
```

Now you understand how it is possible to implement tracking using the mean-shift algorithm. This is only one approach for tracking out of many others on offer. Mean-shift tracking might particularly fail when the objects rapidly change in size, as would be the case if an object of interest were to come straight at the camera.

For such cases, OpenCV has a different algorithm, `cv2.CamShift`, which also takes into account rotations and changes in size, where **CAMShift** stands for **Continuously Adaptive Mean-Shift**. Moreover, OpenCV has a range of available trackers that can be used out of the box and are referred to as the **OpenCV Tracking API**. Let's learn about them in the next section.

Learning about the OpenCV Tracking API

We have applied the mean-shift algorithm on the saliency map for tracking salient objects. Surely, not all the objects in the world are salient, so we can't use that approach for tracking any object. As mentioned previously, we could also use an HSV histogram in combination with the mean-shift algorithm to track objects. The latter does not require a saliency map—if a region is selected, that approach will try to track selected objects throughout the consequent frames.

In this section, we will create a script that is able to track an object throughout a video using the tracking algorithms available in OpenCV. All these algorithms have the same API and are referred to collectively as the OpenCV Tracking API. These algorithms track single objects—once the initial bounding box is provided to the algorithm, it will try to maintain the new positions of the box throughout the consequent frames. Surely, it's also possible to track multiple objects in the scene by creating a new tracker for each object.

First of all, we import the libraries that we will use and define our constants:

```
import argparse
import time

import cv2
import numpy as np

# Define Constants
FONT = cv2.FONT_HERSHEY_SIMPLEX
GREEN = (20, 200, 20)
RED = (20, 20, 255)
```

OpenCV currently has eight built-in trackers. We define a map of the constructors of all trackers:

```
trackers = {
    'BOOSTING': cv2.TrackerBoosting_create,
    'MIL': cv2.TrackerMIL_create,
    'KCF': cv2.TrackerKCF_create,
    'TLD': cv2.TrackerTLD_create,
    'MEDIANFLOW': cv2.TrackerMedianFlow_create,
    'GOTURN': cv2.TrackerGOTURN_create,
    'MOSSE': cv2.TrackerMOSSE_create,
    'CSRT': cv2.TrackerCSRT_create
}
```

Our script will be able to accept the name of the tracker and a path to a video as arguments. In order to achieve this, we create arguments, set their default values, and parse them with the previously imported `argparse` module:

```
# Parse arguments
parser = argparse.ArgumentParser(description='Tracking API demo.')
parser.add_argument(
    '--tracker',
    default="KCF",
    help=f"One of {trackers.keys()}")
parser.add_argument(
    '--video',
    help="Video file to use",
    default="videos/test.mp4")
args = parser.parse_args()
```

Then, we make sure that such a tracker exists and we try to read the first frame from the specified video.

Now that we have set up the script and can accept parameters, the next thing to do is to instantiate the tracker:

1. First of all, it's a good idea to make the script case-insensitive and check whether the passed tracker exists at all:

```
tracker_name = args.tracker.upper()
assert tracker_name in trackers, f"Tracker should be one of
{trackers.keys()}"
```

2. Open the video and read the first `frame`. Then, break the script if the video cannot be read:

```
video = cv2.VideoCapture(args.video)
assert video.isOpened(), "Could not open video"
ok, frame = video.read()
assert ok, "Video file is not readable"
```

3. Select a region of interest (using a bounding box) for tracking throughout the video. OpenCV has a user-interface-based implementation for that:

```
bbox = cv2.selectROI(frame, False)
```

Once this method is called, an interface will appear where you can select a box. Once the *Enter* key is pressed, the coordinates for the selected box are returned.

4. Initiate the tracker with the first frame and the selected bounding box:

```
tracker = trackers[tracker_name]()
tracker.init(frame, bbox)
```

Now we have an instance of the tracker that has been initiated with the first frame and selected a bounding box of interest. We update the tracker with the next frames to find the new location of the object in the bounding box. We also estimate the **frames per second (FPS)** of the selected tracking algorithm using the `time` module:

```
for ok, frame in iter(video.read, (False, None)):
    # Time in seconds
    start_time = time.time()
    # Update tracker
    ok, bbox = tracker.update(frame)
    # Calcurlate FPS
    fps = 1 / (time.time() - start_time)
```

All the calculations are done by this point. Now we illustrate the results for each iteration:

```
if ok:
    # Draw bounding box
    x, y, w, h = np.array(bbox, dtype=np.int)
    cv2.rectangle(frame, (x, y), (x + w, y + w), GREEN, 2, 1)
else:
    # Tracking failure
    cv2.putText(frame, "Tracking failed", (100, 80), FONT, 0.7, RED, 2)
cv2.putText(frame, f"{tracker_name} Tracker",
            (100, 20), FONT, 0.7, GREEN, 2)
cv2.putText(frame, f"FPS : {fps:.0f}", (100, 50), FONT, 0.7, GREEN, 2)
cv2.imshow("Tracking", frame)
```

```
# Exit if ESC pressed
if cv2.waitKey(1) & 0xff == 27:
    break
```

If a bounding box was returned by the algorithm, we draw that box on the frame, otherwise, we illustrate that the tracking failed, which means that the selected algorithm failed to find the object in the current frame. Also, we type the name of the tracker and the current FPS on the frame.

You can run this script on different videos with different algorithms in order to see how the algorithms behave, especially how they handle occlusions, fast-moving objects, and objects that change a lot in appearance. After trying the algorithms, you might also be interested to read the original papers of the algorithms to find out implementation details.

In order to track multiple objects using these algorithms, OpenCV has a convenient wrapper class that combines multiple instances of the tracker and updates them simultaneously. In order to use it, first, we create an instance of the class:

```
multiTracker = cv2.MultiTracker_create()
```

Next, for each bounding box of interest, a new tracker is created (MIL tracker, in this case) and added to the multiTracker object:

```
for bbox in bboxes:
    multiTracker.add(cv2.TrackerMIL_create(), frame, bbox)
```

Finally, the new positions of the bounding boxes are obtained by updating the multiTracker object with a new frame:

```
success, boxes = multiTracker.update(frame)
```

As an exercise, you might want to replace the mean-shift tracking in the application for tracking salient objects with one of the trackers introduced in this chapter. In order to do it, you can use multiTracker with one of the trackers to update the positions of bounding boxes for proto-objects.

Putting it all together

The result of our app can be seen in the following set of screenshots:

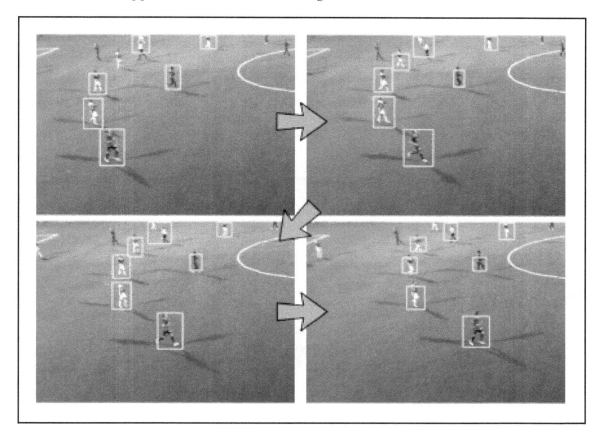

Throughout the video sequence, the algorithm is able to pick up the location of the players and successfully track them frame by frame by using mean-shift tracking.

Summary

In this chapter, we explored a way to label the potentially *interesting* objects in a visual scene, even if their shape and number are unknown. We explored natural image statistics using Fourier analysis and implemented a method for extracting the visually salient regions in the natural scenes. Furthermore, we combined the output of the salience detector with a tracking algorithm to track multiple objects of unknown shape and number in a video sequence of a soccer game.

We have introduced other, more complex tracking algorithms available in OpenCV, which you can use to replace mean-shift tracking in the application or even create your own application. Of course, it would also be possible to replace the mean-shift tracker with a previously studied technique such as feature matching or optic flow.

In the next chapter, we will move on to the fascinating field of machine learning, which will allow us to build more powerful descriptors of objects. Specifically, we will focus on both detection (*the where*) and identification (*the what*) of street signs in images. This will allow us to train a classifier that could be used in a dashboard camera in your car and will familiarize us with the important concepts of machine learning and object recognition.

Dataset attribution

"Soccer video and player position dataset," S. A. Pettersen, D. Johansen, H. Johansen, V. Berg-Johansen, V. R. Gaddam, A. Mortensen, R. Langseth, C. Griwodz, H. K. Stensland, and *P. Halvorsen,* in Proceedings of the International Conference on Multimedia Systems (MMSys), Singapore, March 2014, pp. 18-23.

Learning to Recognize Traffic Signs

7

We have previously studied how to describe objects by means of key points and features, and how to find the correspondence points in two different images of the same physical object. However, our previous approaches were rather limited when it came to recognizing objects in real-world settings and assigning them to conceptual categories. For example, in Chapter 2, *Hand Gesture Recognition Using a Kinect Depth Sensor*, the required object in the image was a hand, and it had to be nicely placed in the center of the screen. Wouldn't it be nice if we could remove these restrictions?

The goal of this chapter is to train a **multiclass classifier** to recognize traffic signs. In this chapter, we will cover the following concepts:

- Planning the app
- Briefing on supervised learning concepts
- Understanding the **German Traffic Sign Recognition Benchmark (GTSRB)** dataset
- Learning about dataset feature extraction
- Learning about **support vector machines (SVMs)**
- Putting it all together
- Improving results with neural networks

In this chapter, you will learn how to apply machine learning models to real-world problems. You will learn how to use already available datasets for training models. You will also learn how to use SVMs for multiclass classification and how to train, test, and improve machine learning algorithms provided with OpenCV to achieve real-world tasks.

We will train an SVM to recognize all sorts of traffic signs. Although SVMs are binary classifiers (that is, they can be used to learn, at most, two categories—positives and negatives, animals and non-animals, and so on), they can be extended to be used in multiclass classification. In order to achieve good classification performance, we will explore a number of color spaces, as well as the **Histogram of Oriented Gradients** (**HOG**) feature. The end result will be a classifier that can distinguish more than 40 different signs from the dataset, with very high accuracy.

Learning the basics of machine learning will be very useful for the future when you would like to make your vision-related applications even smarter. This chapter will teach you the basics of machine learning, on which the following chapters will build.

Getting started

The GTSRB dataset can be freely obtained from `http://benchmark.ini.rub.de/?section=gtsrb&subsection=dataset` (see the *Dataset attribution* section for attribution details).

You can find the code that we present in this chapter at our GitHub repository: `https://github.com/PacktPublishing/OpenCV-4-with-Python-Blueprints-Second-Edition/tree/master/chapter7`.

Planning the app

To arrive at such a multiclass classifier (that can differentiate between more than 40 different signs from the dataset), we need to perform the following steps:

1. **Preprocess the dataset**: We need a way to load our dataset, extract the regions of interest, and split the data into appropriate training and test sets.
2. **Extract features**: Chances are that raw pixel values are not the most informative representation of the data. We need a way to extract meaningful features from the data, such as features based on different color spaces and HOG.
3. **Train the classifier**: We will train the multiclass classifier on the training data using a *one-versus-all* strategy.
4. **Score the classifier**: We will evaluate the quality of the trained ensemble classifier by calculating different performance metrics, such as **accuracy**, **precision**, and **recall**.

We will discuss all these steps in detail in the upcoming sections.

The final app will parse a dataset, train the ensemble classifier, assess its classification performance, and visualize the result. This will require the following components:

- `main`: The main function routine (in `chapter7.py`) is required for starting the application.
- `datasets.gtsrb`: This is a script for parsing the GTSRB dataset. This script contains the following functions:
  - `load_data`: This function is used to load the GTSRB dataset, extract a feature of choice, and split the data into training and test sets.
  - `*_featurize`, `hog_featurize`: These functions are passed to `load_data` for extracting a feature of choice from the dataset. Example functions are as follows:
    - `gray_featurize`: This is a function that creates features based on grayscale pixel values.
    - `surf_featurize`: This is a function that creates features based on **Speeded-Up-Robust Features (SURF)**.

The classification performance will be judged based on accuracy, precision, and recall. The following sections will explain all of these terms in detail.

Briefing on supervised learning concepts

An important subfield of machine learning is **supervised learning**. In supervised learning, we try to learn from a set of labeled data—that is, every data sample has a desired target value or true output value. These target values could correspond to the continuous output of a function (such as y in $y = sin(x)$), or to more abstract and discrete categories (such as *cat* or *dog*).

A supervised learning algorithm uses the already labeled training data, analyzes it, and produces a mapping inferred function from features to a label, which can be used for mapping new examples. Ideally, the inferred algorithm will generalize well and give correct target values for new data.

We divide supervised learning tasks into two categories:

- If we are dealing with continuous output (for example, the probability of rain), the process is called **regression**.
- If we are dealing with discrete output (for example, species of an animal), the process is called **classification**.

In this chapter, we focus on the classification problem of labeling images of the GTSRB dataset, and we will use an algorithm called SVM to infer a mapping function between images and their labels.

Let's first understand how machine learning gives *machines* the ability to *learn like humans*. Here is a hint—we train them.

The training procedure

As an example, we may want to learn what cats and dogs look like. To make this a supervised learning task, first, we have to put it as a question that has either a categorical answer or a real-valued answer.

Here are some example questions:

- Which animal is shown in the given picture?
- Is there a cat in the picture?
- Is there a dog in the picture?

After that, we have to gather an example picture with its corresponding correct answer—**training data**.

Then, we have to pick a learning algorithm (**learner**) and start tweaking its parameters in some way (**learning algorithm**) so that the learner can tell the correct answers when presented with a datum from training data.

We repeat this process until we are satisfied with the learner's performance or **score** (which could be **accuracy**, **precision**, or some other **cost function**) on the training data. If we are not satisfied, we change the parameters of the learner in order to improve the score over time.

This procedure is outlined in the following screenshot:

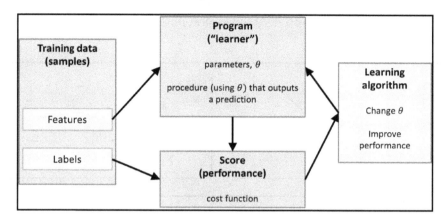

From the previous screenshot, **Training data** is represented by a set of **Features**. For real-life classification tasks, these features are rarely the raw pixel values of an image, since these tend not to represent the data well. Often, the process of finding the features that best describe the data is an essential part of the entire learning task (also referred to as **feature selection** or **feature engineering**).

That is why it is always a good idea to deeply study the statistics and appearances of the training set that you are working with before even thinking about setting up a classifier.

As you are probably aware, there is an entire zoo of learners, cost functions, and learning algorithms out there. These make up the core of the learning procedure. The **learner** (for example, a linear classifier or SVM) defines how input features are converted into a score function (for example, mean-squared error), whereas the **Learning algorithm** (for example, gradient descent) defines how the parameters of the **learner** are changed over time.

The training procedure in a classification task can also be thought of as finding an appropriate **decision boundary**, which is a line that best partitions the training set into two subsets, one for each class. For example, consider training samples with only two features (**x** and **y** values) and a corresponding class label (positive (+), or negative (−)).

At the beginning of the training procedure, the classifier tries to draw a line to separate all positives from all negatives. As the training progresses, the classifier sees more and more data samples. These are used to update the decision boundary, as illustrated in the following screenshot:

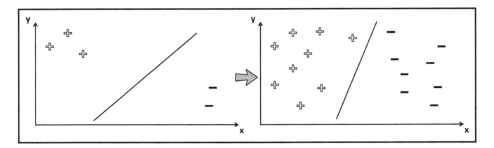

Compared to this simple illustration, an SVM tries to find the optimal decision boundary in a high-dimensional space, so the decision boundary can be more complex than a straight line.

We now move on to understand the testing procedure.

The testing procedure

In order for a trained classifier to be of any practical value, we need to know how it performs when applied to a data sample (also called **generalization**) that has never been seen before. To stick to our example shown earlier, we want to know which class the classifier predicts when we present it with a previously unseen picture of a cat or a dog.

More generally speaking, we want to know which class the **?** sign, in the following screenshot, corresponds to, based on the decision boundary we learned during the training phase:

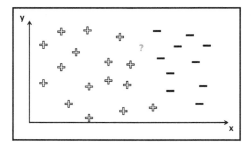

From the preceding screenshot, you can see why this is a tricky problem. If the location of the question mark (**?**) were more to the left, we would be certain that the corresponding class label is **+**.

However, in this case, there are several ways to draw the decision boundary such that all the **+** signs are to the left of it and all the **–** signs are to the right of it, as illustrated in the following screenshot:

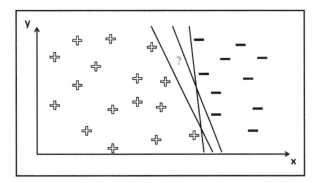

The label of **?** thus depends on the exact decision boundary that was derived during training. If the **?** sign in the preceding screenshot is actually a **–** sign, then only one decision boundary (the leftmost) would get the correct answer. A common problem is that training can result in a decision boundary that works *too well* on the training set (also known as **overfitting**) but also makes a lot of mistakes when applied to unseen data.

In that case, it is likely that the learner imprinted details that are specific to the training set on the decision boundary, instead of revealing general properties about the data that might also be true for unseen data.

 A common technique for reducing the effect of overfitting is called **regularization**.

Long story short: the problem always comes back to finding the boundary that best splits not only the training set but also the test set. That is why the most important metric for a classifier is its generalization performance (that is, how well it classifies data not seen in the training phase).

In order to apply our classifier to traffic-sign recognition, we need a suitable dataset. A good choice might be the GTSRB dataset. Let us learn about it next.

Understanding the GTSRB dataset

The GTSRB dataset contains more than 50,000 images of traffic signs belonging to 43 classes.

This dataset was used by professionals in a classification challenge during the **International Joint Conference on Neural Networks (IJCNN)** in 2011. The GTSRB dataset is perfect for our purposes because it is large, organized, open source, and annotated.

Although the actual traffic sign is not necessarily a square or is in the center of each image, the dataset comes with an annotation file that specifies the bounding boxes for each sign.

A good idea before doing any sort of machine learning is usually to get a feel of the dataset, its qualities, and its challenges. Some good ideas include manually going through the data and understanding what are some characteristics of it, reading a data description—if it's available on the page—to understand which models might work best, and so on.

Here, we present a snippet from `data/gtsrb.py` that loads and then plots a random-15 sample of the training dataset, and does that `100` times, so you can paginate through the data:

```
if __name__ == '__main__':
    train_data, train_labels = load_training_data(labels=None)
    np.random.seed(75)
    for _ in range(100):
        indices = np.arange(len(train_data))
        np.random.shuffle(indices)
        for r in range(3):
            for c in range(5):
                i = 5 * r + c
                ax = plt.subplot(3, 5, 1 + i)
                sample = train_data[indices[i]]
                ax.imshow(cv2.resize(sample, (32, 32)), cmap=cm.Greys_r)
                ax.axis('off')
        plt.tight_layout()
        plt.show()
        np.random.seed(np.random.randint(len(indices)))
```

Another good strategy would be to plot 15 samples from each of the 43 classes and see how images change for the given class. The following screenshot shows some examples of this dataset:

Even from this small data sample, it is immediately clear that this is a challenging dataset for any sort of classifier. The appearance of the signs changes drastically based on viewing angle (orientation), viewing distance (blurriness), and lighting conditions (shadows and bright spots).

For some of these signs—such as the second sign of the third row—it is difficult, even for humans (at least for me), to tell the correct class label right away. It's a good thing we are aspiring experts in machine learning!

Let's now learn to parse the dataset in order to convert to a format suitable for the SVM to use for training.

Parsing the dataset

The GTSRB dataset has 21 files that we can download. We choose to work with the raw data to make it more educational and download the official training data—**Images and annotations** (GTSRB_Final_Training_Images.zip) for training, and the official training dataset that was used at the **IJCNN 2011 competition**—**Images and annotations** (GTSRB-Training_fixed.zip) for scoring.

The following screenshot shows the files from the dataset:

Archive Files

Name	Date	Size
GTSRB-Training_fixed.zip	2019-05-10 11:26:35	187490228
GTSRB_Final_Test_GT.zip	2019-05-10 11:26:35	99620
GTSRB_Final_Test_Haar.zip	2019-05-10 11:26:35	318949368
GTSRB_Final_Test_HOG.zip	2019-05-10 11:26:35	292285317
GTSRB_Final_Test_HueHist.zip	2019-05-10 11:26:35	4798306
GTSRB_Final_Test_Images.zip	2019-05-10 11:26:35	88978620
GTSRB_Final_Training_Haar.zip	2019-05-10 11:26:35	990882445
GTSRB_Final_Training_HOG.zip	2019-05-10 11:26:35	905512002
GTSRB_Final_Training_HueHist.zip	2019-05-10 11:26:35	18175283
GTSRB_Final_Training_Images.zip	2019-05-10 11:26:35	276294756
GTSRB_Online-Test-Haar-Sorted.zip	2019-05-10 11:26:35	319282224
GTSRB_Online-Test-Haar.zip	2019-05-10 11:26:35	319502253
GTSRB_Online-Test-HOG-Sorted.zip	2019-05-10 11:26:35	295572728
GTSRB_Online-Test-HOG.zip	2019-05-10 11:26:35	296231502
GTSRB_Online-Test-HueHist-Sorted.zip	2019-05-10 11:26:35	5245948
GTSRB_Online-Test-HueHist.zip	2019-05-10 11:26:35	5465543
GTSRB_Online-Test-Images-Sorted.zip	2019-05-10 11:26:35	88234254
GTSRB_Online-Test-Images.zip	2019-05-10 12:05:37	88610452
GTSRB_Training_Features_Haar.zip	2019-05-10 11:26:35	623933894
GTSRB_Training_Features_HOG.zip	2019-05-10 11:26:35	553169013
GTSRB_Training_Features_HueHist.zip	2019-05-10 11:26:35	14399826

1 to 21 of 21 rows   25 files per page

We chose to download the train and test data separately instead of constructing our own train/test data from one of the datasets because, after exploring the data, there are usually 30 images of the same sign from different distances that look very much alike. Putting these 30 images in different datasets will skew the problem and lead to great results, even though our model might not generalize well.

The following code is a function that downloads the data from the **University of Copenhagen Data Archive**:

```
ARCHIVE_PATH =
'https://sid.erda.dk/public/archives/daaeac0d7ce1152aea9b61d9f1e19370/'

def _download(filename, *, md5sum=None):
    write_path = Path(__file__).parent / filename
    if write_path.exists() and _md5sum_matches(write_path, md5sum):
        return write_path
    response = requests.get(f'{ARCHIVE_PATH}/{filename}')
    response.raise_for_status()
    with open(write_path, 'wb') as outfile:
        outfile.write(response.content)
    return write_path
```

The previous code takes a filename (you can see the files and their names from the previous screenshot) and checks if the file already exists or not (and checks whether the md5sum matches or not, if provided). This saves a lot of bandwidth and time by not having to download the files again and again. Then, it downloads the file and stores it in the same directory as the file that contains the code.

 The annotation format can be viewed at http://benchmark.ini.rub.de/?section=gtsrbsubsection=dataset#Annotationformat.

After we have downloaded the file, we write a function that unzips and extracts the data using the annotation format provided with the data, as follows:

1. First, we open the downloaded .zip file (this could be either the training or test data), and we iterate over all the files and only open .csv files, which contain the target information of each image in the corresponding class. This is shown in the following code:

```
def _load_data(filepath, labels):
    data, targets = [], []

    with ZipFile(filepath) as data_zip:
        for path in data_zip.namelist():
            if not path.endswith('.csv'):
                continue
            # Only iterate over annotations files
            ...
```

2. Then, we check if the label of the image is in the `labels` array that we are interested in. Then, we create a `csv.reader` that we will use to iterate over the `.csv` file contents, as follows:

```
....
# Only iterate over annotations files
*dir_path, csv_filename = path.split('/')
label_str = dir_path[-1]
if labels is not None and int(label_str) not in labels:
    continue
with data_zip.open(path, 'r') as csvfile:
    reader = csv.DictReader(TextIOWrapper(csvfile),
delimiter=';')
    for img_info in reader:
    ...
```

3. Every line of the file contains the annotation for one data sample. So, we extract the image path, read the data, and convert it to a NumPy array. Usually, the object in these samples is not perfectly cut out but is embedded in its surroundings. We cut the image using the boundary-box information provided in the archive, using a `.csv` file for each of the labels. In the following code, we add the sign to `data` and add the label to `targets`:

```
            img_path = '/'.join([*dir_path,
img_info['Filename']])
            raw_data = data_zip.read(img_path)
            img = cv2.imdecode(np.frombuffer(raw_data,
np.uint8), 1)

            x1, y1 = np.int(img_info['Roi.X1']),
            np.int(img_info['Roi.Y1'])
            x2, y2 = np.int(img_info['Roi.X2']),
            np.int(img_info['Roi.Y2'])

            data.append(img[y1: y2, x1: x2])
            targets.append(np.int(img_info['ClassId']))
```

Often, it is desirable to perform some form of feature extraction, because raw image data is rarely the best description of the data. We will defer this job to another function, which we will discuss in detail later.

As pointed out in the previous subsection, it is imperative to separate the samples that we use to train our classifier from the samples that we use to test it. For this, the following code snippet shows us that we have two different functions that download training and testing data and load them into memory:

```
def load_training_data(labels):
    filepath = _download('GTSRB-Training_fixed.zip',
                         md5sum='513f3c79a4c5141765e10e952eaa2478')
    return _load_data(filepath, labels)

def load_test_data(labels):
    filepath = _download('GTSRB_Online-Test-Images-Sorted.zip',
                         md5sum='b7bba7dad2a4dc4bc54d6ba2716d163b')
    return _load_data(filepath, labels)
```

Now that we know how to convert images into NumPy matrices, we can go on to more interesting parts, namely, we can feed the data to the SVM and train it to make predictions. So, let's move on to the next section, which covers feature extraction.

Learning about dataset feature extraction

Chances are that raw pixel values are not the most informative way to represent the data, as we have already realized in `Chapter 3`, *Finding Objects via Feature Matching and Perspective Transforms*. Instead, we need to derive a measurable property of the data that is more informative for classification.

However, often, it is not clear which features would perform best. Instead, it is often necessary to experiment with different features that the practitioner finds appropriate. After all, the choice of features might strongly depend on the specific dataset to be analyzed or the specific classification task to be performed.

For example, if you have to distinguish between a stop sign and a warning sign, then the most distinctive feature might be the shape of the sign or the color scheme. However, if you have to distinguish between two warning signs, then color and shape will not help you at all, and you will be required to come up with more sophisticated features.

In order to demonstrate how the choice of features affects classification performance, we will focus on the following:

- **A few simple color transformations** (such as grayscale; **red, green, blue (RGB)**; and **hue, saturation, value (HSV)**): Classification based on grayscale images will give us some baseline performance for the classifier. RGB might give us slightly better performance because of the distinct color schemes of some traffic signs.

  Even better performance is expected from HSV. This is because it represents colors even more robustly than RGB. Traffic signs tend to have very bright, saturated colors that (ideally) are quite distinct from their surroundings.

- **SURF**: This should appear very familiar to you by now. We have previously recognized SURF as an efficient and robust method of extracting meaningful features from an image. So, can't we use this technique to our advantage in a classification task?

- **HOG**: This is by far the most advanced feature descriptor to be considered in this chapter. The technique counts occurrences of gradient orientations along a dense grid laid out on the image and is well suited for use with SVMs.

Feature extraction is performed by functions in the `data/process.py` file, from which we will call different functions to construct and compare different features.

Here is a nice blueprint, which—if you follow it—will enable you to easily write your own featurization functions and use with our code, and compare if your `your_featurize` function will yield better results:

```
def your_featurize(data: List[np.ndarry], **kwargs) -> np.ndarray:
    ...
```

The `*_featurize` functions take a list of images and return a matrix (as a 2D `np.ndarray`), where each row is a new sample and each column represents a feature.

For most of the following features, we will be using the (already suitable) default arguments in OpenCV. However, these values are not set in stone, and, even in real-world classification tasks, it is often necessary to search across the range of possible values for both features extracting and feature learning parameters in a process called **hyperparameter exploration**.

Now that we know what we are doing, let's take a look at some featurization functions that we have come up with that build on top of concepts from previous sections and also add some new concepts as well.

Understanding common preprocessing

Before we look at what we have come up with, let's take our time to look at the two most common forms of preprocessing that are almost always applied to any data before machine learning tasks—namely, **mean subtraction** and **normalization**.

Mean subtraction is the most common form of preprocessing (sometimes also referred to as **zero centering** or de-meaning), where the mean value of every feature dimension is calculated across all samples in a dataset. This feature-wise average is then subtracted from every sample in the dataset. You can think of this process as centering the *cloud* of data on the origin.

Normalization refers to the scaling of data dimensions so that they are of roughly the same scale. This can be achieved by either dividing each dimension by its standard deviation (once it has been zero-centered) or scaling each dimension to lie in the range of [-1, 1].

It makes sense to apply this step only if you have reason to believe that different input features have different scales or units. In the case of images, the relative scales of pixels are already approximately equal (and in the range of [0, 255]), so it is not strictly necessary to perform this additional preprocessing step.

Armed with these two concepts, let's take a look at our feature extractors.

Learning about grayscale features

The easiest feature to extract is probably the grayscale value of each pixel. Usually, grayscale values are not very indicative of the data they describe, but we will include them here for illustrative purposes (that is, to achieve baseline performance).

For each image in the input set, we are going to perform the following steps:

1. Resize all images to have the same (usually smaller) size. We use `scale_size=(32, 32)` to make sure we don't make the images too small. At the same time, we want our data to be small enough to work on our personal computer. We can do this with the following code:

   ```
   resized_images = (cv2.resize(x, scale_size) for x in data)
   ```

2. Convert the image to grayscale (values are still in 0-255 range), like this:

   ```
   gray_data = (cv2.cvtColor(x, cv2.COLOR_BGR2GRAY) for x in
   resized_images)
   ```

3. Convert each image to have the pixel value in (0, 1) and flatten, so instead of a matrix of (32, 32) size for each image, we have a vector of size 1024, as follows:

```
scaled_data = (np.array(x).astype(np.float32).flatten() / 255 for x
in gray_data)
```

4. Subtract the average pixel value of the flattened vector, like this:

```
return np.vstack([x - x.mean() for x in scaled_data])
```

We use the returned matrix as our training data for the machine learning algorithm.

Now, let's take a look at another example—*what would happen if we used information in the colors as well?*

Understanding color spaces

Alternatively, you might find that colors contain some information that raw grayscale values cannot capture. Traffic signs often have a distinct color scheme, and it might be indicative of the information it is trying to convey (that is, red for stop signs and forbidden actions; green for informational signs; and so on). We could opt to use the RGB images as input, but, in our case, we do not have to do anything since the dataset is already RGB.

However, even RGB might not be informative enough. For example, a stop sign in broad daylight might appear very bright and clear, but its colors might appear much less vibrant on a rainy or foggy day. A better choice might be the HSV color space, which represents colors using hue, saturation, and value (or brightness).

The most telling feature of traffic signs in this color space might be the hue (a more perceptually relevant description of color or chromaticity), provides an improved ability to distinguish between the color scheme of different sign types. Saturation and value could be equally important, however, as traffic signs tend to use relatively bright and saturated colors that do not typically appear in natural scenes (that is, their surroundings).

In OpenCV, the HSV color space is only a single call to cv2.cvtColor away, as shown in the following code:

```
hsv_data = (cv2.cvtColor(x, cv2.COLOR_BGR2HSV) for x in resized_images)
```

So, to summarize, featurization is almost the same as for grayscale features. For each image, we carry out the following four steps:

1. Resize all images to have the same (usually smaller) size.
2. Convert the image to HSV (values in the 0-255 range).
3. Convert each image to have the pixel value in (0, 1), and flatten it.
4. Subtract the average pixel value of the flattened vector.

Now, let's try to look at a more complex example of a feature extractor that uses SURF.

Using SURF descriptor

But wait a minute! In chapter 3, *Finding Objects via Feature Matching and Perspective Transforms*, you learned that the SURF descriptor is one of the best and most robust ways to describe images independent of scale or rotations. Can we use this technique to our advantage in a classification task?

Glad you asked! To make this work, we need to adjust SURF so that it returns a fixed number of features per image. By default, the SURF descriptor is only applied to a small list of *interesting* key points in the image, the number of which might differ on an image-by-image basis. This is unsuitable for our current purposes because we want to find a fixed number of feature values per data sample.

Instead, we need to apply SURF to a fixed dense grid laid out over the image, for which we create a key points array containing all pixels, as illustrated in the following code block:

```
def surf_featurize(data, *, scale_size=(16, 16)):
    all_kp = [cv2.KeyPoint(float(x), float(y), 1)
                for x, y in itertools.product(range(scale_size[0]),
                                              range(scale_size[1]))]
```

Then, it is possible to obtain SURF descriptors for each point on the grid and append that data sample to our feature matrix. We initialize SURF with a hessianThreshold value of 400, as we did before, like this:

```
surf = cv2.xfeatures2d_SURF.create(hessianThreshold=400)
```

The key points and descriptors can then be obtained via the following code:

```
kp_des = (surf.compute(x, kp) for x in data)
```

Because `surf.compute` has two output arguments, `kp_des` will actually be a concatenation of both key points and descriptors. The second element in the `kp_des` array is the descriptor that we care about.

We select the first `num_surf_features` from each data sample and return it as a feature for the image, as follows:

```
return np.array([d.flatten()[:num_surf_features]
                 for _, d in kp_des]).astype(np.float32)
```

Now, let's take a look at a new concept that is very popular in the community—HOG.

Mapping HOG descriptor

The last feature descriptor to consider is the HOG. HOG features have previously been shown to work exceptionally well in combination with SVMs, especially when applied to tasks such as pedestrian recognition.

The essential idea behind HOG features is that the local shapes and appearance of objects within an image can be described by the distribution of edge directions. The image is divided into small connected regions, within which a histogram of gradient directions (or edge directions) is compiled.

The following screenshot shows such a histogram from a region in a picture. Angles are not directional; that's why the range is (**-180, 180**):

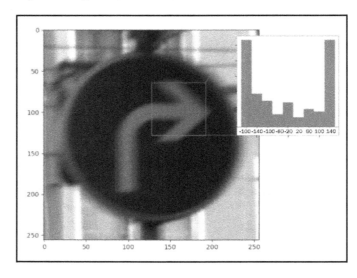

As you can see, it has a lot of edge directions in the horizontal direction (angles around **+180** and **-180** degrees), so this seems like a good feature, especially when we are working with arrows and lines.

Then, the descriptor is assembled by concatenating the different histograms. For improved performance, the local histograms can be contrast normalized, which results in better invariance to changes in illumination and shadowing. You can see why this sort of preprocessing might be just the perfect fit for recognizing traffic signs under different viewing angles and lighting conditions.

The HOG descriptor is fairly accessible in OpenCV by means of `cv2.HOGDescriptor`, which takes the detection window size (32 x 32), the block size (16 x 16), the cell size (8 x 8), and the cell stride (8 x 8) as input arguments. For each of these cells, the HOG descriptor then calculates a HOG using nine bins, like this:

```
def hog_featurize(data, *, scale_size=(32, 32)):
    block_size = (scale_size[0] // 2, scale_size[1] // 2)
    block_stride = (scale_size[0] // 4, scale_size[1] // 4)
    cell_size = block_stride
    hog = cv2.HOGDescriptor(scale_size, block_size, block_stride,
                            cell_size, 9)
    resized_images = (cv2.resize(x, scale_size) for x in data)
    return np.array([hog.compute(x).flatten() for x in resized_images])
```

Applying the HOG descriptor to every data sample is then as easy as calling `hog.compute`.

After we have extracted all the features we want, we return a flattened list for each of the images.

Now, we are finally ready to train the classifier on the preprocessed dataset. So, let's move on to the SVM.

Learning about SVMs

An SVM is a learner for binary classification (and regression) that tries to separate examples from the two different class labels with a decision boundary that maximizes the margin between the two classes.

Let's return to our example of positive and negative data samples, each of which has exactly two features (**x** and **y**) and two possible decision boundaries, as follows:

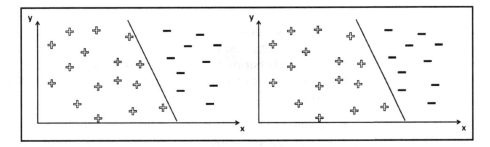

Both of these decision boundaries get the job done. They partition all the samples of positives and negatives with zero misclassifications. However, one of them seems intuitively better. How can we quantify *better* and thus learn the *best* parameter settings?

This is where SVMs come into the picture. SVMs are also called **maximal margin classifiers** because they can be used to do exactly that—define the decision boundary so as to make those two clouds of **+** and **-** as far apart as possible; that is, as far apart from the decision boundary as possible.

For the preceding example, an SVM would find two parallel lines that pass through the data points on the class margins (the *dashed lines* in the following screenshot), and then make the line (that passes through the center of the margins) the decision boundary (the *bold black line* in the following screenshot):

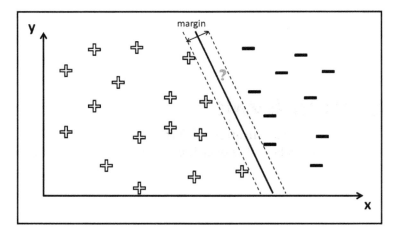

It turns out that to find the maximal margin, it is only important to consider the data points that lie on the class margins. These points are sometimes also called **support vectors**.

 In addition to performing linear classification (that is, when the decision boundary is a straight line), SVMs can also perform a non-linear classification using what is called the **kernel trick**, implicitly mapping their input to high-dimensional feature spaces.

Now, let's take a look at how we can turn this binary classifier into a multiclass classifier that is more appropriate for the 43-class classification problem we are trying to tackle.

Using SVMs for multiclass classification

Whereas some classification algorithms, such as neural networks, naturally lend themselves to using more than two classes, SVMs are binary classifiers by nature. They can, however, be turned into multiclass classifiers.

Here, we will consider two different strategies:

- **One-versus-all**: The *one-versus-all* strategy involves training a single classifier per class, with the samples of that class as positive samples and all other samples as negatives.

  For the k classes, this strategy thus requires the training of k number of different SVMs. During testing, all classifiers can express a +1 vote by predicting that an unseen sample belongs to their class.

  In the end, an unseen sample is classified by the ensemble as the class with the most votes. Usually, this strategy is used in combination with confidence scores instead of predicted labels so that, in the end, the class with the highest confidence score can be picked.

- **One-versus-one**: The *one-versus-one* strategy involves training a single classifier per class pair, with the samples of the first class as positive samples and the samples of the second class as negative samples. For the k classes, this strategy requires the training of k*(k-1)/2 classifiers.

  However, the classifiers have to solve a significantly easier task, so there is a trade-off when considering which strategy to use. During testing, all classifiers can express a +1 vote for either the first or the second class. In the end, an unseen sample is classified by the ensemble as the class with the most votes.

Usually, you would not have to write your own classification algorithms unless you really wanted to dive deep into the algorithms and squeeze the last bit of performance out of your model. And luckily, OpenCV already comes with a good machine learning toolkit that we will use in this chapter. OpenCV uses a one-versus-all approach, and we will focus on that approach.

Now, let's get our hands dirty, and see how we can code this up with OpenCV and get some real results.

Training the SVM

We are going to write the training method in a separate function; it's a good practice if we later wanted to change our training method. First, we define the signature of our function, as follows:

```
def train(training_features: np.ndarray, training_labels: np.ndarray):
```

Thus, we want a function that takes two arguments—`training_features` and `training_labels`—and the correct answers corresponding to each feature. Thus, the first argument will be a matrix in the form of a two-dimensional NumPy array, and the second argument will be a one-dimensional NumPy array.

Then, the function will return an object that should have a `predict` method, which takes new unseen data and labels it. So, let's get started and see how we could train an SVM with OpenCV.

We name our function `train_one_vs_all_SVM`, and do the following:

1. Instantiate an SVM class instance using `cv2.ml.SVM_create`, which creates a multiclass SVM using the one-versus-all strategy, as follows:

```
def train_one_vs_all_SVM(X_train, y_train):
    svm = cv2.ml.SVM_create()
```

2. Set the hyperparameters of the learner. These are called **hyperparameters** because these parameters are out of the control of the learner (versus parameters that the learner changes during the learning process). This can be done with the following code:

```
svm.setKernel(cv2.ml.SVM_LINEAR)
svm.setType(cv2.ml.SVM_C_SVC)
svm.setC(2.67)
svm.setGamma(5.383)
```

3. Call the `train` method on the SVM instance, and OpenCV takes care of training (this takes a couple of minutes on a regular laptop computer with the GTSRB dataset), as follows:

```
svm.train(X_train, cv2.ml.ROW_SAMPLE, y_train)
return svm
```

OpenCV will take care of the rest. What happens under the hood is that the SVM training uses **Lagrange multipliers** to optimize some constraints that lead to the maximum margin decision boundary.

The optimization process is usually performed until some termination criteria are met, which can be specified via the SVM's optional arguments.

Now that we have looked at training the SVM, let's look at testing it.

Testing the SVM

There are many ways to evaluate a classifier, but most often, we are simply interested in the accuracy metric—that is, how many data samples from the test set were classified correctly.

In order to arrive at this metric, we need to get the prediction results out of the SVM—and again, OpenCV has us covered, by providing the `predict` method that takes a matrix of features and returns an array of predicted labels. We thus need to proceed as follows:

1. So, we have to first featurize our testing data:

```
x_train = featurize(train_data)
```

2. Then, we feed the featurized data to the classifier and get the predicted labels, like this:

```
y_predict = model.predict(x_test)
```

3. After that, we can try to see how many of the labels the classifier got correctly, by running the following code:

```
num_correct = sum(y_predict == y_test)
```

Now, we are ready to calculate the desired performance metrics, as described in detail in later sections. For the purpose of this chapter, we choose to calculate accuracy, precision, and recall.

The `scikit-learn` machine learning package (which can be found at `http://scikit-learn.org`) supports the three metrics—which are accuracy, precision, and recall (as well as others)—straight out of the box, and also comes with a variety of other useful tools. For educational purposes (and to minimize software dependencies), we will derive the three metrics ourselves.

Accuracy

The most straightforward metric to calculate is probably accuracy. This metric simply counts the number of test samples that have been predicted correctly, and returns the number as a fraction of the total number of test samples, as shown in the following code block:

```
def accuracy(y_predicted, y_true):
    return sum(y_predicted == y_true) / len(y_true)
```

The previous code shows that we have extracted `y_predicted` by calling `model.predict(x_test)`. This was quite simple, but, again, to make things reusable, we put this inside a function that takes `predicted` and `true` labels. And now, we will go on to implement slightly more complicated metrics that are useful to measure classifier performance.

Confusion matrix

A confusion matrix is a 2D matrix of size equal to (`num_classes`, `num_classes`), where the rows correspond to the predicted class labels, and the columns correspond to the actual class labels. Then, the [`r`, `c`] matrix element contains the number of samples that were predicted to have label `r`, but in reality, have label `c`. Having access to a confusion matrix will allow us to calculate precision and recall.

Now, let's implement a very simple way to calculate the confusion matrix. Similar to accuracy, we create a function with the same arguments, so it's easy to reuse, by following the next steps:

1. Assuming our labels are non-negative integers, we can figure out `num_classes` by taking the highest integer and adding 1 to account for zero, as follows:

```
def confusion_matrix(y_predicted, y_true):
    num_classes = max(max(y_predicted), max(y_true)) + 1
    . . .
```

2. Next, we instantiate an empty matrix, where we will fill the counts, like this:

```
conf_matrix = np.zeros((num_classes, num_classes))
```

3. Next, we iterate over all data, and, for each datum, we take predicted value r and actual value c, and we increment the appropriate value in the matrix. There are much faster ways to achieve this, but nothing is simpler than counting everything one by one. We do this with the following code:

```
for r, c in zip(y_predicted, y_true):
    conf_matrix[r, c] += 1
```

4. After we have accounted for all the data in the training set, we can return our confusion matrix, as follows:

```
return conf_matrix
```

5. Here is our confusion matrix for the GTSRB dataset test data:

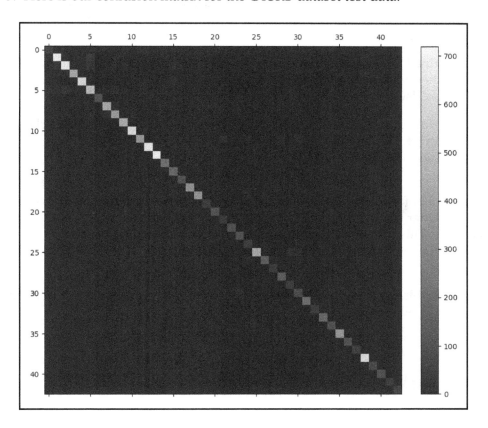

As you can see, most of the values are in the diagonal. This means that at first glance, our classifier is doing pretty well.

6. It is also easy to calculate the accuracy from the confusion matrix as well. We just take the number of elements in the diagonal, and divide by the number of elements overall, like this:

```
cm = confusion_matrix(y_predicted, y_true)
accuracy = cm.trace() / cm.sum()  # 0.95 in this case.
```

Note that we have a different number of elements in each of the classes. Each class contributes to accuracy differently, and our next metric will focus on per-class performance.

Precision

Precision in binary classification is a useful metric for measuring the fraction of retrieved instances that are relevant (also called the **positive predictive value**). In a classification task, the number of **true positives** is defined as the number of items correctly labeled as belonging to the positive class.

Precision is defined as the number of true positives divided by the total number of positives. In other words, out of all the pictures in the test set that a classifier thinks to contain a cat, precision is the fraction of pictures that actually do contain a cat.

 Note that here, we have a positive label; thus, precision is a per-class value. We usually talk about the precision of one class or the precision of cats, and so on.

The total number of positives can also be calculated as the sum of **true positives** and **false positives**, the latter being the number of samples incorrectly labeled as belonging to a particular class. This is where the confusion matrix comes in handy because it will allow us to quickly calculate the number of false positives and true positives by following the next steps:

1. So, in this case, we have to change our function arguments, and add the positive class label, like this:

```
def precision(y_predicted, y_true, positive_label):
    ...
```

2. Let's use our confusion matrix, and calculate the number of true positives, which will be the element at `[positive_label, positive_label]`, as follows:

```
cm = confusion_matrix(y_predicted, y_true)
true_positives = cm[positive_label, positive_label]
```

3. Now, let's calculate the number of true and false positives, which will be the sum of all elements on the `positive_label` row since the row indicates the predicted class label, as follows:

```
total_positives = sum(cm[positive_label])
```

4. And finally, return the ratio of true positives and all positives, like this:

```
return true_positives / total_positives
```

Based on different classes, we get very different values of precision. Here is a histogram of the precision scores for all 43 classes:

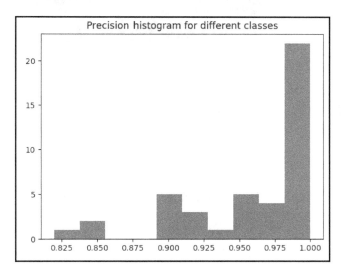

The class with lower precision is **30**, which means that a lot of other signs are mistaken to be the sign shown in the following screenshot:

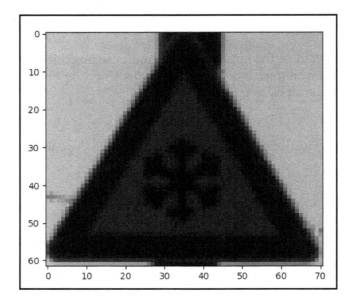

In this case, it's alright if we are extra cautious while driving on the icy road, but it's possible that we missed something important. So, let's look at recall values for different classes.

Recall

Recall is similar to precision in the sense that it measures the fraction of relevant instances that are retrieved (as opposed to the fraction of retrieved instances that are relevant). Thus, it will tell us the probability that we will not notice it for a given positive class (given sign).

In a classification task, the number of false negatives is the number of items that are not labeled as belonging to the positive class but should have been labeled.

Recall is the number of true positives divided by the sum of true positives and false negatives. In other words, out of all the pictures of cats in the world, recall is the fraction of pictures that have been correctly identified as pictures of cats.

Here is how to calculate recall of a given positive label using true and predicted labels:

1. Again, we have the same signature as for the precision, and we retrieve true positives the same way, as follows:

```
def recall(y_predicted, y_true, positive_label):
    cm = confusion_matrix(y_predicted, y_true)
    true_positives = cm[positive_label, positive_label]
```

Now, notice that the sum of true positives and false negatives is the total number of points in the given data class.

2. Thus, we just have to count the number of elements in that class, which means we sum the `positive_label` column of the confusion matrix, as follows:

```
class_members = sum(cm[:, positive_label])
```

3. Then, we return the ratio as for the precision function, like this:

```
return true_positives / class_members
```

Now, let's look at the distribution of recall values for all 43 classes of traffic signs, shown in the following screenshot:

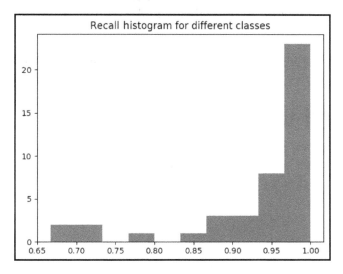

The recall values are a lot more spread out, with class 21 having a value of 0.66. Let's check out which class has a value of 21:

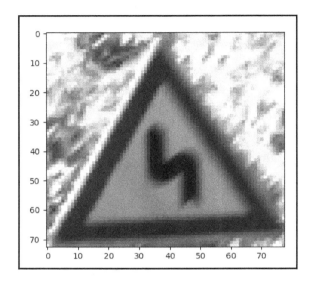

Now, this is not as harmful as driving on a road covered with snowflakes/ice, but it's very important not to miss dangerous curves ahead on the road. Missing this sign could have bad consequences.

The next section will demonstrate the main() function routine needed to run our app.

Putting it all together

To run our app, we will need to execute the main function routine (in chapter6.py). This loads the data, trains the classifier, evaluates its performance, and visualizes the result:

1. First, we need to import all the relevant modules and set up the main function, as follows:

```
import cv2
import numpy as np
import matplotlib.pyplot as plt

from data.gtsrb import load_training_data
from data.gtsrb import load_test_data
from data.process import grayscale_featurize, hog_featurize
```

2. Then, the goal is to compare classification performance across feature extraction methods. This includes running the task using a list of different feature extraction approaches. So, we first load the data, and repeat the process for each of the featurizing functions, as follows:

```
def main(labels):
    train_data, train_labels = load_training_data(labels)
    test_data, test_labels = load_test_data(labels)
    y_train, y_test = np.array(train_labels), np.array(test_labels)
    accuracies = {}
    for featurize in [hog_featurize, grayscale_featurize,
hsv_featurize,
    surf_featurize]:
        . . .
```

For each of the `featurize` functions, we perform the following steps:

1. `Featurize` the data, so we have a matrix of features, like this:

```
x_train = featurize(train_data)
```

2. Train a model using our `train_one_vs_all_SVM` method, as follows:

```
model = train_one_vs_all_SVM(x_train, y_train)
```

3. Predict test labels for the training data, by featurizing the test data and passing to the `predict` method (we have to featurize test data separately to make sure we don't have information leakage), as follows:

```
x_test = featurize(test_data)
res = model.predict(x_test)
y_predict = res[1].flatten()
```

4. We score the predicted labels against the true labels, using the `accuracy` function, and store the score in a dictionary, to plot after we have results for all the `featurize` functions, like this:

```
accuracies[featurize.__name__] = accuracy(y_predict,
y_test)
```

3. Now, it's time to plot the results, and for this, we choose the `bar` plot functionality of `matplotlib`. We also make sure to scale the bar plot accordingly to visually understand the scale of difference. Since the accuracy is a number between 0 and 1, we limit the *y* axis to [0, 1], as follows:

```
plt.bar(accuracies.keys(), accuracies.values())
plt.ylim([0, 1])
```

4. We add some nice formatting to the plot by rotating labels on the horizontal axis, adding a `grid` and a `title` to the plot, like this:

```
plt.axes().xaxis.set_tick_params(rotation=20)
plt.grid()
plt.title('Test accuracy for different featurize functions')
plt.show()
```

5. And after the last line of `plt.show()` has executed, the plot shown in the following screenshot pops up in a separate window:

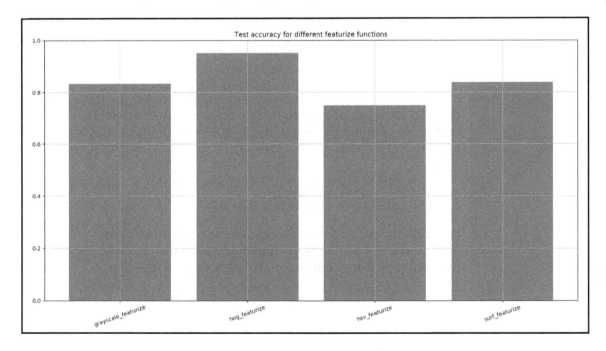

So, we see that `hog_featurize` is a winner on this dataset, but we are far from having perfect results—slightly above 95%. To understand how good a result it's possible to get, you could do a quick Google search, and you will come across a lot of papers achieving 99%+ accuracy. So, even though we are not getting cutting-edge results, we did pretty well with an off-the-shelf classifier and an easy `featurize` function.

Another interesting fact is that even though we thought that traffic signs having bright colors should lead to **hsv_featurize** (it being more important than grayscale features), it turns out that's not the case.

So, a good takeaway is that you should experiment with your data to develop better intuition about which features work for your data and which don't.

Speaking of experimentation, let's use a neural network to increase the efficiency of our obtained results.

Improving results with neural networks

Let's do a quick teaser of how good we could get if we were to use some fancy **deep neural networks (DNNs)**, and give you a sneak peek of what is to come in the future chapters of this book.

If we use the following *"not quite so deep"* neural network, which takes about 2 minutes to train on my laptop (where it takes 1 *minute* to train the SVM), we get an accuracy of around 0.964!

Here is a snippet of the training method (you should be able to plug it into the preceding code, and play with some parameters to see if you could do it later):

```
def train_tf_model(X_train, y_train):
    model = tf.keras.models.Sequential([
        tf.keras.layers.Conv2D(20, (8, 8),
                            input_shape=list(UNIFORM_SIZE) + [3],
                            activation='relu'),
        tf.keras.layers.MaxPooling2D(pool_size=(4, 4), strides=4),
        tf.keras.layers.Dropout(0.15),
        tf.keras.layers.Flatten(),
        tf.keras.layers.Dense(64, activation='relu'),
        tf.keras.layers.Dropout(0.15),
        tf.keras.layers.Dense(43, activation='softmax')
    ])
```

```
model.compile(optimizer='adam',
              loss='sparse_categorical_crossentropy',
              metrics=['accuracy'])
model.fit(x_train, np.array(train_labels), epochs=10)
return model
```

The code uses the high-level Keras API of TensorFlow (we will see more of this in the upcoming chapters) and creates a neural network with the following:

- **Convolutional layer** with max pooling that is followed by a dropout—which is there only during the training.
- **Hidden Dense layer** that is followed by a dropout—which is there only during the training.
- **Final Dense layer** that spits out the final result; it should identify which class (among the 43 classes) the input data belongs to.

Note that we only have one convolutional layer, which is very similar to HOG featurize. If we were to add more convolutional layers, the performance would improve quite a lot, but let's leave that for the next chapters to explore.

Summary

In this chapter, we trained a multiclass classifier to recognize traffic signs from the GTSRB database. We discussed the basics of supervised learning, explored the intricacies of feature extraction, and sneaked a peek into DNNs.

Using the approach we took in this chapter, you should be able to formulate real-life problems as machine learning models, use your Python skills to download a sample labeled dataset from the internet, write your featurizing functions that convert images to feature vectors, and use OpenCV for training off-the-shelf machine learning models that help you solve your real-life problems.

Notably, we left out some details along the way, such as attempting to fine-tune the hyperparameters of the learning algorithm (as they were out of the scope of this book). We only looked at accuracy scores and didn't do much feature engineering by trying to combine all sets of different features.

With this functional setup and a good understanding of the underlying methodology, you can now classify the entire GTSRB dataset to get accuracies higher than 0.97! How about 0.99? It is definitely worth taking a look at their website, where you will find classification results for a variety of classifiers. Maybe your own approach will soon be added to the list.

In the next chapter, we will move even deeper into the field of machine learning. Specifically, we will focus on recognizing emotional expressions in human faces using **convolutional neural networks (CNNs)**. This time, we will combine the classifier with a framework for object detection, which will allow us to find a human face in an image, and then focus on identifying the emotional expression contained in that face.

Dataset attribution

J. Stallkamp, M. Schlipsing, J. Salmen, and C. Igel, The German Traffic Sign Recognition Benchmark—A multiclass classification competition, in *Proceedings of the IEEE International Joint Conference on Neural Networks*, 2011, pages 1453–1460.

8
Learning to Recognize Facial Emotions

We previously familiarized ourselves with the concepts of object detection and object recognition. In this chapter, we will develop an app that does both together. The app will be able to detect your own face in each captured frame of a webcam live stream, recognize your facial emotion, and label it on the **Graphical User Interface (GUI)**.

The goal of this chapter is to develop an app that combines both **face detection** and **face recognition**, with a focus on recognizing emotional expressions for the detected face. After reading the chapter, you will be able to use both face detection and recognition in different applications of your own.

We will be covering the following topics in this chapter:

- Planning the app
- Learning about face detection
- Collecting data for machine learning tasks
- Understanding facial emotion recognition
- Putting it all together

We will touch upon two classic algorithms that come bundled with OpenCV—**Haar cascade classifiers** and **MLPs**. While the former can be used to rapidly detect (or to locate, and to answer the question *Where?*) objects of various sizes and orientations in an image, the latter can be used to recognize them (or to identify, and answer the question *What?*).

Learning MLPs is also the first step toward learning one of the most trendy algorithms these days—**deep neural networks (DNNs)**. We will use PCA to speed up and improve the accuracy of the algorithm when we have not got a huge amount of data, to improve the accuracy of our model.

We will collect our training data ourselves to show you how that process is done, in order for you to be able to train machine learning models for tasks that don't have data readily available. Unfortunately, not having the right data is still one of the biggest obstacles to the widespread adoption of machine learning these days.

Now, let's take a look at how to get started before we get our hands dirty.

Getting started

You can find the code that we present in this chapter at our GitHub repository, at `https://github.com/PacktPublishing/OpenCV-4-with-Python-Blueprints-Second-Edition/tree/master/chapter8`.

Other than that, you should download the **Haar cascade** files from the official OpenCV repository at `https://github.com/opencv/opencv/blob/master/data/haarcascades/`, or copy them from the installation directory of your machine to the project repository.

Planning the app

The reliable recognition of faces and facial expressions is a challenging task for **artificial intelligence** (**AI**), yet humans are able to perform these kinds of tasks with ease. To make our task feasible, we will limit ourselves to the following limited emotional expressions:

- Neutral
- Happy
- Sad
- Surprised
- Angry
- Disgusted

Today's state-of-the-art models range all the way from 3D deformable face models fitting over **convolutional neural networks** (**CNNs**), to deep learning algorithms. Granted, these approaches are significantly more sophisticated than our approach.

Yet, an **MLP** is a classic algorithm that has helped transform the field of machine learning, so for educational purposes, we will stick to a set of algorithms that come bundled with OpenCV.

To arrive at such an app, we need to solve the following two challenges:

- **Face detection**: We will use the popular Haar cascade classifier by Viola and Jones, for which OpenCV provides a whole range of pre-trained exemplars. We will make use of face cascades and eye cascades to reliably detect and align facial regions from frame to frame.

- **Facial expression recognition**: We will train an MLP to recognize the six different emotional expressions listed earlier, in every detected face. The success of this approach will crucially depend on the training set that we assemble, and the preprocessing that we choose to apply to each sample in the set.

    In order to improve the quality of our self-recorded training set, we will make sure that all data samples are aligned using **affine transformations**, and will reduce the dimensionality of the feature space by applying **PCA**. The resulting representation is sometimes also referred to as **Eigenfaces**.

We will combine the algorithms mentioned earlier in a single end-to-end app that annotates a detected face with the corresponding facial expression label in each captured frame of a video live stream. The end result might look something like the following screenshot, capturing my sample reaction when the code first ran:

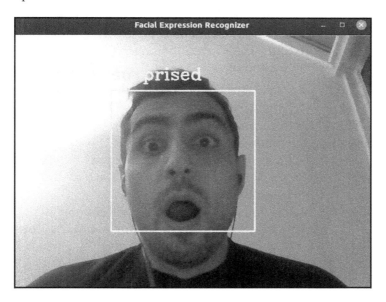

The final app will consist of the main script that integrates the process flow end to end—that is, from face detection to facial expression recognition, as well as some utility functions to help along the way.

Thus, the end product will require several components that are located in the `chapter8/` directory of the book's GitHub repository, listed as follows:

- `chapter8.py`: This is the main script and entry point for the chapter, and we will use this for both data collection and demo. It will have the following layouts:
    - `chapter8.FacialExpressionRecognizerLayout`: This is a custom layout based on `wx_gui.BaseLayout` that will detect a face in each video frame and predict the corresponding class label by using a pre-trained model.
    - `chapter8.DataCollectorLayout`: This is a custom layout based on `wx_gui.BaseLayout` that will collect image frames, detect a face therein, assign a label using a user-selected facial expression label, and will save the frames into the `data/` directory.
- `wx_gui.py`: This is a link to our `wxpython` GUI file that we developed in `Chapter 1`, *Fun with Filters*.
- `detectors.FaceDetector`: This is a class that will encompass all the code for face detection based on Haar cascades. It will have the following two methods:
    - `detect_face`: This method detects faces in a grayscale image. Optionally, the image is downscaled for better reliability. Upon successful detection, the method returns the extracted head region.
    - `align_head`: This method preprocesses an extracted head region with affine transformations, such that the resulting face appears centered and upright.
- `params/`: This is a directory that contains the default Haar cascades that we use for the book.
- `data/`: We will write all the code to store and process our custom data here. The code is split into the following files:
    - `store.py`: This is a file where we put all the helper functions to write the data to disk and to load the data from the disk into computer memory.
    - `process.py`: This is a file that will contain all the code to preprocess the data before saving. It will also contain the code to construct features from the raw data.

In the following sections, we will discuss these components in detail. First, let's look at the face detection algorithm.

Learning about face detection

OpenCV comes preinstalled with a range of sophisticated classifiers for general-purpose object detection. These all have very similar APIs and are easy to use, once you know what you are looking for. Perhaps the most commonly known detector is the **cascade of Haar-based feature detectors** for face detection, which was first introduced by Paul Viola and Michael Jones in their paper *Rapid Object Detection using a Boosted Cascade of Simple Features* in 2001.

A Haar-based feature detector is a machine learning algorithm that is trained on a lot of positive and negative labeled samples. What will we do in our application is take a pre-trained classifier that comes with OpenCV (you can find the link in the *Getting started* section). But first, let's take a closer look at how the classifier works.

Learning about Haar-based cascade classifiers

Every book on OpenCV should at least mention the Viola-Jones face detector. Invented in 2001, this cascade classifier disrupted the field of computer vision, as it finally allowed real-time face detection and face recognition.

The classifier is based on **Haar-like features** (similar to **Haar basis functions**) that sum up the pixel intensities in small regions of an image, as well as capture the difference between adjacent image regions.

The following screenshot visualizes four rectangle features. The visualization works to calculate the value of the feature applied at a location. You should sum up all pixel values in the dark gray rectangle and subtract this value from the sum of all pixel values in the white rectangle:

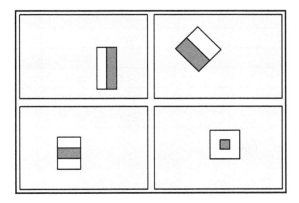

In the previous screenshot, the top row shows two examples of an edge feature (that is, you can detect edges with them), either vertically oriented (top left) or oriented at a 45° angle (top right). The bottom row shows a line feature (bottom left) and a center-surround feature (bottom right).

Applying these filters at all possible locations allows the algorithm to capture certain details of human faces, such as the fact that eye regions are usually darker than the region surrounding the cheeks.

Thus, a common Haar feature would have a dark rectangle (representing the eye region) atop a bright rectangle (representing the cheek region). Combining this feature with a bank of rotated and slightly more complicated **wavelets**, Viola and Jones arrived at a powerful feature descriptor for human faces. In an additional act of brilliance, these guys came up with an efficient way to calculate these features, making it possible for the first time to detect faces in real time.

The final classifier is a weighted sum of small weaker classifiers, each of whose binary classifiers are based on a single feature described previously. The hardest part is to figure out which combinations of features are helpful for detecting different types of objects. Luckily, OpenCV contains a collection of such classifiers. Let's take a look at some of these in the following section.

Understanding pre-trained cascade classifiers

Even better, this approach not only works for faces but also for eyes, mouths, full bodies, company logos; you name it. In the following table, a number of pre-trained classifiers are shown that can be found under the OpenCV install path in the `data` folder:

Cascade classifier types	XML filenames
Face detector (default)	`haarcascade_frontalface_default.xml`
Face detector (fast Haar)	`haarcascade_frontalface_alt2.xml`
Eye detector	`haarcascade_eye.xml`
Mouth detector	`haarcascade_mcs_mouth.xml`
Nose detector	`haarcascade_mcs_nose.xml`
Full body detector	`haarcascade_fullbody.xml`

In this chapter, we will only use `haarcascade_frontalface_default.xml` and `haarcascade_eye.xml`.

If you are wearing glasses, make sure to use `haarcascade_eye_tree_eyeglasses.xml` for eye detection instead.

We will first look at how to use a cascade classifier.

Using a pre-trained cascade classifier

A cascade classifier can be loaded and applied to an image (grayscale) using the following code, where we first read the image, then convert it to grayscale, and finally detect all the faces using a cascade classifier:

```
import cv2

gray_img = cv2.cvtColor(cv2.imread('example.png'), cv2.COLOR_RGB2GRAY)

cascade_clf = cv2.CascadeClassifier('haarcascade_frontalface_default.xml')
faces = cascade_clf.detectMultiScale(gray_img,
                                     scaleFactor=1.1,
                                     minNeighbors=3,
                                     flags=cv2.CASCADE_SCALE_IMAGE)
```

From the previous code, the `detectMultiScale` function comes with a number of options:

- `minFeatureSize` is the minimum face size to consider—for example, 20 x 20 pixels.
- `searchScaleFactor` is the amount by which we rescale the image (scale pyramid). For example, a value of `1.1` will gradually reduce the size of the input image by 10 %, making it more likely for a face (image) with a larger value to be found.
- `minNeighbors` is the number of neighbors that each candidate rectangle will have to retain. Typically, we choose 3 or 5.
- `flags` is an options object used to tweak the algorithm—for example, whether to look for all faces or just the largest face (`cv2.cv.CASCADE_FIND_BIGGEST_OBJECT`).

If detection is successful, the function will return a list of bounding boxes (`faces`) that contain the coordinates of the detected face regions, as follows:

```
for (x, y, w, h) in faces:
    # draw bounding box on frame
    cv2.rectangle(frame, (x, y), (x + w, y + h), (100, 255, 0),
                  thickness=2)
```

In the previous code, we iterate through the returned faces and add a rectangle outline with a thickness of 2 pixels to each of the faces.

 If your pre-trained face cascade does not detect anything, a common reason is usually that the path to the pre-trained cascade file could not be found. In this case, `CascadeClassifier` will fail silently. Thus, it is always a good idea to check whether the returned classifier `casc = cv2.CascadeClassifier(filename)` is empty, by checking `casc.empty()`.

This is what you should get if you run the code on the `Lenna.png` picture:

Image credit—Lenna.png by Conor Lawless is licensed under CC BY 2.0

From the previous screenshot, on the left, you see the original image, and on the right is the image that was passed to OpenCV, and the rectangle outline of the detected face.

Now, let's try to wrap this detector into a class to make it usable for our application.

Understanding the FaceDetector class

All relevant face detection code for this chapter can be found as part of the FaceDetector class in the detectors module. Upon instantiation, this class loads two different cascade classifiers that are needed for preprocessing—namely, a face_cascade classifier and an eye_cascade classifier, as follows:

```
import cv2
import numpy as np


class FaceDetector:

    def __init__(self, *,
                 face_cascade='params/haarcascade_frontalface_default.xml',
                 eye_cascade='params/haarcascade_lefteye_2splits.xml',
                 scale_factor=4):
```

Because our preprocessing requires a valid face cascade, we make sure that the file can be loaded. If not, we throw a ValueError exception, so the program will terminate and notify the user what went wrong, as shown in the following code block:

```
# load pre-trained cascades
self.face_clf = cv2.CascadeClassifier(face_cascade)
if self.face_clf.empty():
    raise ValueError(f'Could not load face cascade
    "{face_cascade}"')
```

We do the same thing for the eye classifier as well, like this:

```
self.eye_clf = cv2.CascadeClassifier(eye_cascade)
if self.eye_clf.empty():
    raise ValueError(
        f'Could not load eye cascade "{eye_cascade}"')
```

Face detection works best on low-resolution grayscale images. This is why we also store a scaling factor (`scale_factor`) so that we can operate on downscaled versions of the input image if necessary, like this:

```
self.scale_factor = scale_factor
```

Now that we have set up the class initialization, let's take a look at the algorithm that detects the faces.

Detecting faces in grayscale images

Now, we will put what we learned in the previous section into a method that will take an image and return the biggest face in the image. We are returning the biggest face to simplify things since we know that, in our application, there is going to be a single user sitting in front of the webcam. As a challenge, you could try to expand this to work with more than one face!

We call the method to detect the biggest face (`detect_face`). Let's go through it step by step:

1. As in the last section, first, we convert the argument RGB image to grayscale and scale it by `scale_factor` by running the following code:

```
def detect_face(self, rgb_img, *, outline=True):
    frameCasc = cv2.cvtColor(cv2.resize(rgb_img, (0, 0),
                                        fx=1.0 /
                                        self.scale_factor,
                                        fy=1.0 /
                                        self.scale_factor),
                             cv2.COLOR_RGB2GRAY)
```

2. Then, we detect the faces in the grayscale image, like this:

```
faces = self.face_clf.detectMultiScale(
        frameCasc,
        scaleFactor=1.1,
        minNeighbors=3,
        flags=cv2.CASCADE_SCALE_IMAGE) * self.scale_factor
```

3. We iterate over the detected faces and outline if the `outline=True` keyword argument was passed to `detect_face`. OpenCV returns us `x`, `y` coordinates of the top-left location and `w`, `h` width and height of the head. So, in order to construct the outline, we just calculate the bottom and right coordinates of the outline, and call the `cv2.rectangle` function, as follows:

```
for (x, y, w, h) in faces:
        if outline:
            cv2.rectangle(rgb_img, (x, y), (x + w, y + h),
                        (100, 255, 0), thickness=2)
```

4. We crop the head out of the original RGB image. This will be handy if we want to do more processing on the head (for example, recognize the facial expression). Run the following code:

```
head = cv2.cvtColor(rgb_img[y:y + h, x:x + w],
                    cv2.COLOR_RGB2GRAY)
```

5. We return the following 4-tuple:
   - A Boolean value to check whether the detection was successful or not
   - The original image with the outline of the faces added (if requested)
   - A cropped image of the head to use as needed
   - Coordinates of the location of the head in the original image

6. In the case of success, we return the following:

```
return True, rgb_img, head, (x, y)
```

In the case of failure, we return that no head was found, and return `None` for anything that is undetermined, like this:

```
return False, rgb_img, None, (None, None)
```

Now, let's look at what happens after we detect the faces, to get them ready for machine learning algorithms.

Preprocessing detected faces

After a face has been detected, we might want to preprocess the extracted head region before applying classification to it. Although the face cascade is fairly accurate, for the recognition, it is important that all the faces are upright and centered on the image.

Here is what we want to accomplish:

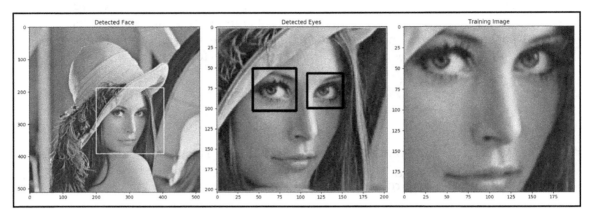

Image credit—Lenna.png by Conor Lawless is licensed under CC BY 2.0

As you can see from the preceding screenshot, as this is not a passport photo, the model has her head slightly tilted to the side while looking over her shoulder. The facial region, as extracted by the face cascade, is shown in the middle thumbnail in the preceding screenshot.

In order to compensate for the head orientation and position in the detected box, we aim to rotate, move, and scale the face so that all data samples will be perfectly aligned. This is the job of the `align_head` method in the `FaceDetector` class, shown in the following code block:

```
def align_head(self, head):
    desired_eye_x = 0.25
    desired_eye_y = 0.2
    desired_img_width = desired_img_height = 200
```

In the previous code, we have hardcoded some parameters that are used to align the heads. We want all eyes to be 25 % below the top of the final image and 20 % from the left and right edges, and this function is going to return a processed image of the head that has a fixed size of 200 x 200 pixels.

The first step of the process is to detect where the eyes are in the image, after which we will use their location to construct the necessary transformation.

Detecting the eyes

Fortunately, OpenCV comes with a few eye cascades that can detect both open and closed eyes, such as `haarcascade_eye.xml`. This allows us to calculate the angle between the line that connects the center of the two eyes and the horizon so that we can rotate the face accordingly.

In addition, adding eye detectors will reduce the risk of having false positives in our dataset, allowing us to add a data sample only if both the head and the eyes have been successfully detected.

After loading the eye cascade from the file in the `FaceDetector` constructor, it is applied to the input image (`head`), as follows:

```
try:
    eye_centers = self.eye_centers(head)
except RuntimeError:
    return False, head
```

If we are unsuccessful and the cascade classifier couldn't find an eye, OpenCV will throw a `RuntimeError`. Here, we are catching it and returning a (`False, head`) tuple, indicating that we failed to align the head.

Next, we try to order the references to the eyes that the classifier has found. We set `left_eye` to be the eye with the lower first coordinate—that is, the one on the left, as follows:

```
if eye_centers[0][0] < eye_centers[0][1]:
    left_eye, right_eye = eye_centers
else:
    right_eye, left_eye = eye_centers
```

Now that we have the location of both of the eyes, we want to figure out what kind of transformation we want to make in order to put the eyes in the hardcoded positions—that is, 25% from the sides and 25% below the top of the image.

Transforming the face

Transforming the face is a standard process that can be achieved by warping the image using cv2.warpAffine (recall Chapter 3, *Finding Objects via Feature Matching and Perspective Transforms*). We will follow the next steps to achieve this transformation:

1. First, we calculate the angle (in degrees) between the line that connects the two eyes and a horizontal line, as follows:

```
eye_angle_deg = 180 / np.pi * np.arctan2(right_eye[1]
                                         - left_eye[1],
                                         right_eye[0]
                                         - left_eye[0])
```

2. Then, we derive a scaling factor that will scale the distance between the two eyes to be exactly 50% of the image width, like this:

```
eye_dist = np.linalg.norm(left_eye - right_eye)
eye_size_scale = (1.0 - desired_eye_x * 2) *
desired_img_width / eye_dist
```

3. With the two parameters (eye_angle_deg and eye_size_scale) in hand, we can now come up with a suitable rotation matrix that will transform our image, as follows:

```
eye_midpoint = (left_eye + right_eye) / 2
rot_mat = cv2.getRotationMatrix2D(tuple(eye_midpoint),
                                  eye_angle_deg,
                                  eye_size_scale)
```

4. Next, we will make sure that the center of the eyes will be centered in the image, like this:

```
rot_mat[0, 2] += desired_img_width * 0.5 - eye_midpoint[0]
rot_mat[1, 2] += desired_eye_y * desired_img_height -
eye_midpoint[1]
```

5. Finally, we arrive at an upright scaled version of the facial region that looks like the third image (named as **Training Image**) in the previous screenshot (eye regions are highlighted only for the demonstration), as follows:

```
res = cv2.warpAffine(head, rot_mat, (desired_img_width,
                                     desired_img_width))
return True, res
```

After this step, we know how to extract nicely aligned, cropped, and rotated images from unprocessed images. Now, it's time to take a look at how to use these images to identify facial expressions.

Collecting data

The facial-expression-recognition pipeline is encapsulated in `chapter8.py`. This file consists of an interactive GUI that operates in two modes (**training** and **testing**), as described earlier.

Our entire application is divided into parts, mentioned as follows:

1. Running the application in the `collect` mode using the following command from the command line:

   $ python chapter8.py collect

   The previous command will pop up a GUI in the data collection mode to assemble a training set,
   training an MLP classifier on the training set via `python train_classifier.py`. Because this step can take a long time, the process takes place in its own script. After successful training, store the trained weights in a file, so that we can load the pre-trained MLP in the next step.

2. Then, again running the GUI in the `demo` mode as follows, we will be able to see how good the facial recognition is on the real data:

   $ python chapter8.py demo

   In this mode, you will have a GUI to classify facial expressions on a live video stream in real time. This step involves loading several pre-trained cascade classifiers as well as our pre-trained MLP classifier. These classifiers will then be applied to every captured video frame.

Now, let's take a look at how you can build an application to collect training data.

Assembling a training dataset

Before we can train an MLP, we need to assemble a suitable training set. This is done because chances are that your face is not yet part of any dataset out there (the **National Security Agency's** (**NSA's**) private collection doesn't count), thus we will have to assemble our own. This is done most easily by returning to our GUI application from the previous chapters that can access a webcam, and operate on each frame of a video stream.

We are going to subclass the `wx_gui.BaseLayout` and tweak the **user interface** (**UI**) to our liking. We will have two classes for the two different modes.

The GUI will present the user with the option of recording one of the following six emotional expressions—namely, neutral, happy, sad, surprised, angry, and disgusted. Upon clicking a button, the app will take a snapshot of the detected facial region and add it to the data collection in a file.

These samples can then be loaded from the file and used to train a machine learning classifier in `train_classifier.py`, as described in *Step 2* (given earlier).

Running the application

As we have seen in the previous chapters with a **wxpython GUI**, in order to run this app (`chapter8.py`), we need to set up a screen capture by using `cv2.VideoCapture`, and pass the handle to the `FaceLayout` class. We can do this by following the next steps:

1. First, we create a `run_layout` function that will work with any `BaseLayout` subclass, as follows:

```
def run_layout(layout_cls, **kwargs):
    # open webcam
    capture = cv2.VideoCapture(0)
    # opening the channel ourselves, if it failed to open.
    if not(capture.isOpened()):
        capture.open()

    capture.set(cv2.CAP_PROP_FRAME_WIDTH, 640)
    capture.set(cv2.CAP_PROP_FRAME_HEIGHT, 480)

    # start graphical user interface
    app = wx.App()
    layout = layout_cls(capture, **kwargs)
    layout.Center()
    layout.Show()
    app.MainLoop()
```

As you can see, the code is very similar to the code from previous chapters that used wxpython. We open the webcam, set the resolution, initialize the layout, and start the main loop of the application. This type of optimization is good when you have to use the same function multiple times.

2. Next, we set up an argument parser that will figure out which of the two layouts needs to be run and run it with the appropriate arguments.

To make use of the run_layout function in both modes, we add a command-line argument to our script using the argparse module, like this:

```
if __name__ == '__main__':
    parser = argparse.ArgumentParser()
    parser.add_argument('mode', choices=['collect', 'demo'])
    parser.add_argument('--classifier')
    args = parser.parse_args()
```

We have used the argparse module that comes with Python to set up an argument parser and add an argument with collect and demo options. We have also added an optional --classifier argument that we will use for demo mode only.

3. Now, we use all the arguments that the user passed, to call the run_layout function with appropriate arguments, as follows:

```
if args.mode == 'collect':
    run_layout(DataCollectorLayout, title='Collect Data')
elif args.mode == 'demo':
    assert args.svm is not None, 'you have to provide --svm'
    run_layout(FacialExpressionRecognizerLayout,
               title='Facial Expression Recognizer',
               classifier_path=args.classifier)
```

As you can see in the previous code, we have set it up to pass an extra classifier_path argument when we are in the demo mode. We will see how it is being used when we talk about FacialExpresssionRecognizerLayout in the later sections of this chapter.

Now that we have established how to run our application, let's build the GUI elements.

Implementing the data collector GUI

Analogous to some of the previous chapters, the GUI of the app is a customized version of the generic `BaseLayout`, as shown in the following code block:

```
import wx
from wx_gui import BaseLayout

class DataCollectorLayout(BaseLayout):
```

We start building the GUI by calling the constructor of the parent class to make sure it's correctly initialized, like this:

```
def __init__(self, *args,
             training_data='data/cropped_faces.csv',
             **kwargs):
    super().__init__(*args, **kwargs)
```

Notice that we have added some extra arguments in the previous code. Those are for all extra attributes that our class has and that the parent class doesn't.

Next, before we go on to adding UI components, we also initialize a `FaceDetector` instance and a reference to the file to store data, as follows:

```
self.face_detector = FaceDetector(
    face_cascade='params/haarcascade_frontalface_default.xml',
    eye_cascade='params/haarcascade_eye.xml')
self.training_data = training_data
```

Notice that we are using the hardcoded cascade XML files. Feel free to experiment with these as well.

Now, let's take a look at how we construct the UI using `wxpython`.

Augmenting the basic layout

The creation of the layout is again deferred to a method called `augment_layout`. We keep the layout as simple as possible. We create a panel for the acquired video frame and draw a row of buttons below it.

The idea is to then click one of the six radio buttons to indicate which facial expression you are trying to record, then place your head within the bounding box, and click the `Take Snapshot` button.

So, let's have a look at how to build the six buttons, and correctly place them on a `wx.Panel` object. The code for this is shown in the following block:

```
def augment_layout(self):
    pnl2 = wx.Panel(self, -1)
    self.neutral = wx.RadioButton(pnl2, -1, 'neutral', (10, 10),
                                  style=wx.RB_GROUP)
    self.happy = wx.RadioButton(pnl2, -1, 'happy')
    self.sad = wx.RadioButton(pnl2, -1, 'sad')
    self.surprised = wx.RadioButton(pnl2, -1, 'surprised')
    self.angry = wx.RadioButton(pnl2, -1, 'angry')
    self.disgusted = wx.RadioButton(pnl2, -1, 'disgusted')
    hbox2 = wx.BoxSizer(wx.HORIZONTAL)
    hbox2.Add(self.neutral, 1)
    hbox2.Add(self.happy, 1)
    hbox2.Add(self.sad, 1)
    hbox2.Add(self.surprised, 1)
    hbox2.Add(self.angry, 1)
    hbox2.Add(self.disgusted, 1)
    pnl2.SetSizer(hbox2)
```

You can see that even if there is a lot of code, what we wrote is mostly repetitive. We create a `RadioButton` for each emotion and add the button to a `pnl2` panel.

The `Take Snapshot` button is placed below the radio buttons and will bind to the `_on_snapshot` method, as follows:

```
# create horizontal layout with single snapshot button
pnl3 = wx.Panel(self, -1)
self.snapshot = wx.Button(pnl3, -1, 'Take Snapshot')
self.Bind(wx.EVT_BUTTON, self._on_snapshot, self.snapshot)
hbox3 = wx.BoxSizer(wx.HORIZONTAL)
hbox3.Add(self.snapshot, 1)
pnl3.SetSizer(hbox3)
```

As the comment suggests, we created a new panel and added a regular button with the `Take Snapshot` label. The important part is that we bind the click on the button to the `self._on_snapshot` method, which will process each captured image once we click on the `Take Snapshot` button.

The layout will look like the following screenshot:

To make these changes take effect, the created panels need to be added to the list of existing panels, like this:

```
# arrange all horizontal layouts vertically
self.panels_vertical.Add(pnl2, flag=wx.EXPAND | wx.BOTTOM,
                         border=1)
self.panels_vertical.Add(pnl3, flag=wx.EXPAND | wx.BOTTOM,
                         border=1)
```

The rest of the visualization pipeline is handled by the `BaseLayout` class.

Now, let's see how we add boundary boxes to the faces once they appear in the video capture, using the `process_frame` method.

Processing the current frame

The `process_frame` method is called on all the images, and we'd like to show a frame around a face when it appears in the video feed. This is illustrated in the following code block:

```
def process_frame(self, frame_rgb: np.ndarray) -> np.ndarray:
    _, frame, self.head, _ = self.face_detector.detect_face(frame_rgb)
    return frame
```

We have just called the `FaceDetector.detect_face` method of the `self.face_detector` object we created in the constructor of the layout class. Remember from the previous section that it detects faces in a downscaled grayscale version of the current frame using Haar cascades.

So, we are adding a frame if we recognize a face; that's it. Now, let's look at how we store training images inside the `_on_snapshot` method.

Storing the data

We will store the data once the user clicks on the **Take Snapshot** button, and the `_on_snapshot` event listener method is called, as shown in the following code block:

```
def _on_snapshot(self, evt):
    """Takes a snapshot of the current frame

    This method takes a snapshot of the current frame, preprocesses
    it to extract the head region, and upon success adds the data
    sample to the training set.
    """
```

Let's take a look at the code inside this method, as follows:

1. First, we figure out the label of the image by finding out which of the radio buttons was selected, like this:

```
if self.neutral.GetValue():
    label = 'neutral'
elif self.happy.GetValue():
    label = 'happy'
elif self.sad.GetValue():
    label = 'sad'
elif self.surprised.GetValue():
    label = 'surprised'
elif self.angry.GetValue():
    label = 'angry'
elif self.disgusted.GetValue():
    label = 'disgusted'
```

As you can see, it's very straightforward, once we realize that each radio button has a `GetValue()` method that returns `True` only if it was selected.

2. Next, we need to look at the detected facial region of the current frame (stored in `self.head` by `detect_head`) and align it with all the other collected frames. That is, we want all the faces to be upright and the eyes to be aligned.

   Otherwise, if we do not align the data samples, we run the risk of having the classifier compare eyes to noses. Because this computation can be costly, we do not apply it on every frame in the `process_frame` method, but instead only upon taking a snapshot in the `_on_snapshot` method, as follows:

   ```
   if self.head is None:
       print("No face detected")
   else:
       success, aligned_head =
       self.face_detector.align_head(self.head)
   ```

   Since this happened after `process_frame` was called, we already had access to `self.head`, which stored the image of the head present in the current frame.

3. Next, if we have successfully aligned the head (that is, if we have found the eyes), we will store the datum. Otherwise, we notify the user, using a `print` command to the Terminal, as follows:

   ```
   if success:
       save_datum(self.training_data, label, aligned_head)
       print(f"Saved {label} training datum.")
   else:
       print("Could not align head (eye detection
                                    failed?)")
   ```

Actual saving is done in the `save_datum` function, which we have abstracted away since it is not part of the UI. Also, this is handy in case you want to add a different dataset to your file, as illustrated in the following code block:

```
def save_datum(path, label, img):
    with open(path, 'a', newline='') as outfile:
        writer = csv.writer(outfile)
        writer.writerow([label, img.tolist()])
```

As you can see in the previous code, we use a `.csv` file to store the data, where each of the images is a `newline`. So, if you want to go back and delete an image (maybe you had forgotten to comb your hair), you just have to open the `.csv` file with a text editor and delete that line.

Now, let's move to more interesting parts, and find out how we are going to use the data we collect to be able to train a machine learning model to detect emotions.

Understanding facial emotion recognition

In this section, we will train an MLP to recognize facial emotions in the pictures.

We have previously made the point that finding the features that best describe the data is often an essential part of the entire learning task. We have also looked at common preprocessing methods, such as **mean subtraction** and **normalization**.

Here, we will look at an additional method that has a long tradition in face recognition—that is, PCA. We are hoping that, even if we don't collect thousands of training pictures, PCA will help us get good results.

Processing the dataset

Analogous to Chapter 7, *Learning to Recognize Traffic Signs*, we write a new dataset parser in data/emotions.py that will parse our self-assembled training set.

We define a load_data function that will load the training data and return a tuple of collected data and their corresponding labels, as follows:

```
def load_collected_data(path):
    data, targets = [], []
    with open(path, 'r', newline='') as infile:
        reader = csv.reader(infile)
        for label, sample in reader:
            targets.append(label)
            data.append(json.loads(sample))
    return data, targets
```

This code, similar to all the processing codes, is self-contained and resides in the data/process.py file, similar to Chapter 7, *Learning to Recognize Traffic Signs*.

Our featurization function in this chapter is going to be the pca_featurize function that will perform PCA on all samples. But unlike Chapter 7, *Learning to Recognize Traffic Signs*, our featurization function takes into account the characteristics of the entire dataset, instead of operating on each of the images separately.

Now, instead of returning only the featurized data (as in Chapter 7, *Learning to Recognize Traffic Signs*), it will return a tuple of training data, and all parameters necessary to apply the same function to the test data, as follows:

```
def pca_featurize(data) -> (np.ndarray, List)
```

Now, let's figure out what is PCA, and why we need it.

Learning about PCA

PCA is a dimensionality-reduction technique that is helpful whenever we are dealing with high-dimensional data. In a sense, you can think of an image as a point in a high-dimensional space. If we flatten a 2D image of height m and width n (by concatenating either all rows or all columns), we get a (feature) vector of length $m \times n$. The value of the ith element in this vector is the grayscale value of the ith pixel in the image.

To describe every possible 2D grayscale image with these exact dimensions, we will need an $m \times n$-dimensional vector space that contains $256^{m \times n}$ vectors. Wow!

An interesting question that comes to mind when considering these numbers is—*Could there be a smaller, more compact vector space (using less-than m x n features) that describes all these images equally well?* After all, we have previously realized that grayscale values are not the most informative measures of content.

This is where PCA comes into the picture. Consider a dataset from which we extracted exactly two features. These features could be the grayscale values of pixels at some x and y positions, but they could also be more complex than that. If we plot the dataset along these two feature axes, the data might be mapped within some multivariate Gaussian distribution, as shown in the following screenshot:

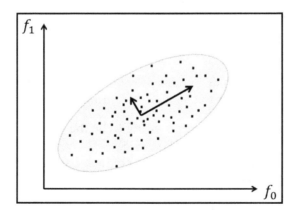

What PCA does is *rotate* all data points until the data is mapped aligned with the two axes (the two inset vectors) that explain most of the *spread* of the data. PCA considers these two axes to be the most informative because, if you walk along with them, you can see most of the data points separated. In more technical terms, PCA aims to transform the data to a new coordinate system by means of an orthogonal linear transformation.

The new coordinate system is chosen such that if you project the data onto these new axes, the first coordinate (called the **first principal component**) observes the greatest variance. In the preceding screenshot, the small vectors drawn correspond to the eigenvectors of the covariance matrix, shifted so that their tails come to lie at the mean of the distribution.

If we had previously calculated a set of basis vectors (top_vecs) and mean (center), transforming the data would be straightforward, as stated in the previous paragraph—we subtract the center from each datum, then multiply those vectors by principal components, as follows:

```
def _pca_featurize(data, center, top_vecs):
    return np.array([np.dot(top_vecs, np.array(datum).flatten() - center)
                    for datum in data]).astype(np.float32)
```

Notice that the previous code will work for any number of top_vecs; thus, if we only supply a num_components number of top vectors, it will reduce the dimensionality of the data to num_components.

Now, let's construct a pca_featurize function that takes only the data, and returns both the transformation and the list of arguments necessary to replicate the transformation—that is, center and top_vecs— so we can apply _pcea_featurize on the testing data as well, as follows:

```
def pca_featurize(training_data) -> (np.ndarray, List)
```

Fortunately, someone else has already figured out how to do all this in Python. In OpenCV, performing PCA is as simple as calling cv2.PCACompute, but we have to pass correct arguments rather than re-format what we get from OpenCV. Here are the steps:

1. First, we convert training_data into a NumPy 2D array, like this:

```
x_arr = np.array(training_data).reshape((len(training_data),
-1)).astype(np.float32)
```

2. Then, we call `cv2.PCACompute`, which computes the center of the data, and the principal components, as follows:

```
mean, eigvecs = cv2.PCACompute(x_arr, mean=None)
```

3. We can limit ourselves to the most informative components of `num_components` by running the following code:

```
# Take only first num_components eigenvectors.
top_vecs = eigvecs[:num_components]
```

The beauty of PCA is that the first principal component, by definition, explains most of the variance of the data. In other words, the first principal component is the most informative of the data. This means that we do not need to keep all of the components to get a good representation of the data.

4. We also convert `mean` to create a new `center` variable that is a 1D vector that represents the center of the data, as follows:

```
center = mean.flatten()
```

5. Finally, we return the training data processed by the `_pca_featurize` function, and the arguments necessary to pass to the `_pca_featurize` function, to replicate the same transformation so that the test data could be *featurized* in the exact same way as the train data, as follows:

```
args = (center, top_vecs)
return _pca_featurize(training_data, *args), args
```

Now we know how to clean and featurize our data, it's time to look at the training method we use to learn to recognize facial emotions.

Understanding MLPs

MLPs have been around for a while. MLPs are **artificial neural networks** (**ANNs**) used to convert a set of input data into a set of output data.

At the heart of an MLP is a **perceptron**, which resembles (yet overly simplifies) a biological neuron. By combining a large number of perceptrons in multiple layers, the MLP is able to make nonlinear decisions about its input data. Furthermore, MLPs can be trained with **backpropagation**, which makes them very interesting for supervised learning.

The following section explains the concept of a perceptron.

Understanding a perceptron

A perceptron is a binary classifier that was invented in the 1950s by Frank Rosenblatt. A perceptron calculates a weighted sum of its inputs, and, if this sum exceeds a threshold, it outputs a 1; else, it outputs a 0.

In some sense, a perceptron is integrating evidence that its afferents signal the presence (or absence) of some object instance, and if this evidence is strong enough, the perceptron will be active (or silent). This is loosely connected to what researchers believe biological neurons are doing (or can be used to do) in the brain, hence the term *ANN*.

A sketch of a perceptron is depicted in the following screenshot:

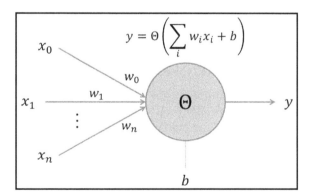

Here, a perceptron computes a weighted (w_i) sum of all its inputs (x_i), combined with a bias term (b). This input is fed into a nonlinear activation function (θ) that determines the output of the perceptron (y). In the original algorithm, the activation function was the **Heaviside step function**.

In modern implementations of ANNs, the activation function can be anything ranging from sigmoid to hyperbolic tangent functions. The Heaviside step function and the sigmoid function are plotted in the following screenshot:

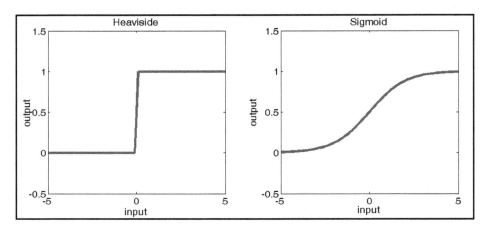

Depending on the activation function, these networks might be able to perform either classification or regression. Traditionally, one only talks of MLPs when nodes use the Heaviside step function.

Knowing about deep architectures

Once you have the perceptron figured out, it would make sense to combine multiple perceptrons to form a larger network. MLPs usually consist of at least three layers, where the first layer has a node (or neuron) for every input feature of the dataset, and the last layer has a node for every class label.

The layer in between the first and the last layer is called the hidden layer. An example of this feed-forward neural network is shown in the following screenshot:

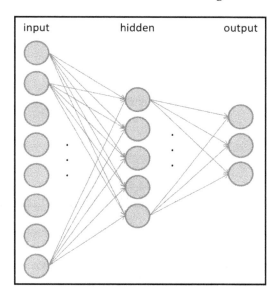

In a feed-forward neural network, some or all of the nodes in the input layer are connected to all the nodes in the hidden layer, and some or all of the nodes in the hidden layer are connected to some or all of the nodes in the output layer. You would usually choose the number of nodes in the input layer to be equal to the number of features in the dataset so that each node represents one feature.

Analogously, the number of nodes in the output layer is usually equal to the number of classes in the data, so that when an input sample of class c is presented, the cth node in the output layer is active, and all others are silent.

It is also, of course, possible to have multiple hidden layers. Often, it is not clear beforehand what the optimal size of the network should be.

Typically, you will see the error rate on the training set decrease when you add more neurons to the network, as is depicted in the following screenshot (*thinner, red curve*):

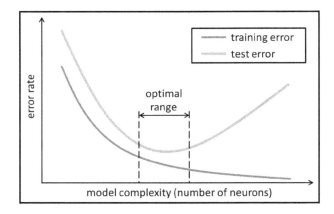

This is because the expressive power or complexity (also referred to as the **Vapnik-Chervonenkis** or **VC dimension**) of the model increases with the increasing size of the neural network. However, the same cannot be said for the error rate on the test set shown in the preceding screenshot (*thicker, blue curve*).

Instead, you will find that, with increasing model complexity, the test error goes through its minimum, and adding more neurons to the network will not improve the performance on the test data anymore. Therefore, you would want to keep the size of the neural network to what is labeled the optimal range in the preceding screenshot, which is where the network achieves the best generalization performance.

You can think of it in this way—a model of weak complexity (on the far left of the plot) is probably too small to really understand the dataset that it is trying to learn, thus yielding large error rates on both the training and the test sets. This is commonly referred to as **underfitting**.

On the other hand, a model on the far right of the plot is probably so complex that it begins to memorize the specifics of each sample in the training data, without paying attention to the general attributes that make a sample stand apart from the others. Therefore, the model will fail when it has to predict data that it has never seen before, effectively yielding a large error rate on the test set. This is commonly referred to as **overfitting**.

Instead, what you want is to develop a model that neither is underfitting nor overfitting. Often, this can only be achieved by *trial and error*; that is, by considering the network size as a hyperparameter that needs to be tweaked and tuned, depending on the exact task to be performed.

An MLP learns by adjusting its weights so that when an input sample of class c is presented, the cth node in the output layer is active and all the others are silent. MLPs are trained by means of the **backpropagation** method, which is an algorithm to calculate the partial derivative of a **loss function** with respect to any synaptic weight or neuron bias in the network. These partial derivatives can then be used to update the weights and biases in the network in order to reduce the overall loss step by step.

A loss function can be obtained by presenting training samples to the network and by observing the network's output. By observing which output nodes are active and which are dormant, we can calculate the relative error between the output of the last layer and the true labels we provided with the loss function.

We then make corrections to all the weights in the network so that the error decreases over time. It turns out that the error in the hidden layer depends on the output layer, and the error in the input layer depends on the error in both the hidden layer and the output layer. Thus, in a sense, the error backpropagates through the network. In OpenCV, backpropagation is used by specifying cv2.ANN_MLP_TRAIN_PARAMS_BACKPROP in the training parameters.

Gradient descent comes in two common flavors—that is, in **stochastic gradient descent** and **batch learning**.

In stochastic gradient descent, we update the weights after each presentation of a training example, whereas, in batch learning, we present training examples in batches and update the weights only after each batch is presented. In both scenarios, we have to make sure that we adjust the weights only slightly per sample (by adjusting the **learning rate**) so that the network slowly converges to a stable solution over time.

Now, after learning the theory behind MLPs, let's get our hands dirty and code this up using OpenCV.

Crafting an MLP for facial expression recognition

Analogous to Chapter 7, *Learning to Recognize Traffic Signs*, we will use the machine learning class that OpenCV provides, which is ml.ANN_MLP. Here are the steps to create and configure an MLP in OpenCV:

1. Instantiate an empty ANN_MLP object, like this:

```
mlp = cv2.ml.ANN_MLP_create()
```

2. Set the network architecture—the first layer equal to the dimensionality of the data, and the last layer equal to the output size of 6 required for the number of possible emotions, as follows:

```
mlp.setLayerSizes(np.array([20, 10, 6], dtype=np.uint8)
```

3. We set the training algorithm to backpropagation, and use the symmetric sigmoid function for activation, as we discussed in the previous sections, by running the following code:

```
mlp.setTrainMethod(cv2.ml.ANN_MLP_BACKPROP, 0.1)
mlp.setActivationFunction(cv2.ml.ANN_MLP_SIGMOID_SYM)
```

4. Finally, we set the termination criteria to either after 30 iterations or when the loss reaches values smaller than 0.000001, as follows, and we are ready to train the MLP:

```
mlp.setTermCriteria((cv2.TERM_CRITERIA_COUNT |
                     cv2.TERM_CRITERIA_EPS, 30, 0.000001 ))
```

In order to train the MLP, we need training data. We would also like to have an idea of how well our classifier is doing, so we need to split the collected data into training and test sets.

 The best way to split the data would be to make sure that we don't have near-identical images in the training and testing sets—for example, the user double-clicked on the **Take Snapshot** button, and we have two images that were taken milliseconds apart, thus are almost identical. Unfortunately, that is a tedious and manual process and out of the scope of this book.

We define the signature of the function, as follows. We want to get indices of an array of size n and we want to specify a ratio of the train data to all the data:

```
def train_test_split(n, train_portion=0.8):
```

Geared with the signature, let's go over the `train_test_split` function step by step, as follows:

1. First, we create a list of `indices` and `shuffle` them, like this:

```
indices = np.arange(n)
np.random.shuffle(indices)
```

2. Then, we calculate the number of training points that need to be in the N training dataset, like this:

```
N = int(n * train_portion)
```

3. After that, we create a selector for the first N indices for the training data, and create a selector for the rest of `indices` to be used for the test data, as follows:

```
return indices[:N], indices[N:]
```

Now we have a model class and a training data generator, let's take a look at how to train the MLP.

Training the MLP

OpenCV provides all the training and predicting methods, so we have to figure out how to format our data to fit the OpenCV requirements.

First, we split the data into train/test, and featurize the training data, as follows:

```
train, test = train_test_split(len(data), 0.8)
x_train, pca_args = pca_featurize(np.array(data)[train])
```

Here, `pca_args` are the arguments that we will need to store if we wanted to featurize any future data (for example, live frames during the demo).

Because the `train` method of the `cv2.ANN_MLP` module does not allow integer-valued class labels, we need to first convert `y_train` into one-hot encoding, consisting only of 0s and 1s, which can then be fed to the `train` method, as follows:

```
encoded_targets, index_to_label = one_hot_encode(targets)
y_train = encoded_targets[train]
mlp.train(x_train, cv2.ml.ROW_SAMPLE, y_train)
```

The one-hot encoding is taken care of in the `one_hot_encode` function in `train_classifiers.py`, in the following way:

1. First, we determine how many points there are in the data, like this:

```
def one_hot_encode(all_labels) -> (np.ndarray, Callable):
    unique_lebels = list(sorted(set(all_labels)))
```

2. Each c class label in `all_labels` needs to be converted into a
   (`len(unique_labels)`) long vector of 0s and 1s, where all entries are zeros
   except the cth, which is a 1. We prepare this operation by allocating a vector of
   zeros, like this:

```
y = np.zeros((len(all_labels),
    len(unique_lebels))).astype(np.float32)
```

3. Then, we create dictionaries mapping indices of columns to labels, and vice
   versa, as follows:

```
index_to_label = dict(enumerate(unique_lebels))
label_to_index = {v: k for k, v in index_to_label.items()
```

4. The vector elements at these indices then need to be set to 1, as follows:

```
for i, label in enumerate(all_labels):
    y[i, label_to_index[label]] = 1
```

5. We also return `index_to_label` so we are able to recover the label from the
   prediction vector, as follows:

```
return y, index_to_label
```

We now move on to the testing of the MLP that we just trained.

Testing the MLP

Analogous to Chapter 7, *Learning to Recognize Traffic Signs*, we will evaluate the
performance of our classifier in terms of accuracy, precision, and recall.

To reuse our previous code, we just need to calculate `y_hat` and pass `y_true` alongside it
to the metric functions by doing the following:

1. First, we featurize our test data using the `pca_args` we stored when we
   featurized the training data, and the `_pca_featurize` function, like this:

```
x_test = _pca_featurize(np.array(data)[test], *pca_args)
```

2. Then, we predict the new labels, like this:

```
_, predicted = mlp.predict(x_test)
    y_hat = np.array([index_to_label[np.argmax(y)] for y
    in predicte
```

3. Finally, we extract the true test labels using indices we stored for testing, as follows:

```
y_true = np.array(targets)[test]
```

The only things that are left to pass to a function are both `y_hat` and `y_true`, to calculate the accuracy of our classifier.

It took me 84 pictures (10-15 of each emotion) to get to a training accuracy of `0.92` and have a good enough classifier to be able to show off my software to my friends. *Can you beat it?*

Now, let's see how we run the training script, and save the output in a manner that the demo application will be able to use.

Running the script

The MLP classifier can be trained and tested by using the `train_classifier.py` script, which does the following:

1. The script first sets up the command-line options of `--data` to the location of the saved data, and `--save` to the location of a directory where we want to save the trained model (this argument is optional), as follows:

```
if __name__ == '__main__':
    parser = argparse.ArgumentParser()
    parser.add_argument('--data', required=True)
    parser.add_argument('--save', type=Path)
    args = parser.parse_args()
```

2. Then, we load the saved data, and follow the training procedure described in the previous section, as follows:

```
data, targets = load_collected_data(args.data)

mlp = cv2.ml.ANN_MLP_create()
...
mlp.train(...
```

3. Finally, we check if the user wants us to save the trained model, by running the following code:

```
if args.save:
    print('args.save')
    x_all, pca_args = pca_featurize(np.array(data))
    mlp.train(x_all, cv2.ml.ROW_SAMPLE, encoded_targets)
```

```
mlp.save(str(args.save / 'mlp.xml'))
pickle_dump(index_to_label, args.save / 'index_to_label')
pickle_dump(pca_args, args.save / 'pca_args')
```

The previous code saves the trained model, the `index_to_label` dictionary so that we can display human-readable labels in the demo, and `pca_args` so that we can featurize live camera feed frames in the demo.

The saved `mlp.xml` file contains the network configuration and learned weights. OpenCV knows how to load it. So, let's see what the demo application looks like.

Putting it all together

In order to run our app, we will need to execute the main function routine (`chapter8.py`) that loads the pre-trained cascade classifier and the pre-trained MLP and applies them to each frame of the webcam live stream.

However, this time, instead of collecting more training samples, we will start the program with a different option, shown here:

```
$ python chapter8.py demo --classifier data/clf1
```

This will start the application with a new `FacialExpressionRecognizerLayout` layout, which is a subclass of `BasicLayout` without any extra UI elements. Let's go over the constructor first, as follows:

1. It reads and initializes all the data that was stored by the training script, like this:

```
class FacialExpressionRecognizerLayout(BaseLayout):
    def __init__(self, *args,
                 clf_path=None,
                 **kwargs):
        super().__init__(*args, **kwargs)
```

2. It loads the pre-trained classifier using ANN_MLP_load, as follows:

```
self.clf = cv2.ml.ANN_MLP_load(str(clf_path / 'mlp.xml'))
```

3. It loads the Python variables that we want to pass from training, like this:

```
self.index_to_label = pickle_load(clf_path
                                  / 'index_to_label')
self.pca_args = pickle_load(clf_path / 'pca_args')
```

4. It initializes a `FaceDetector` class to be able to do face recognition, as follows:

```
self.face_detector = FaceDetector(
    face_cascade='params/
    haarcascade_frontalface_default.xml',
    eye_cascade='params/haarcascade_lefteye_2splits.xml')
```

Once we have all the pieces from training in place, we can go ahead and put some code in place to add labels to faces. In this demo, we don't have any use of extra buttons; so, the only method we have to implement is `process_frame`, which first tries to detect a face in the live feed and place a label on top of it, We will proceed as follows:

1. First, we try to detect if there is a face present in the video stream or not, by running the following code:

```
def process_frame(self, frame_rgb: np.ndarray) -> np.ndarray:
    success, frame, self.head, (x, y) =
    self.face_detector.detect_face(frame_rgb)
```

2. If there is no face, we do nothing and `return` an unprocessed `frame`, as follows:

```
if not success:
    return frame
```

3. Once there is a face, we try to align the face (the same as when collecting the training data), like this:

```
success, head = self.face_detector.align_head(self.head)
if not success:
    return frame
```

4. If we are successful, we featurize the head and predict the label using the MLP, as follows:

```
_, output = self.clf.predict(self.featruize_head(head))
label = self.index_to_label[np.argmax(output)]
```

5. Finally, we put the text with the label on top of the face's bounding box and show that to the user, by running the following code:

```
cv2.putText(frame, label, (x, y - 20),
            cv2.FONT_HERSHEY_COMPLEX, 1, (0, 255, 0), 2)

return frame
```

In the previous method, we made use of `featurize_head`, which is a convenient function to call `_pca_featurize`, as shown in the following code block:

```
def featurize_head(self, head):
    return _pca_featurize(head[None], *self.pca_args)
```

The end result looks like the following:

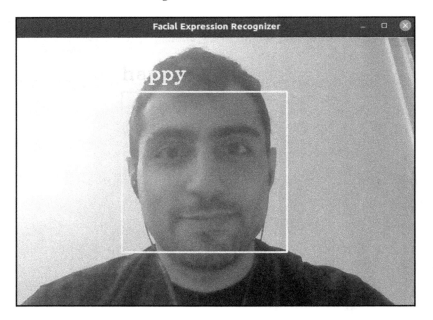

Although the classifier has only been trained on (roughly) 100 training samples, it reliably detects my various facial expressions in every frame of the live stream, no matter how distorted my face seemed to be at the given moment.

This is a good indication that the neural network that was trained previously is neither underfitting nor overfitting the data since it is capable of predicting the correct class labels, even for new data samples.

Summary

This chapter of the book has really rounded up our experience and made us combine a variety of our skills to arrive at an end-to-end app that consists of both object detection and object recognition. We became familiar with a range of pre-trained cascade classifiers that OpenCV has to offer, and we collected and created our very own training dataset, learned about MLPs, and trained them to recognize emotional expressions in faces (well, at least my face).

The classifier undoubtedly benefited from the fact that I was the only subject in the dataset, but, with all the knowledge and experience that you have gathered throughout this book, it is now time to overcome these limitations.

After learning the techniques in this chapter, you can start with something smaller, and train the classifier on images of you (indoors and outdoors, at night and day, during summer and winter). Or, you can take a look at **Kaggle's Facial Expression Recognition Challenge**, which has a lot of nice data you could play with.

If you are into machine learning, you might already know that there is a variety of accessible libraries out there, such as **Pylearn**, **scikit-learn**, and **PyTorch**.

In the next chapter, you will start your deep learning journey and will put your hands on deep CNNs. You will get acquainted with multiple deep learning concepts, and you will create and train your own classification and localization networks using transfer learning. To accomplish this, you will use one of the pre-trained classification CNNs available in **Keras**. Throughout the chapter, you will extensively use **Keras** and **TensorFlow,** which are a couple of the most popular deep learning frameworks at the time of writing.

Further reading

- **Kaggle's Facial Expression Recognition Challenge**: https://www.kaggle.com/c/challenges-in-representation-learning-facial-expression-recognition-challenge.
- **Pylearn**: https://github.com/lisa-lab/pylearn2.
- **scikit-learn**: http://scikit-learn.org.
- **pycaffe**: http://caffe.berkeleyvision.org.

- **Theano**: http://deeplearning.net/software/theano.
- **Torch**: http://torch.ch.
- **UC Irvine Machine Learning Repository**: http://archive.ics.uci.edu/ml.

Attributions

Lenna.png—Image Lenna is available at http://www.flickr.com/photos/15489034@N00/ 3388463896 by Conor Lawless under attribution CC 2.0 Generic.

Learning to Classify and Localize Objects

9

So far, we have studied a range of algorithms and approaches where you have learned how to solve real-world problems with the help of computer vision. In recent years, in parallel with the considerable hardware computational power that is provided with devices such as **Graphical Processing Units (GPUs)**, a lot of algorithms arose that utilized this power and achieved state-of-the-art results in computer vision tasks. Usually, these algorithms are based on neural networks, which enable the creator of the algorithm to squeeze quite a lot of meaningful information from data.

Meanwhile, in contrast to the classical approaches, this information is often quite hard to interpret. From that point of view, you might say that we are getting closer to artificial intelligence—that is, we are giving a computer an approach and it figures out how to do the rest. In order for all of this to not appear so mysterious, let's learn about deep learning models in this chapter.

As you have already seen, a few of the classical problems in computer vision include object detection and localization. Let's look at how to classify and localize objects with the help of deep learning models in this chapter.

The goal of this chapter is to learn important deep learning concepts such as transfer learning and how to apply them to build your own object classifier and localizer. Specifically, we will cover the following topics:

- Preparing a large dataset for training a deep learning model
- Understanding **Convolutional Neural Networks (CNNs)**
- Classifying and localizing with CNNs
- Learning about transfer learning
- Implementing activation functions
- Understanding backpropagation

We will start by preparing a dataset for training. Then, we will go on to understand how to use a pretrained model for creating a new classifier. Once you have understood how it is done, we will move forward and build more complex architectures that will perform localization.

During these steps, we will use the **Oxford-IIIT-Pet** dataset. Finally, we will run the app that will use our trained localizer network for inference. Although the network will be trained only using the bounding boxes of the heads of pets, you will see that it will also be good for localization of the human head position. The latter will show the power of generalization of our model.

Learning about these concepts of deep learning and seeing them in action will be very useful in the future when you make your own applications using deep learning models or when you start to work on completely new deep learning architectures.

Getting started

As we have mentioned in all of the chapters of this book, you will need to have OpenCV installed. Besides that, you will need to install TensorFlow.

The Oxford-IIIT-Pet dataset is available for download at `https://www.robots.ox.ac.uk/~vgg/data/pets/`, along with our dataset preparation script, which will be downloaded automatically for you.

You can find the code that we present in this chapter (from the GitHub repository) at `https://github.com/PacktPublishing/OpenCV-4-with-Python-Blueprints-Second-Editi on`. You can also use the Docker files available in the repository to run the code in the chapter. Refer to the `Appendix B`, *Setting Up a Docker Container*, for more information on the Docker files.

Planning the app

The final app will consist of modules to prepare the dataset, train the models, and run an inference with the models using input from your camera. This will require the following components:

- `main.py`: This is the main script for starting the application and localizing the head (of the pets) in real time.

- `data.py`: This is a module to download and prepare the dataset for training.
- `classification.py`: This is a script to train a classifier network.
- `localization.py`: This is a script to train and save a localization network.

After preparing the dataset for training, we will do the following to complete our app:

1. We will first train a classification network using transfer learning.
2. Next, we will train an object localization network, again using transfer learning.
3. After we create and train our localization network, we will run our `main.py` script to localize the heads in real time.

Let's start by learning how to prepare the inference script that will run our app. The script will connect to your camera, find a head position in each frame of the video stream using the localization model that we will create, and then illustrate the results in real time.

Preparing an inference script

Our inference script is quite simple. It will first prepare a drawing function, then load the model and connect it to the camera. Then, it will loop over the frames from the video stream. In the loop, for each frame of the stream, it will use the imported model to make an inference and the drawing function to display the results. Let's create a complete script using the following steps:

1. First, we import the required modules:

   ```
   import numpy as np
   import cv2
   import tensorflow.keras as K
   ```

   In this code, besides importing NumPy and OpenCV, we have also imported **Keras**. We are going to use Keras to make predictions in this script; additionally, we will use it to create and train our models throughout the chapter.

2. Then, we define a function to draw localization bounding boxes on a frame:

   ```
   def draw_box(frame: np.ndarray, box: np.ndarray) -> np.ndarray:
       h, w = frame.shape[0:2]
       pts = (box.reshape((2, 2)) * np.array([w, h])).astype(np.int)
       cv2.rectangle(frame, tuple(pts[0]), tuple(pts[1]), (0, 255, 0),
   2)
       return frame
   ```

The preceding `draw_box` function accepts `frame` and the normalized coordinates of the two corners of a bounding box as an array of four numbers. The function first reshapes the one-dimensional array of the box into a two-dimensional array, where the first index represents the point and the second represents the *x* and *y* coordinates. Then, it transforms the normalized coordinates to the coordinates of the image by multiplying them with an array composed of the width and height of the image and translates the result into integer values in the same line. Finally, it draws the bounding box with the color green using the `cv2.rectangle` function and returns `frame`.

3. Then, we import the model that we will prepare throughout the chapter and connect to the camera:

```
model = K.models.load_model("localization.h5")
cap = cv2.VideoCapture(0)
```

`model` will be stored in a binary file, which is imported using a convenient function from Keras.

4. After that, we iterate over the frames from the camera, resize each `frame` to a standard size (that is, the default image size for the models that we will create), and convert `frame` to the **RGB (red, green, blue)** color space as we will train our models on RGB images:

```
for _, frame in iter(cap.read, (False, None)):
    input = cv2.resize(frame, (224, 224))
    input = cv2.cvtColor(input, cv2.COLOR_BGR2RGB)
```

5. In the same loop, we normalize the image and add one to the shape of the frame as the model accepts batches of images. Then, we pass the result to `model` for inference:

```
box, = model.predict(input[None] / 255)
```

6. We continue the loop by drawing the predicted bounding box using the previously defined function, show the results, and then set the termination criteria:

```
cv2.imshow("res", frame)
if(cv2.waitKey(1) == 27):
    break
```

Now that we have our inference script ready, let's start the journey of creating our model by first preparing the dataset in the next section.

Preparing the dataset

As mentioned previously, in this chapter, we are going to use the Oxford-IIIT-Pet dataset. It will be a good idea to encapsulate the preparation of the dataset in a separate `data.py` script, which can then be used throughout the chapter. As with any other script, first of all, we have to import all the required modules, as shown in the following code snippet:

```
import glob
import os

from itertools import count
from collections import defaultdict, namedtuple

import cv2
import numpy as np
import tensorflow as tf
import xml.etree.ElementTree as ET
```

In order to prepare our dataset for use, we will first download and parse the dataset into memory. Then, out of the parsed data, we will create a TensorFlow dataset, which allows us to work with a dataset in a convenient manner as well as prepare the data in the background so that the preparation of the data does not interrupt the neural network training process. So, let's move on to download and parse the dataset in the next section.

Downloading and parsing the dataset

In this section, we first download the dataset from the official website and then parse it into a convenient format. During this stage, we will leave out the images, which occupy quite a lot of memory. We cover this procedure in the following steps:

1. Define where we want to store our pets dataset and download it using a convenient `get_file` function in Keras:

```
DATASET_DIR = "dataset"
for type in ("annotations", "images"):
    tf.keras.utils.get_file(
        type,
        f"https://www.robots.ox.ac.uk/~vgg/data/pets/data/{type}.tar.gz",
        untar=True,
        cache_dir=".",
        cache_subdir=DATASET_DIR)
```

As our dataset resides in an archive, we have also extracted it by passing `untar=True`. We also pointed `cache_dir` to the current directory. Once the files are saved, consequent executions of the `get_file` function will result in no action.

 The dataset weighs more than half a gigabyte, and, on the first run, you will need a stable internet connection with good bandwidth.

2. Once we have downloaded and extracted our dataset, let's define constants for the dataset and annotation folders and set the image size that we want to resize our images to:

```
IMAGE_SIZE = 224
IMAGE_ROOT = os.path.join(DATASET_DIR,"images")
XML_ROOT = os.path.join(DATASET_DIR,"annotations")
```

Size `224` is often the default size on which image classification networks are trained. Hence, it's a good idea to keep to that size for better accuracy.

3. Annotations of this dataset contain information about the image in XML format. Before parsing the XML, let's first define what data we want to have:

```
Data = namedtuple("Data","image,box,size,type,breed")
```

`namedtuple` is an extension of a standard tuple in Python and allows you to refer to an element of a tuple by its name. The names that we have defined correspond to the data elements that we are interested in. Namely, those are the image itself (`image`), the head bounding box of the pet (`box`), the image size, `type` (cat or dog), and `breed` (there are 37 breeds).

4. `breeds` and `types` are strings in the annotation; what we want are numbers corresponding to `breeds`. For that purpose, we define two dictionaries:

```
types = defaultdict(count().__next__ )
breeds = defaultdict(count().__next__ )
```

`defaultdict` is a dictionary that returns default values for the undefined keys. Here, it will return the next number starting from zero when requested.

5. Next, we define a function that, given a path to an XML file, will return an instance of our data:

```
def parse_xml(path: str) -> Data:
```

The previously defined function covers the following steps:

1. Open the XML file and parse it:

```
with open(path) as f:
    xml_string = f.read()
root = ET.fromstring(xml_string)
```

The contents of the XML file are parsed using the `ElementTree` module, which represents the XML in a format that is convenient to navigate through.

2. Then, get the name of the corresponding image and extract the name of the breed:

```
img_name = root.find("./filename").text
breed_name = img_name[:img_name.rindex("_")]
```

3. After that, convert the breed to a number using `breeds` that was previously defined, which assigns the next number for each undefined key:

```
breed_id = breeds[breed_name]
```

4. Similarly, get the ID of `types`:

```
type_id = types[root.find("./object/name").text]
```

5. Then, extract the bounding box and normalize it:

```
box =
np.array([int(root.find(f"./object/bndbox/{tag}").text)
               for tag in
"xmin,ymin,xmax,ymax".split(",")])
size = np.array([int(root.find(f"./size/{tag}").text)
               for tag in "width,height".split(",")])
normed_box = (box.reshape((2, 2)) / size).reshape((4))
```

Return the results as an instance of `Data`:

```
return Data(img_name,normed_box,size,type_id,breed_id)
```

6. Now that we have downloaded the dataset and prepared a parser, let's go on to parse the dataset:

```
xml_paths = glob.glob(os.path.join(XML_ROOT,"xmls","*.xml"))
xml_paths.sort()
parsed = np.array([parse_xml(path) for path in xml_paths])
```

We have also sorted the paths so that they appear in the same order in different runtime environments.

As we have parsed our dataset, we might want to print out available breeds and types for illustration:

```
print(f"{len(types)} TYPES:", *types.keys(), sep=", ")
print(f"{len(breeds)} BREEDS:", *breeds.keys(), sep=", ")
```

The previous code snippet outputs two types, namely `cat` and `dog`, and their `breeds`:

```
2 TYPES:, cat, dog
37 BREEDS:, Abyssinian, Bengal, Birman, Bombay, British_Shorthair,
Egyptian_Mau, Maine_Coon, Persian, Ragdoll, Russian_Blue, Siamese, Sphynx,
american_bulldog, american_pit_bull_terrier, basset_hound, beagle, boxer,
chihuahua, english_cocker_spaniel, english_setter, german_shorthaired,
great_pyrenees, havanese, japanese_chin, keeshond, leonberger,
miniature_pinscher, newfoundland, pomeranian, pug, saint_bernard, samoyed,
scottish_terrier, shiba_inu, staffordshire_bull_terrier, wheaten_terrier,
yorkshire_terrier
```

Later on in this chapter, we will have to split the dataset on training and test sets. In order to perform a good split, we should randomly pick data elements from the dataset in order to have a proportional number of `breeds` in the train and test sets.

We can mix the dataset now so that we don't have to worry about it later, as follows:

```
np.random.seed(1)
np.random.shuffle(parsed)
```

The previous code first sets a random seed, which is required to get the same result every time we execute the code. The `seed` method accepts one argument, which is a number specifying a random sequence.

Once the `seed` method is set, we have the same sequence of random numbers in functions that use random numbers. Such numbers are called **pseudorandom**. This means that, although they look random, they are predefined. In our case, we use the `shuffle` method, which mixes the order of elements in the `parsed` array.

Now that we have parsed our dataset into a convenient NumPy array, let's move on and create a TensorFlow dataset out of it.

Creating a TensorFlow dataset

We are going to use the TensorFlow dataset adapter in order to train our models. Of course, we could create a NumPy array from our dataset, but imagine how much memory it would require to keep all the images in the memory.

In contrast, the dataset adapter allows you to load the data into memory when required. Moreover, the data is loaded and prepared in the background so that it will not be a bottleneck in our training process. We transform our parsed array as follows:

```
ds = tuple(np.array(list(i)) for i in np.transpose(parsed))
ds_slices = tf.data.Dataset.from_tensor_slices(ds)
```

From the previous code snippet, `from_tensor_slices` creates `Dataset` whose elements are slices of the given tensors. In our case, the tensors are NumPy arrays of labels (box, breed, image location, and more).

Under the hood, it is a similar concept to the Python `zip` function. First, we have prepared the input accordingly. Let's now print one element from the dataset to see how it looks:

```
for el in ds_slices.take(1):
    print(el)
```

This gives the following output:

```
(<tf.Tensor: id=14, shape=(), dtype=string,
numpy=b'american_pit_bull_terrier_157.jpg'>, <tf.Tensor: id=15, shape=(4,),
dtype=float64, numpy=array([0.07490637, 0.07 , 0.58426966, 0.44333333])>,
<tf.Tensor: id=16, shape=(2,), dtype=int64, numpy=array([267, 300])>,
<tf.Tensor: id=17, shape=(), dtype=int64, numpy=1>, <tf.Tensor: id=18,
shape=(), dtype=int64, numpy=13>)
```

It is the TensorFlow—`tensor` that contains all the information that we have parsed from a single XML file. Given the dataset, we can check whether all our bounding boxes are correct:

```
for el in ds_slices:
    b = el[1].numpy()
    if(np.any((b>1) |(b<0)) or np.any(b[2:]-b[:2] < 0)):
        print(f"Invalid box found {b} image: {el[0].numpy()}")
```

As we have normalized the boxes, they should be in the range of [0,1]. Additionally, we make sure that the coordinates of the first point of the box are less than or equal to the coordinates of the second point.

Now, we define a function that will transform our data element so that we can feed it into a neural network:

```
def prepare(image,box,size,type,breed):
    image = tf.io.read_file(IMAGE_ROOT+"/"+image)
    image = tf.image.decode_png(image,channels=3)
    image = tf.image.resize(image,(IMAGE_SIZE,IMAGE_SIZE))
    image /= 255
    return
Data(image,box,size,tf.one_hot(type,len(types)),tf.one_hot(breed,len(breeds
))))
```

The function first loads the corresponding image and resizes it to the standard size and normalizes it to [0,1]. Then, it creates a one_hot vector out of types and breeds using the tf.one_hot method and returns the result as an instance of Data.

Now what remains is to map our dataset with the function, and we are ready to go:

```
ds = ds_slices.map(prepare).prefetch(32)
```

We have also called the prefetch method, which makes sure that some amount of data is prefetched so that our networks will not have to wait for the data to be loaded from the hard drive.

If we are running the data preparation script directly, it might be a good idea to illustrate some samples of the data. First, we create a function that creates an illustration image when it is given a sample of data:

```
if __name__ == "__main__":
    def illustrate(sample):
        breed_num = np.argmax(sample.breed)
        for breed, num in breeds.items():
            if num == breed_num:
                break
        image = sample.image.numpy()
        pt1, pt2 = (sample.box.numpy().reshape(
            (2, 2)) * IMAGE_SIZE).astype(np.int32)
        cv2.rectangle(image, tuple(pt1), tuple(pt2), (0, 1, 0))
        cv2.putText(image, breed, (10, 10),
                    cv2.FONT_HERSHEY_SIMPLEX, 0.4, (0, 1, 0))
        return image
```

The function converts the `breed` one-hot vector back to a number, finds the name of the breed in the `breeds` dictionary, and plots the bounding box of the head together with the breed name.

Now, we concatenate several such illustrations and show the resulting image:

```
samples_image = np.concatenate([illustrate(sample)
                                for sample in ds.take(3)], axis=1)
cv2.imshow("samples", samples_image)
cv2.waitKey(0)
```

The result is shown in the following screenshot:

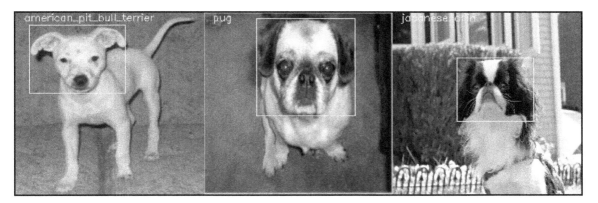

The preceding screenshot shows nice pets with the bounding boxes around their heads as expected. Note that, although we have used random numbers to mix the dataset in our script, you obtain the same result as illustrated previously. So, you can now see the power of pseudorandom numbers.

Now that we have prepared the dataset, let's move on to creating and training classifiers in the next section. We will build two classifiers—one for the pet type and the other for the breed.

Classifying with CNNs

To start with the classification, first of all, we have to import the required modules:

```
import tensorflow.keras as K
from data import ds
```

We have to import our prepared dataset and Keras, which we will use to build our classifier.

However, before we build our classifier, let's first learn about convolutional networks, as we are going to use them to build our classifier.

Understanding CNNs

In Chapter 1, *Fun with Filters*, you learned about filters and convolution. In particular, you learned how filters can be used to create a pencil sketch image. In the pencil sketch, you could see the points in the image that had a sharp change in value, that is, they were darker than those that had a smooth change.

From that point of view, the filters that we applied can be thought of as filters for edge detection. In other words, the filters act as a feature detector, where the feature is an edge. Alternatively, you could compose a different filter that is activated on the corners or that is activated when there is no change in the color value.

The filters that we have used act on a single-channel image and have two dimensions; however, we can extend the filter with the third dimension, which can then be applied to a multichannel image. For example, if a single-channel filter has size *3 x 3*, the corresponding 3-channel (for example, RGB) filter will have size *3 x 3 x 3*, where the last value is the depth of the filter.

Such filters can already be used for more complex features. For example, you might think of a filter that works with the color green, meanwhile ignoring the values in red and blue by setting zeros in the corresponding elements of the filter.

Once you come up with a good set of filters, you can apply them to the original image and then stack them into a new multichannel image. For example, if we apply 100 filters on an image, we will obtain 100 single-channel images, which will result in a 100-channel image after stacking. Hence, we have built a layer that accepts 3 channels and outputs 100 channels.

Next, we can compose new filters that have a depth of 100 and act on the composed 100-channel image. These filters can also be activated on more complex features. For example, if there were filters in previous layers that are activated on edges, we can compose a filter that is activated on an intersection of edges.

After a range of layers, we might see filters that are activated, for example, on the noses of people, heads, the wheels of vehicles, or so on. That is actually how the convolutional network works. Surely, a question arises: how do we compose those filters? The answer is we don't, because they are learned.

We provide the data and the network learns which filters it needs to make good predictions. Another difference between the convolutional filters that you have used is that, besides the learnable parameter of the filters, there is one more learnable value called, which is a constant term added to the output of a filter.

Besides that, after the convolutional filters in each layer, usually, a nonlinear function is applied to the output of the filters called the **activation function**. As a result of the nonlinearity, the network represents quite a wider class of functions so that there is a relatively higher chance of building a good model.

Now that we have some understanding of how a convolutional network works, let's start by building a classifier. While building the networks in this chapter, you will see how the convolutional layers are built and used. As mentioned previously, we use a pretrained model for our new models, or, in other words, we use transfer learning. Let's understand what this is in the next section.

Learning about transfer learning

Usually, a CNN has millions of parameters. Let's make an estimation to find out where all of those parameters come from.

Suppose we have a 10-layer network and each layer has 100 filters of size *3 x 3*. These numbers are quite low and networks that have good performance usually have dozens of layers and hundreds of filters in each layer. For our case, each filter has a depth of 100.

Hence, each filter has 3 x 3 x 3 = 900 parameters (excluding biases, the number of which is 100), which results in *900 x 100* parameters for each layer and, therefore, about 900,000 parameters for the complete network. To learn so many parameters from scratch without overfitting would require quite a large annotated dataset. A question arises: what can we do instead?

You have learned that layers of a network act as feature extractors. Besides this, natural images have quite a lot in common. Therefore, it would be a good idea to use the feature extractors of a network that was trained on a large dataset to achieve good performance on a different, smaller dataset. This technique is called **transfer learning**.

Let's pick a pretrained model as our base model, which is a single line of code with Keras:

```
base_model = K.applications.MobileNetV2(input_shape=(224,224, 3),
include_top=False)
```

Here, we use the `MobileNetV2` pretrained network, which is a robust and lightweight network. Of course, you can use other available models instead, which can be found on the Keras website or by simply listing them with `dir(K.applications)`.

We have taken the version of the network that excludes the top layers responsible for classification by passing in `include_top=False`, as we are going to build a new classifier on top of it. But still, the network includes all the other layers that were trained on **ImageNet**. ImageNet is a dataset that includes millions of images and each of the images is annotated with one of 1,000 classes of the dataset.

Let's take a look at the shape of the output of our base model:

```
print(base_model.output.shape)
```

The result is as follows:

(None, 7, 7, 1280)

The first number is undefined and denotes the batch size or, in other words, the number of input images. Suppose we simultaneously pass a stack of 10 images to the network; then, the output here would have a shape of `(10,7,7,1280)` and the first dimension of the tensor will correspond to the input image number.

The next two indexes are the size of the output shape and the last is the number of channels. In the original model, this output represents features from the input images that are later used to classify the images of the ImageNet dataset.

Therefore, they are quite a good representation of all the images so that the network can classify the images of ImageNet based on them. Let's try to use these features to classify the types and breeds of our pets. In order to do this, let's first prepare a classifier in the next section.

Preparing the pet type and breed classifier

As we are going to use the features as they are, let's first freeze the weights of the network layers so that they don't update during the training process:

```
for layer in base_model.layers:
    layer.trainable = False
```

In general, each location of an activation map specifies whether there is a feature of the corresponding type in that location. As we work on the last layers of the network, we can suppose that different locations on the activation map contain similar information and reduce the dimensionality of our features by averaging the activation maps:

```
x = K.layers.GlobalAveragePooling2D()(base_model.output)
```

The operation is called `AveragePooling2D`—we pool the average of the tensor in two dimensions of our feature tensor. You can see the results by printing the shapes of the input and output of the operation:

```
print(base_model.output.shape, x.shape)
```

This shows the following output:

```
(None, 7, 7, 1280) (None, 1280)
```

Now that we have just `1280` features per image, let's add the classification layer right away and prepare our dataset for training either on the types or the breeds:

```
is_breeds = True
if is_breeds:
    out = K.layers.Dense(37,activation="softmax")(x)
    inp_ds = ds.map(lambda d: (d.image,d.breed))
else:
    out = K.layers.Dense(2,activation="softmax")(x)
    inp_ds = ds.map(lambda d: (d.image,d.type))
```

Training on the types and `breeds` differs only by the number of output neurons and the labels. In the case of `breeds`, the number of labels is `37`, and, in the case of types, this is `2` (namely cat or dog), which you can see in the code. A dense layer represents densely connected neurons. The latter means that each neuron in the layer is connected to all 1,280 inputs to the layer.

Hence, each neuron has *1280 + 1* learnable parameters, where 1 is for the bias. Mathematically, for the complete layer, the weights of the kernel are represented with a matrix that has a size (1,280 for the number of classes) and a column of height 1280.

The linear part of the layer can be written as follows:

$$(a * x + b),$$

Here, **x** is the output of the previous layer (1,280 averaged features, in our case), **a** is the matrix, and **b** is the column.

Also, we have set a **softmax** function as the activation, which is a good choice with classification tasks. The latter is defined as follows:

$$softmax(x)_i = \frac{exp(x_i)}{\sum_j exp(x_j))}$$

Here, **x** is the input to the activation (output of the linear part).

You can see that it sums up to one across all outputs; hence, the output can be thought of as the probability of the corresponding class.

The mapping that we defined on the dataset will set the image as data and the breeds or types as the label.

Now we are ready to define our model:

```
model = K.Model(inputs=base_model.input, outputs=out)
```

Here, you can see that the input of the network is our base model and the output is our classifier layer. Hence, we have successfully built our classification network.

So, now that we have prepared our classifier network, let's train and evaluate it in the next section:

Training and evaluating the classifier

In order to train the classifier, we have to configure it for training. We have to specify an objective function (the `loss` function) and a training method. Additionally, we might want to specify some metrics in order to see how the model performs. We can configure the classifier using the `compile` method of the model:

```
model.compile(loss="categorical_crossentropy", optimizer="adam",
metrics=["categorical_accuracy","top_k_categorical_accuracy"])
```

We have passed `metrics` as `categorical_accuracy`, which will show which part of the dataset is classified with the right class. Besides this, we have passed one more metric called `top_k_categorical_accuracy`, which shows which part of the dataset is correct in the top `k` prediction of the network.

The default value of `k` is five, so the metric shows which part of the dataset is in the most probable five classes predicted by the neural network. We have also passed `optimizer="adam"`, which forces the model to use **Adam Optimizer** as a training algorithm. You will learn how neural networks are usually trained in the *Understanding backpropagation* section.

Before training, we also split the dataset into training and test sets in order to see how the network performs on unseen data:

```
evaluate = inp_ds.take(1000)
train = inp_ds.skip(1000).shuffle(10**4)
```

Here, we take the first `1000` elements of the dataset for test purposes. And the remaining part is used for training.

The training part is mixed by calling the `shuffle` method, which will make sure that we have a different order of the data in each epoch of training. Finally, we train our network by calling the `fit` method of the dataset and then evaluate this on the validation set:

```
model.fit(train.batch(32), epochs=4)
model.evaluate(valid.batch(1))
```

First, the `fit` method accepts the dataset itself, which we pass with batches of `32`. The latter means that, on each step of the training process, `32` images from the dataset will be used.

We have also passed a number of `epochs`, which means that our dataset will be iterated for 4 times until the training procedure stops. The output of the last `epoch` looks as follows:

```
Epoch 4/4
 84/84 [==============================] - 13s 156ms/step - loss: 0.0834 -
categorical_accuracy: 0.9717 - top_k_categorical_accuracy: 1.0000
```

Our categorical accuracy on the train set is more than 97%. So, we are pretty good at differentiating between cats and dogs. Of course, the **top-K accuracy** will be 100 percent as we have just two classes. Now, let's see how we are performing on the validation set.

After training, the model is evaluated and you should obtain results similar to the test set:

```
model.evaluate(valid.batch(1))
```

The output is given as follows:

```
1000/1000 [==============================] - 9s 9ms/step - loss: 0.0954 -
categorical_accuracy: 0.9730 - top_k_categorical_accuracy: 1.0000
```

We again get the categorical accuracy of more than 97%. Therefore, our model does not overfit and performs well on the test set.

If we train on breeds, the same output for training looks as follows:

```
Epoch 4/4
 84/84 [==============================] - 13s 155ms/step - loss: 0.3272 -
categorical_accuracy: 0.9233 - top_k_categorical_accuracy:
 0.9963
```

Meanwhile, the output for testing looks like this:

```
1000/1000 [==============================] - 11s 11ms/step - loss: 0.5646 -
categorical_accuracy: 0.8080 - top_k_categorical_accuracy: 0.9890
```

For breeds, we get worse results, which is expected as it is much more difficult to differentiate a breed than just state whether it is a cat or a dog. In any case, the model does not perform too badly. Its first-attempt guess is more than 80 percent right, and we can also be about 99 percent sure that it will guess the breed if it has 5 attempts.

In this section, we have learned how to use a pretrained classifier network to build a new classifier. In the next section, let's move ahead with our deep learning journey and create an object localization network using the same base model—a task that the base model was never trained to accomplish.

Localizing with CNNs

Being able to create your own localizer is a good way to acquire intuition on how an object detection network might work. This is because the only conceptual difference between object detection and localization networks is that a localization network predicts a single bounding box, while an object detection network predicts multiple boxes. Also, it is a good way to start understanding how to build a neural network that accomplishes other regression tasks.

In this section, we are going to use the same pretrained classifier network, `MobileNetV2`, as the previous section. However, this time we are going to use the network for localizing objects instead of classifying. Let's import the required modules and the base model in the same way that we did in the previous section—although, this time, we are not going to freeze the layers of the base model:

```
import tensorflow.keras as K

from data import ds

base_model = K.applications.MobileNetV2(
    input_shape=(224, 224, 3), include_top=False)
```

Now that we have everything ready, let's go on to prepare our localizer model.

Preparing the model

First, let's think about how we can make a localizer using the output of the base model.

As mentioned previously, the output tensor of the base model has a shape of (`None`, `7`, `7`, `1280`). The output tensor represents features obtained using a convolutional network. We can suppose that some spatial information is encoded in the spatial indexes *(7,7)*.

Let's try to reduce the dimensionality of our feature map using a couple of convolutional layers and create a regressor that should predict the corner coordinates of the pets' head bounding boxes provided by the dataset.

Our convolutional layers will have several options that are the same:

```
conv_opts = dict(
    activation='relu',
    padding='same',
    kernel_regularizer="l2")
```

First of all, they will both use the **Rectified Linear Unit** (**ReLU**) as an activation function. The latter is a simple function, which is zero when the input is less than zero and is equal to the input when the input is greater than or equal to zero.

`padding=same` specifies that we do not want the convolution operation to reduce the size of the feature map. The feature maps will be padded with zeros such that the feature maps do not reduce size. This is in contrast to `padding='valid'`, which applies the convolutional kernel only up to the margins of the feature maps.

It is often a good idea to regularize trained parameters, normalize them, or do both. The latter often allows you to train easier, faster, and generalize better. Regularizers allow you to apply penalties on layer parameters during optimization. These penalties are incorporated in the loss function that the network optimizes.

In our case, we use the `l2` kernel regularizer, which regularizes the **Euclidian** norm of the convolutional kernel weights. The regularization is accomplished by adding the $\lambda\|w\|^2$ term to the loss function (the objective function). Here, λ is a small constant and $\|w\|$ is the *L2* norm, which is equal to the square root of the sum of squares of the parameters of the layer.

This is one of the most widely used regularization terms. Now we are ready to define our convolutional layers. The first layer is shown as follows:

```
x = K.layers.Conv2D(256, (1, 1), **conv_opts)(base_model.output)
```

Here, the first parameter is the number of output channels, which is also the number of convolutional filters. The second parameter describes the size of the convolutional filters. At first glance, it might seem that a single-pixel convolutional kernel does not make much sense as it cannot encode the contextual information of a feature map.

That is surely correct; however, in this case, it is used for a different purpose. It is a fast operation that allows encoding the depth of the input feature maps in a lower dimensionality. The depth is reduced from 1280 to `256`.

The next layer looks as follows:

```
x = K.layers.Conv2D(256, (3, 3), strides=2, **conv_opts)(x)
```

Here, besides the default options that we use, we use strides, which specify the number of pixels shifts over the input. In Chapter 1, *Fun with Filters,* the convolutional operation was applied in each location, which means the filter was moved one pixel at a time and is equivalent to strides equal to one.

When the `strides` option is 2, then we move the filters by two pixels at each step. The option is in plural form as we might want to have different strides in different directions, which can be done by passing a tuple of numbers. The application of a `stride` with a value greater than 1 is a means to reduce the size of the activation map without losing spatial information.

Of course, there are other operations that can reduce the size of the activation maps. For example, an operation called **max pooling** can be used, which is one of the most widely used operations in modern convolutional networks. The latter takes a small window size (for example, 2 x 2), picks a single maximal value from that window, moves by a specified number of pixels (for example, 2), and repeats the procedure throughout the activation map. Therefore, as a result of this procedure, the size of the activation map will be reduced by a factor of 2.

In contrast to the approach with strides, the max-pooling operation is more suitable for tasks where we are not very interested in spatial information. Such tasks are, for example, classification tasks, in which we are not interested where an object is exactly but are simply interested in what it is. The loss of the spatial information in max pooling happens when we simply take the maximal value in a window without considering its position in the window.

The last thing that we want to do is to connect a dense layer of four neurons to the convolutional layer, which will be regressed to the two corner coordinates of the bounding boxes ((x, y) for each corner):

```
out = K.layers.Flatten()(x)
out = K.layers.Dense(4, activation="sigmoid")(out)
```

As the coordinates of bounding boxes are normalized, it's a good idea to use an activation function, which has values in the range of (0,1) such as a sigmoid function, in our case.

All the required layers are ready. Now, let's define the model with the new layers and compile it for training:

```
model = K.Model(inputs=base_model.input, outputs=out)
model.compile(
    loss="mean_squared_error",
    optimizer="adam",
    metrics=[
        K.metrics.RootMeanSquaredError(),
        "mae"])
```

We use the **Mean Squared Error (MSE)** as a loss function, which is the squared difference between the ground truth and the predicted value. During training, this value will be minimized; hence, the model is supposed to predict the corner coordinates after training.

The regularization terms that we have added to the convolutional layers are also added to loss as discussed. The latter is done automatically by Keras. Also, we use the **Root of MSE (RMSE)** along with the **Mean Absolute Error (MAE)**, which measures the average magnitude of the errors, as our metrics.

Let's now split the dataset, in the same way that we did in the previous section:

```
inp_ds = ds.map(lambda d: (d.image,d.box))
valid = inp_ds.take(1000)
train = inp_ds.skip(1000).shuffle(10000)
```

What is left to do is to train our model, just like we did in the previous section. However, before proceeding with our training, you might be interested in learning how exactly the training of our new layers is accomplished. In multilayer neural networks, training is usually done using the **backpropagation algorithm**, so let's first learn about that in the next section.

Understanding backpropagation

A neural network is considered to be trained when we have some optimal weights of the network so that the network makes good predictions on our data. So, the question is how do we reach these optimal weights? Neural networks are usually trained using a **gradient descent** algorithm. This might be either the pure gradient descent algorithm or some improved optimization method such as **Adam optimizer**, which is again based on computing the gradient.

In all of these algorithms, we need to compute the gradient of the loss function relative to all the weights. As a neural network is a complex function, it might not appear to be straightforward. This is where the backpropagation algorithm jumps in, which allows us to calculate the gradients easily in complex networks and understand what the gradient looks like. Let's dive into the details of the algorithm.

Suppose we have a neural network consisting of an N sequential layer. Generally speaking, the ith layer in such a network is a function that can be defined as follows:

$$f_i = f_i(w_i, f_{i-1})$$

 Here, w_i is the weight of the layer and f_{i-1} is the function corresponding to the previous layer.

We can define f_0 to be the input of our network so that the formula holds for the complete neural network including the first layer.

We can also define f_{N+1} to be our loss function so that the formula defines not only all the layers but also the loss function. Of course, such a generalization excludes the weight normalization term that we have already used. However, this is a simple term that just adds up to the loss and hence can be omitted for simplicity.

We can compute the gradient of the loss function by setting $i = N + 1$ and using the chain rule as follows:

$$\frac{\partial f_i}{\partial w_{1..i}} = \frac{\partial f_i}{\partial f_{i-1}} \times \frac{\partial f_{i-1}}{\partial w_{1..i-1}} + \frac{\partial f_i}{\partial w_i}$$

According to our definition, this formula holds not only for the loss function, but it is also general for all of the layers. In this formula, we can see that the partial derivative of a certain layer with respect to all the weight in the previous layer including the current layer is expressed in terms of the same derivative of the previous layer, which is the $\partial f_{i-1} / \partial w_{1..i-1}$ term in the formula, and terms that can be calculated using only the current layer, namely, $\partial f_i / \partial f_{i-1}$ and $\partial f_i / \partial w_i$.

Using the formula, we can now numerically compute the gradient. In order to do that, we first define a variable representing an error signal and assign its initial value to one. It should be clear in a moment why it represents an error signal. Then, we start from the last layer (the loss function, in our case) and repeat the following steps until we reach the input of the network:

1. Compute the partial derivative of the current layer with respect to its weights and multiply by the error signal. This will be the part of the gradient corresponding to the weights of the current layer.
2. Compute the partial derivative with respect to the previous layer, multiply by the error signal, and then update the error signal with the resulting value.
3. If the input of the network is not reached, move to the previous layer and repeat the steps.

Once we reach the input, we have all the partial derivatives of the loss with respect to the learnable weights; therefore, we have the gradient of our loss function. Now we can note that this is the partial derivative of a layer with respect to the previous layer that propagates backward throughout the network during the gradient computation process.

That is a **propagating signal**, which influences the contribution of each layer to the gradient of the loss function. For example, if it becomes all zero somewhere during the propagation, then the contribution of all the remaining layers to the gradient will also be zero. Such a phenomenon is called a **vanishing-gradient problem**. This algorithm can be generalized to acyclic networks with different kinds of branches.

In order to train our network, all that is left to do is to update our weight in the direction of the gradient and repeat the procedure until convergence. If the pure gradient descent algorithm is used, we simply subtract the gradient multiplied by some small constant from the weights; however, usually, more advanced optimization algorithms are used such as Adam optimizer.

The problem with the pure gradient descent algorithm is that, first, we should find some optimal value for the small constant so that the update of the weights is neither too small, which will result in slow learning, or too large, as too large a value results in instability. Another problem is that once we have found an optimal value, we have to start to decrease it once the network starts to converge. What is more important, it's often wise to update different weights with different factors as different weights might be at different distances from their optimal values.

These are some of the reasons why we might want to use more advanced optimization techniques such as Adam optimizer or **RMSProp**, which take some or all of these mentioned issues, and even some unmentioned issues, into account. Meanwhile, while creating your networks, you should note that there is still ongoing research in the field of optimization algorithms and that one of the existing optimizers might be better in some cases than others, although the Adam optimizer should be a good choice for many tasks.

You might also note that in the algorithm, we did not mention exactly how the partial derivatives in a layer can be computed. Of course, they can be numerically computed by varying the values and measuring the response as is done with numerical methods for computing a derivative. The problem is that such computations would be heavy and error-prone. A better way to do it is to define a symbolic representation for each operation used and then, again, use the chain rule as in the backpropagation.

So, we now understand how the complete gradient is calculated. Actually, most of the modern deep learning frameworks do the differentiation for you. You usually don't need to worry about how exactly it is accomplished, but understanding the backgrounds of the computation might be very helpful if you are planning to work on new, that is, your own, models.

But for now, let's train our prepared model in the next section and see how it performs.

Training the model

Before we proceed with the actual training, it is a good idea to have some means to save the model with the best weights. For that purpose, we will use a callback from Keras:

```
checkpoint = K.callbacks.ModelCheckpoint("localization.h5",
    monitor='val_root_mean_squared_error',
    save_best_only=True, verbose=1)
```

The callback will be called after each epoch of training; it will calculate the `root_mean_square_error` metric of predictions on the validation data and will save the model to `localization.h5` if the metric has improved.

Now, we train our model in the same way that we did with classification:

```
model.fit(
    train.batch(32),
    epochs=12,
    validation_data=valid.batch(1),
    callbacks=[checkpoint])
```

Here, the difference is that we train with more `epochs` this time, as well as pass our callbacks and the validation dataset.

During training, you will first see a gradual decrease in the loss and metrics, both on the train and validation data. After several `epochs`, you might see that the metrics on the validation data increase. The latter might be thought of as a sign of overfitting, but after more `epochs`, you might see that the metrics on `validation_data` suddenly drop. The latter phenomenon is because the model switches to a better minimum metric during the optimization process.

Here is the result of the lowest value of the monitored metric:

```
Epoch 8/12
 83/84 [============================>.] - ETA: 0s - loss: 0.0012 -
root_mean_squared_error: 0.0275 - mae: 0.0212
 Epoch 00008: val_root_mean_squared_error improved from 0.06661 to 0.06268,
saving model to best_model.hdf5
 84/84 [=============================] - 39s 465ms/step - loss: 0.0012 -
root_mean_squared_error: 0.0275 - mae: 0.0212 - val_loss: 0.0044 -
val_root_mean_squared_error: 0.0627 - val_mae: 0.0454
```

You can note that, in this case, it was the eighth `epoch` that performed best on the validation data. You can note that the RMSE deviation on the validation data is about 6 percent. The MAE is less than 6 percent. We can interpret this result as follows—given an image from the validation data, the corner coordinates of the bounding box are usually shifted by a factor of 1/20 of the size of the image, which is not a bad result as the size of the bounding box is comparable with the size of the image.

You might also want to try to train the model with the frozen layers of the base models. If you do so, you will notice a far worse performance than with an unfrozen model. It will perform about twice as badly on the validation dataset according to the metrics. Given these numbers, we can conclude that the layers of the base model were able to learn on the dataset so that our model performs better on the localization task.

So, now that we have our model ready, let's use our inference script to see what it can do in the next section.

Seeing inference in action

Once we run our inference script, it will connect to the camera and localize a box on each frame, as depicted in the following photograph:

Although the model was trained on the location of heads of pets, we can see that it's quite good at localizing the head of a person. This is where you can note the power of generalization of the model.

When you create your own deep learning apps, you might discover that you have a lack of data for your particular application. However, if you relate your specific case to other available datasets, you might be able to find some applicable dataset that, although different, might allow you to successfully train your model.

Summary

Throughout this chapter, we have created and trained classification and localization models using the Oxford-IIIT-Pet dataset. We have learned how to create deep learning classifiers and localizers using transfer learning.

You have started to understand how to solve real-world problems using deep learning. You have understood how CNNs work and you know how to create a new CNN using a base model.

We have also covered the backpropagation algorithm for computing gradients. Understanding this algorithm will allow you to make wiser decisions on the architecture of models that you might want to build in the future.

In the next chapter, we will continue our deep learning journey. We will create an application that will detect and track objects with high accuracy.

Dataset attribution

Oxford-IIIT-Pet dataset: *Cats and Dogs*, O. M. Parkhi, A. Vedaldi, A. Zisserman, C. V. Jawahar in IEEE Conference on Computer Vision and Pattern Recognition, 2012.

10
Learning to Detect and Track Objects

In the previous chapter, you got your hands on deep convolutional neural networks and built deep classification and localization networks using transfer learning. You have started your deep learning journey and have familiarized yourself with a range of deep learning concepts. You now understand how deep models are trained and you are ready to learn about more advanced deep learning concepts.

In this chapter, you will continue your deep learning journey, first using object detection models to detect multiple objects of different types in a video of a relevant scene such as a street view with cars and people. After that, you will learn how such models are built and trained.

In general, robust object detection models have a wide range of applications nowadays. Those areas include but are not limited to medicine, robotics, surveillance, and many others. Understanding how they work will allow you to use them for building your own real-life applications, as well as elaborating on new models on top of them.

After we cover object detection, we will implement the **Simple Online and Realtime Tracking (Sort)** algorithm, which is able to robustly track detected objects throughout frames. During the implementation of the Sort algorithm, you will also get acquainted with the **Kalman filter**, which in general is an important algorithm when working with time series.

A combination of a good detector and tracker finds multiple applications in industrial problems. In this chapter, we'll limit the applications by counting the total objects by their type as they appear throughout the video of the relevant scene. Once you understand how this specific task is achieved, you will probably have your own usage ideas that will end up in your own applications.

For example, having a good object tracker allows you to answer statistical questions such as which part of the scene appears more condensed? And, where do objects move more slowly or quickly during the observation time? In some scenarios, you might be interested in monitoring the trajectories of specific objects, estimating their speed or the time that they spend in different areas of the scene. Having a good tracker is the solution for all of these things.

In this chapter, we will cover the following topics:

- Preparing the app
- Preparing the main script
- Detecting objects with SSD
- Understanding object detectors
- Tracking detected objects
- Implementing a Sort tracker
- Understanding the Kalman filter
- Seeing the app in action

Let's start the chapter by pointing out the technical requirements and planning the app.

Getting started

As mentioned in all of the chapters of the book, you need an appropriate installation of **OpenCV**, **SciPy**, and **NumPY**.

You can find the code that we present in this chapter at the GitHub repository at `https://github.com/PacktPublishing/OpenCV-4-with-Python-Blueprints-Second-Edition/tree/master/chapter10`.

When running the app with Docker, the Docker container should have appropriate access to the **X11 server**. This app cannot run in **headless mode**. The best environment to run the app with Docker is a **Linux** desktop environment. On **macOS**, you can use **xQuartz** (refer, to `https://www.xquartz.org/`) in order to create an accessible X11 server.

You can also use one of the available Docker files in the repository in order to run the app.

Planning the app

As mentioned previously, the final app will be able to detect, track, and count objects in a scene. This will require the following components:

- `main.py`: This is the main script for detecting, tracking, and counting objects in real time.
- `sort.py`: This is the module that implements the tracking algorithm.

We will first prepare the main script. During the preparation, you will learn how to use detection networks, as well as how they work and how they are trained. In the same script, we will use the tracker to track and count objects.

After preparing the main script, we will prepare the tracking algorithm and will be able to run the app. Let's now start with the preparation of the main script.

Preparing the main script

The main script will be responsible for the complete logic of the app. It will process a video stream and use an object-detection deep convolutional neural network combined with the tracking algorithm that we will prepare later in this chapter.

The algorithm is used to track objects from frame to frame. It will also be responsible for illustrating results. The script will accept arguments and have some intrinsic constants, which are defined in the following initialization steps of the script:

1. As with any other script, we start by importing all the required modules:

```
import argparse

import cv2
import numpy as np

from classes import CLASSES_90
from sort import Sort
```

We will use `argparse` as we want our script to accept arguments. We store the object classes in a separate file in order not to contaminate our script. Finally, we import our `Sort` tracker, which we will build later in the chapter.

2. Next, we create and parse arguments:

```
parser = argparse.ArgumentParser()
parser.add_argument("-i", "--input",
                    help="Video path, stream URI, or camera ID ",
default="demo.mkv")
parser.add_argument("-t", "--threshold", type=float, default=0.3,
                    help="Minimum score to consider")
parser.add_argument("-m", "--mode", choices=['detection',
'tracking'], default="tracking",
                    help="Either detection or tracking mode")

args = parser.parse_args()
```

Our first argument is the input, which can be a path to a video, the ID of a camera (0 for the default camera), or a video stream **Universal Resource Identifier (URI)**. For example, you will be able to connect the app to a remote IP camera using the **Real-time Transport Control Protocol (RTCP)**.

The networks that we will use will predict the bounding boxes of objects. Each bounding box will have a score, which will specify how probable it is that the bounding box contains an object of a certain type.

The next parameter is threshold, which specifies the minimal value of the score. If the score is below threshold, then we will not consider the detection. The last parameter is mode, in which we want to run the script. If we run it in detection mode, the flow of the algorithm will stop after detecting objects and will not proceed further with tracking. The results of object detections will be illustrated in the frame.

3. OpenCV accepts the ID of a camera as an integer. If we specify the ID of a camera, the input argument will be a string instead of an integer. Hence, we need to convert it to an integer if required:

```
if args.input.isdigit():
    args.input = int(args.input)
```

4. Next, we define the required constants:

```
TRACKED_CLASSES = ["car", "person"]
BOX_COLOR = (23, 230, 210)
TEXT_COLOR = (255, 255, 255)
INPUT_SIZE = (300,300)
```

In this app, we will track cars and people. We will illustrate bounding boxes in a yellowish color and write text in white. We'll also define the standard input size of the **Single Shot Detector (SSD)** model that we are going to use for detection.

Detecting objects with SSD

OpenCV has methods for importing models built with deep learning frameworks. We load the TensorFlow SSD model as follows:

```
config = "./ssd_mobilenet_v1_coco_2017_11_17.pbtxt.txt"
model = "frozen_inference_graph.pb"
detector = cv2.dnn.readNetFromTensorflow(model,config)
```

The first parameter of the `readNetFromTensorflow` method accepts a path to a file that contains a TensorFlow model in binary **Protobuf (Protocol Buffers)** format. The second parameter is optional. It is a path to a text file that contains a graph definition of the model, again in Protobuf format.

Surely, the model file itself might contain the graph definition and OpenCV can read that definition from the model file. But, with many networks, it might be required to create a separate definition, as OpenCV cannot interpret all operations available in TensorFlow and those operations should be replaced with operations that OpenCV can interpret.

Let's now define functions that will be useful for illustrating detections. The first function is for illustrating a single bounding box:

```
def illustrate_box(image: np.ndarray, box: np.ndarray, caption: str) ->
None:
```

From the previous code, the `illustrate_box` function accepts an image, a normalized bounding box as an array of four coordinates specifying two opposite corners of the box. It also accepts a caption for the box. Then, the following steps are covered in the function:

1. It first extracts the size of the image:

```
rows, cols = frame.shape[:2]
```

2. It then extracts the two points, scales them by the size of the image, and converts them into integers:

```
points = box.reshape((2, 2)) * np.array([cols, rows])
p1, p2 = points.astype(np.int32)
```

3. After that, we draw the corresponding `rectangle` using the two points:

```
cv2.rectangle(image, tuple(p1), tuple(p2), BOX_COLOR, thickness=4)
```

4. Finally, we put the caption near the first point:

```
cv2.putText(
    image,
    caption,
    tuple(p1),
    cv2.FONT_HERSHEY_SIMPLEX,
    0.75,
    TEXT_COLOR,
    2)
```

The second function will illustrate all `detections`, given as follows:

```
def illustrate_detections(dets: np.ndarray, frame: np.ndarray) ->
np.ndarray:
    class_ids, scores, boxes = dets[:, 0], dets[:, 1], dets[:, 2:6]
    for class_id, score, box in zip(class_ids, scores, boxes):
        illustrate_box(frame, box, f"{CLASSES_90[int(class_id)]}
{score:.2f}")
    return frame
```

From the preceding code snippet, the second function accepts detections as a two-dimensional `numpy` array and a frame on which it illustrates the detections. Each detection consists of the class ID of the detected object, a score specifying the probability that the bounding box contains an object of the specified class, and the bounding box of the detection itself.

The function first extracts the previously stated values for all detections, then illustrates each bounding box of the detection using the `illustrate_box` methods. The class name and `score` are added as the caption for the box.

Let's now connect to the camera:

```
cap = cv2.VideoCapture(args.input)
```

We pass the `input` argument to `VideoCapture`, which, as mentioned previously, can be a video file, stream, or camera ID.

Now that we have loaded the network, defined the required functions for illustration, and opened the video capture, we are ready to iterate over frames, detect objects, and illustrate the results. We use a `for` loop for this purpose:

```
for res, frame in iter(cap.read, (False, None)):
```

The body of the loop contains the following steps:

1. It sets the frame as the input of the `detector` network:

```
detector.setInput(
    cv2.dnn.blobFromImage(
        frame,
        size=INPUT_SIZE,
        swapRB=True,
        crop=False))
```

`blobFromImage` creates a four-dimensional input for the network from the provided image. It also resizes the image to the input size and swaps the red and blue channels of the image as the network is trained on RGB images, whereas OpenCV reads frames in BGR.

2. Then it makes a prediction with the network and gets the output in the desired format:

```
detections = detector.forward()[0, 0, :, 1:]
```

From the previous code, `forward` stands for forward propagation. The result is a two-dimensional `numpy` array. The first index of the array specifies the detection number, and the second index represents a specific detection, which is expressed by the object class, score, and four values specifying two corner coordinates of the bounding box.

3. After that, it extracts `scores` from `detections`, and filters out the ones that have a very low score:

```
scores = detections[:, 1]
detections = detections[scores > 0.3]
```

4. In the cases when the script is running in `detection` mode, illustrate `detections` right away:

```
if args.mode == "detection":
    out = illustrate_detections(detections, frame)
    cv2.imshow("out", out)
```

5. Then we have to set termination criteria:

```
if cv2.waitKey(1) == 27:
    exit()
```

Now we have everything ready to run our script in detection mode. A sample result is shown in the image that follows:

You can note in the frame from the preceding image that the SSD model has successfully detected all the cars and the single individual (person) visible in the scene. Let's now look at how we can use other object detectors.

Using other detectors

In this chapter, we are using an object detector to get bounding boxes with their object types, which will be further processed by the Sort algorithm for tracking. In general, it does not matter by what exact means the boxes are obtained. In our case, we have used an SSD pre-trained model. Let's now understand how to replace it with a different model.

Let's first understand how we can use YOLO for this purpose. YOLO is also a single-stage detector and stands for **You Only Look Once (YOLO)**. The original YOLO models are based on **Darknet**, which is another open-source neural network framework and is written in C++ and CUDA. OpenCV has the ability to load networks based on Darknet, similarly to how it loads TensorFlow models.

In order to load a YOLO model, you should first download the files containing the network configuration and the network weights.

 The latter can be done by visiting `https://pjreddie.com/darknet/yolo/`. In our case, as an example, we will use **YOLOv3-tiny**, which is the most lightweight one at the time of writing.

Once you have downloaded the network configuration and weights, you can load them similarly to how you loaded the SSD model:

```
detector = cv2.dnn.readNetFromDarknet("yolov3-tiny.cfg", "yolov3-tiny.weights")
```

The difference is that the `readNetFromDarknet` function is used instead of `readNetFromTensorflow`.

In order to use this detector instead of the SSD, we have several things to do:

- We have to change the size of the input:

```
INPUT_SIZE = (320, 320)
```

  The network is originally trained in with the specified size. If you have a high-resolution input video stream and you want the network to detect small objects in the scene, you can set the input to a different size, which is a multiplier of 160, for example, size (640, 480). The larger the input size, the more small objects will be detected, but the network will make predictions slower.

- We have to change class names:

```
with open("coco.names") as f:
    CLASSES_90 = f.read().split("\n")
```

  Although the YOLO network is trained on the **COCO** dataset, the IDs of the objects are different. You can still run with the previous class names, but you will have the wrong names of the classes in that case.

 You can download the file from the darknet repository `https://github.com/pjreddie/darknet`.

- We have to slightly change the input:

```
detector.setInput(
    cv2.dnn.blobFromImage(
        frame,
        scalefactor=1 / 255.0,
        size=INPUT_SIZE,
        swapRB=True,
        crop=False))
```

In comparison with the input for SSD, we add `scalefactor`, which normalizes the input.

Now we are ready to successfully make predictions. Although, we are not completely ready to display the results with this detector. The problem is that the predictions of the YOLO model have a different format.

Each detection consists of the coordinates of the center of the bounding box: the width, the height of the bounding box, and a one-hot vector representing the probabilities of each type of object in the bounding box. In order to finalize the integration, we have to bring the detections in the format that we use in the app. The latter can be accomplished with the following steps:

1. We extract the center coordinates of the bounding boxes:

   ```
   centers = detections[:, 0:2]
   ```

2. We then also extract the width and height of the bounding boxes:

   ```
   sizes = detections[:, 2:4]
   ```

3. Then, we extract `scores_one_hot`:

   ```
   scores_one_hot = detections[:, 5:]
   ```

4. Then, we find the `class_ids` of the maximum scores:

   ```
   class_ids = np.argmax(scores_one_hot, axis=1)
   ```

5. After that, we extract the maximum scores:

   ```
   scores = np.max(scores_one_hot, axis=1)
   ```

6. Then, we construct `detections` in the format consumed by the rest of the app using the results obtained in the previous steps:

```
detections = np.concatenate(
    (class_ids[:, None], scores[:, None], centers - sizes / 2,
centers + sizes / 2), axis=1)
detections = detections[scores > 0.3]
```

Now we can successfully run the app with the new detector. Depending on your needs, the available resources, and the required accuracy, you might want to use other detection models, such as other versions of SSD or **Mask-RCNN**, which is one of the most accurate object detection networks at the time of writing, although it is much slower than the SSD models.

You can try to load your model of choice with OpenCV, as we have done for both YOLO and SSD in this chapter. With this approach, you might encounter difficulties loading the model. For example, you might have to adapt the network configuration such that all the operations in the network can be processed by OpenCV.

The latter is particularly due to the fact that modern deep learning frameworks develop quite fast and OpenCV at least needs time to catch up to include all new operations. Another approach that you might prefer is to run a model using the original framework, similarly to what we did in Chapter 9, *Learning to Classify and Localize Objects*.

So now that we understand how to use detectors, let's look at how they work in the next section.

Understanding object detectors

In Chapter 9, *Learning to Classify and Localize Objects*, we learned how to use the feature maps of a certain layer of a convolutional neural network to predict the bounding box of an object in the scene, which in our case was a head.

You might note that the difference between the localization network that we composed and the detection networks (that we used in this chapter) is that the detection networks predict multiple bounding boxes instead of a single one, as well as assigning a class to each of the bounding boxes.

Let's now make a smooth transition between the two architectures so that you can understand how object detection networks like YOLO and SSD work.

The single-object detector

First of all, let's look at how to predict the class in parallel with the box. In `Chapter 9`, *Learning to Classify and Localize Objects*, you also learned how to make a classifier. Nothing limits us to combining classification with localization in a single network. That is done by connecting the classification and localization blocks to the same feature map of the base network and training it all together with a loss function, which is a sum of localization and classification losses. You can create and train such a network as an exercise.

The question remains, *what if there is no object in the scene?* To resolve this, we can simply add one more class that corresponds to the background and assign zero to the loss of the bounding box predictor when training. As a result, you will have a detector that detects multiple classes of objects but can only detect one object in the scene. Let's now look at how we can predict multiple boxes instead of one, and hence, arrive at a complete architecture of an object detector.

The sliding-window approach

One of the earliest approaches to create an architecture that can detect multiple objects in the scene was the **sliding-window** approach. With this approach, you first build a classifier for objects of interest. Then, you pick a rectangle (a window) of a size that is several or many times smaller than the image where you want to detect an object. After that, you slide it across all possible locations in the image and classify whether there is an object of the chosen type in each position of the rectangle.

During sliding, a sliding size of between a fraction of the box size and the complete box size is used. The procedure is repeated with different sizes of the sliding window. Finally, you pick the window positions that have a class score above some threshold and you report that those window positions with their sizes are the bounding boxes of the chosen object classes.

The problem with this approach is, first of all, that a lot of classifications should be done on a single image, and hence the architecture of the detector will be quite heavy. Another problem is that the objects are localized only with the precision of the sliding size. Also, the sizes of the detection bounding boxes have to be equal to the sizes of the sliding windows. Surely, the detection could be improved if the slide size was reduced and the number of window sizes was increased, but this would result in an even greater computational cost.

One of the ideas you already might have come up with is to combine the single-object detector with the sliding-window approach and take advantage of both. For example, you could split the image into regions. For example, we could take a 5 x 5 grid and run the single-object detector in each cell of the grid.

You could go even further by creating more grids with a larger or smaller size, or by making the grid cells overlap. As a mini-project to get a deep understanding of the ideas covered, you might like to implement them and play with the results. Still, with these approaches, we make the architectures heavier, that is, once we enlarge the grid size or the number of grids in order to improve the accuracy.

Single-pass detectors

In the previously stated ideas, we have used single-object classification or detection networks to achieve multiple-object detection. In all scenarios, for each predefined region, we feed the network with the complete image or part of it multiple times. In other words, we have multiple passes that result in heavy architecture.

Wouldn't it be nice to have a network that, once fed with an image, detects all the objects in the scene in a single pass? An idea that you could try is to make more outputs for our single-object detector so that it predicts multiple boxes instead of one. This is a good idea, but there is a problem. Suppose we have multiple dogs in the scene that could appear in different locations and in different numbers.

How should we make an invariant correspondence between the dogs and the outputs? If we make an attempt to train such a network by assigning boxes to the outputs, for example, from left to right, we will simply end up with predictions that are close to the average value of all positions.

Networks such as SSD and YOLO tackle the issues and implement multiscale and multibox detection in a single pass. We can sum up their architecture with the following three components:

- First of all, they have a position-aware multibox detector connected to a feature map. We have discussed the training problem that arises when connecting several box predictors to the complete feature map. The problem with SSD and YOLO is solved by having a predictor that is connected to a small region of the feature map instead of a complete feature map.

  It predicts boxes in the region of the image that corresponds to just that exact region of the feature map. Then, the same predictor predicts across all possible locations of the feature map. This operation is implemented using convolutional layers. There are convolutional kernels, with their activations, that slide across the feature map and have coordinates and classes as their output feature maps.

For example, you can obtain a similar operation if you go back to the code of the localization model and replace the last two layers, which flatten the output and create four fully connected neurons for predicting box coordinates with a convolutional layer with four kernels. Also, since the predictors act in a certain region and are aware only about that region, they predict coordinates that are relative to that region, instead of predicting coordinates that are relative to the complete image.

- Both YOLO and SSD predict several boxes in each location instead of a single one. They predict offset coordinates from several **default boxes**, which are also called **anchor boxes**. These boxes are chosen sizes and shapes that are close to the objects in the dataset or the natural scene, so that relative coordinates have small values and even the default boxes match the object bounding boxes pretty well.

  For example, a car usually appears as a wide box and a person usually appears as a tall box. Multiple boxes allow you to achieve better accuracy as well as to have multiple predictions in the same area. For example, if a person is sitting on a bike somewhere in the image and we have a single box, then we would omit one of the objects. With multiple anchor boxes, the objects will correspond to different anchor boxes.

- Besides having multisize anchor boxes, they use several feature maps with different sizes to accomplish multiscale prediction. If the prediction module is connected to the top feature maps of the network with a small size, it is responsible for large objects.

  If it is connected to one of the bottom feature maps, it is responsible for small objects. Once all the multibox predictions in the chosen feature maps are made, the results are translated to the absolute coordinates of the image and concatenated. As a result, we obtain the predictions in the form that we used in this chapter.

 If you are interested in more implementation details, we advise you to read corresponding papers, as well as to analyze the corresponding implementation code.

So now that you understand how the detectors work, you are probably also interested in the principles of their training. However, before we understand those principles, let's understand the metric called **Intersection over Union**, which is heavily used when training and evaluating these networks as well as filtering their predictions.

We will also implement a function to compute this metric, which we will use when building the Sort algorithm for tracking. Hence, you should note that understanding this metric is important not only for object detection but also for tracking.

Learning about Intersection over Union

Intersection over Union (IoU), which is also called the **Jaccard index**, is defined as the size of the intersection divided by the size of the union and has the following formula:

$$J(A, B) = \frac{|A \cap B|}{|A \cup B|}$$

That formula is equivalent to the following:

$$\frac{|A \cap B|}{|A| + |B| - |A \cap B|}$$

In the following diagram, we illustrate IoU for two boxes:

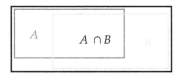

In the previous diagram, the union is the total area of the complete figure and the intersection is the part where the boxes overlap. The IoU can have a value in the range of (0,1) and reaches the maximal value only when the boxes match exactly. Once the boxes are separated, it becomes zero.

Let's define a function that accepts two bounding boxes and returns their `iou` value:

```
def iou(a: np.ndarray, b: np.ndarray) -> float:
```

In order to calculate the `iou` value, the following steps are necessary:

1. We first extract the top-left and bottom-right coordinates of both bounding boxes:

```
a_tl, a_br = a[:4].reshape((2, 2))
b_tl, b_br = b[:4].reshape((2, 2))
```

2. Then, we get the element-wise `maximum` of the two top-left corners:

```
int_tl = np.maximum(a_tl, b_tl)
```

The two arrays are compared element-wise and the result will be a new array containing the larger values of the corresponding indexes in the array. In our case, maximum *x* and *y* coordinates are obtained and stored in `int_tl`. If the boxes intersect, this is the top-left corner of the intersection.

3. Then, we get the element-wise `minimum` of the bottom-right corners:

```
int_br = np.minimum(a_br, b_br)
```

Similar to the previous case, this is the bottom-right corner of the intersection if the boxes intersect.

4. Then, we calculate areas of the bounding boxes:

```
a_area = np.product(a_br - a_tl)
b_area = np.product(b_br - b_tl)
```

The difference between the bottom-right and the top-left corner coordinates of a box is the width and height of the box, hence the product of the elements of the resulting array is the area of the bounding box.

5. After that, we calculate the intersection area:

```
int_area = np.product(np.maximum(0., int_br - int_tl))
```

If the boxes do not overlap, at least one element of the resulting array will be negative. Negative values are replaced with zeros. Hence, in such cases, the area is zero, as expected.

6. And at last, we calculate IoU and `return` the result:

```
return int_area / (a_area + b_area - int_area)
```

So, now that you have understood what IoU is and have built a function to compute it, you are ready to learn how the detection networks used are trained.

Training SSD- and YOLO-like networks

You are already aware that networks such as YOLO and SSD predict objects with predefined anchor boxes. Out of all available boxes, only one box is chosen, which corresponds to the object. During prediction time, the box is assigned with the class of the object and the offsets are predicted.

So, the question is, how do we choose that single box? You might already have guessed that IoU is used for that purpose. The correspondence between the ground truth boxes and anchor boxes can be made as follows:

1. Create a matrix that contains all IoU values of all possible ground truth and anchor box pairs. Say, the row corresponds to the ground truth box and the column corresponds to anchor box.
2. Find the maximal element in the matrix and assign the corresponding boxes to each other. Remove the row and column of the maximal element from the matrix.
3. Repeat *step 2* until there are no ground truth boxes available, or in other words, until all the rows of the matrix are removed.

Once the assignment is done, all that is left to do is to define a loss function for each box, sum the results as the total loss and train the network. The loss for the box offsets bounding boxes which contain objects can be simply defined as IoU—the greater the IoU, the closer the bounding box is to the ground truth, hence, it's negated value should be reduced.

The anchor boxes that do not contain objects do not contribute to the loss. The loss of object classes is also straightforward—the anchor boxes that do not have assignments are trained with the background class and the ones that do have assignments are trained with their corresponding classes.

Each of the considered networks has some modifications to the described loss so that it achieves better performance on the specific network. You can pick a network and define the loss described here on your own, which will be a good exercise for you. If you are building your own app and you need the corresponding trained network with relatively high accuracy in a limited amount of time, you might consider using the training methods that come with the code base of the corresponding network.

So, now that you have understood how to train these networks, let's continue the `main` script of the app and integrate it with the Sort tracker in the next section.

Tracking detected objects

Once we can successfully detect objects in each frame, we can track them by associating detections between frames. As mentioned previously, in this chapter, we are using the Sort algorithm for multiple-object tracking, which stands for **Simple Online and Realtime Tracking**.

Given sequences of multiple bounding boxes, this algorithm associates the boxes of sequence elements and fine-tunes the bounding box coordinates based on physical principles. One of the principles is that a physical object cannot rapidly change its speed or direction of movement. For example, under normal conditions, a moving car cannot reverse its movement direction between two consequent frames.

We suppose that the detector annotates the objects correctly and we instantiate one **Multiple Object Trackers** (mots) for each class of objects that we want to track:

```
TRACKED_CLASSES = ["car", "person"]
mots = {CLASSES_90.index(tracked_class): Sort()
        for tracked_class in TRACKED_CLASSES}
```

We store the instances in a dictionary. The keys in the dictionary are set to the corresponding class IDs. We will track the detected objects using the following function:

```
def track(dets: np.ndarray,
          illustration_frame: np.ndarray = None):
    for class_id, mot in mots.items():
```

The function accepts detections and an optional illustration frame. The main loop of the function iterates over the multi-object trackers that we have instantiated. Then, for each multi-object tracker, the following steps are covered:

1. We first extract detections of the object type of the current multi-object tracker from all the passed detections:

    ```
    class_dets = dets[dets[:, 0] == class_id]
    ```

2. Then, we update the tracker by passing the bounding boxes of the current object type to the update method of the tracker:

    ```
    sort_boxes = mot.update(class_dets[:, 2:6])
    ```

The update method returns the bounding box coordinates of the tracked objects associated with the IDs of the object.

3. If the illustration frame is provided, illustrate the boxes in the frame:

```
if illustration_frame is not None:
    for box in sort_boxes:
        illustrate_box(illustration_frame, box[:4],
            f"{CLASSES_90[class_id]} {int(box[4])}")
```

For each returned result, the corresponding bounding box will be drawn using our previously defined illustrate_box function. Each box will be annotated with the class name and the ID of the box.

We also want to define a function that will print general information about tracking on the frame:

```
def illustrate_tracking_info(frame: np.ndarray) -> np.ndarray:
    for num, (class_id, tracker) in enumerate(trackers.items()):
        txt = f"{CLASSES_90[class_id]}:Total:{tracker.count}
Now:{len(tracker.trackers)}"
        cv2.putText(frame, txt, (0, 50 * (num + 1)),
                    cv2.FONT_HERSHEY_SIMPLEX, 0.75, TEXT_COLOR, 2)
    return frame
```

For each class of tracked objects, the function will write the total number of tracked objects and the number of currently tracked objects.

Now that we have defined the functions for tracking and illustration, we are ready to modify the main loop, which iterates over frames, so that we can run our app in tracking mode:

```
if args.mode == "tracking"
    out = frame
    track(detections, frame)
    illustrate_tracking_info(out)
```

From the previous snippet, if the app runs in tracking mode, the detected objects of the chosen classes will be tracked throughout frames using our track function and tracking information will be shown on the frame.

What's left to do is to elaborate on the tracking algorithm in order to finalize the complete app. We will do that in the next section with the help of the Sort tracker.

Implementing a Sort tracker

The Sort algorithm is a simple yet robust real-time tracking algorithm for the multiple-object tracking of detected objects in video sequences. The algorithm has a mechanism to associate detections and trackers that results in a maximum of one detection box for each tracked object.

For each tracked object, the algorithm creates an instance of a single object-tracking class. Based on physical principles such as an object cannot rapidly change size or speed, the class instance can predict the feature location of the object and maintain tracking from frame to frame. The latter is achieved with the help of the **Kalman** filter.

We import the modules that we will use in the implementation of the algorithm as follows:

```
import numpy as np
from scipy.optimize import linear_sum_assignment
from typing import Tuple
import cv2
```

As usual, the main dependencies are `numpy` and OpenCV. The unfamiliar `linear_sum_assignment` method will be used when associating detected objects with tracked ones.

Let's now dive into the algorithm by first understanding what the Kalman Filter is, which is used in the implementation of a single box tracker in the next section.

Understanding the Kalman filter

The Kalman filter is a statistical model that has a wide range of applications in signal processing, control theory, and statistics. The Kalman filter is a complex model, but it could be thought of as an algorithm to **de-noise** the observations of an object that contain a lot of noise over time when we know the dynamics of the system with certain accuracy.

Let's look at an example, to illustrate how the Kalman filter works. Imagine we want to find the location of a train that moves on rails. The train will have a velocity, but unfortunately, the only measurements we have are from radar, which only shows the location of the train.

We would like to accurately measure the location of the train. If we were to look at each radar measurement, we could learn the location of the train from it, but what if the radar is not very reliable and has high measurement noise. For example, the locations that radar reported are as shown in the following diagram:

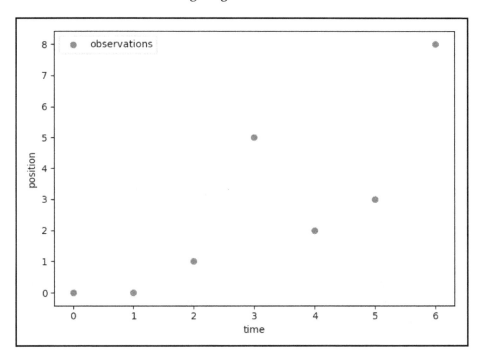

What can we tell about the real location of the train at 3 p.m.? Well, there is a possibility that the train was at **position 5**, but since we know that trains are heavy and change their speed very slowly, it would be very hard for the train to reverse its direction of travel twice in quick succession, to go to **position 5** and back. So, we can use some knowledge of how things work, and the previous observations, to make more reliable predictions about the location of the train.

For example, if we assumed that we could describe the train by its location and velocity, we would define the state to be the following:

$$s = (x, v)^T$$

Here, x is the location of the train and v is the velocity of the train.

Now we need a way to describe our model of the world, which is called the **state-transition model**—for a train, it is simple:

$$x[t] = x[t-1] + v$$
$$v[t] = v[t-1]$$

We could write this in a matrix form using the state variable, s:

$$s[t] = F \cdot s[t-1] = \begin{pmatrix} 1 & 1 \\ 0 & 1 \end{pmatrix} \begin{pmatrix} x[t-1] \\ v[t-1] \end{pmatrix}$$

The matrix, F, is called the **state-transition matrix**.

As such, we believe that the train doesn't change its velocity and moves at a constant speed. This means that there should be a straight line on the graph of observations, but that's too restrictive and we know that no real system behaves that way, so we allow for some noise being present in the system, that is, **process noise**:

$$s[t] = F \cdot s[t-1] + \omega[t]$$

Once we make statistical assumptions about the nature of the process noise, this will become a statistical framework, which is usually what happens. But, this way, if we are uncertain about our state transition model, but certain about observations, surely the best solution would still be what the instruments reported. So, we need to tie our state to our observations. Notice that we are observing x, so the observation could be recovered by multiplying the state by a simple row matrix:

$$o[t] = H \cdot s[t] = \begin{pmatrix} 1 & 0 \end{pmatrix} \begin{pmatrix} x[t] \\ v[t] \end{pmatrix}$$

But, as we said, we have to allow for the observations being imperfect (maybe our radar is very old, and sometimes has erroneous readings), that is, we need to allow for **observation noise**; thus, the final observation is the following:

$$o[t] = H \cdot s[t] + \epsilon[t]$$

Now, if we can characterize process noise and observation noise, the Kalman filter will be able to give us good predictions for the locations of the train at each point, using only the observations *before* that time. The best way to parametrize noise is with a covariance matrix:

$$\omega[t] \sim N(0, Q)$$
$$\epsilon[t] \sim N(0, R)$$

The Kalman filter has a recursive **state-transition model**, so we have to supply the initial value of the state. If we pick it to be (0, 0), and if we assume that **process noise** and **measurement noise** are equally probable (this is a terrible assumption in real life), the Kalman filter will give us the following predictions for each point in time:

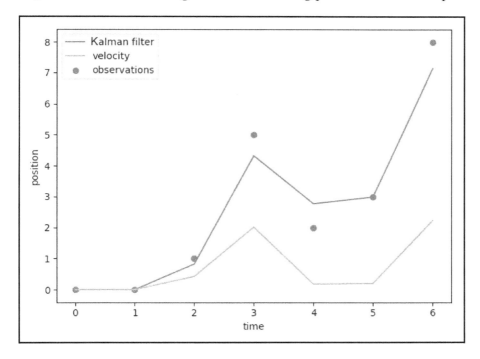

Since we believe our observations as much as our assumption that the velocity doesn't change, we got a smoothed curve (blue) that is not as extreme, but it is still not that convincing. So, we have to make sure that we encode our intuition in the variables that we pick.

Now, if we say that the **signal-to-noise ratio**, that is, the square root of the ratio of covariances, is 10, we will get the following results:

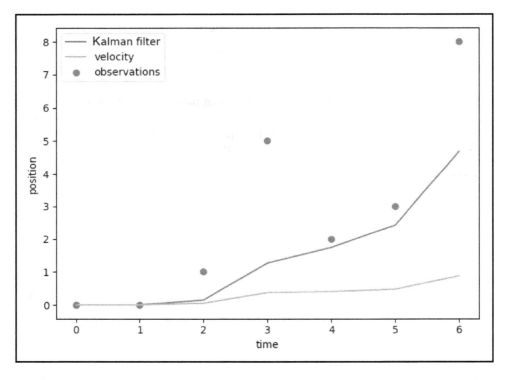

As you can see, the velocity does indeed move very slowly, but we seem to have underestimated how far the train has gone. *Or have we?*

It's a really hard task to tune the Kalman filter, and there are many algorithms for doing that, but unfortunately, none are perfect. For this chapter, we will not cover those; we will try to pick parameters that make sense, and we will see that those parameters give decent results.

Now let's revisit our single car tracking model, and see how we should model our system dynamics.

Using a box tracker with the Kalman filter

First, we have to figure out how to model each car's state. It might be better to start with the observation model; that is, *what can we measure about each car?*

Well, the object detectors give us boxes, but the way they are presented is not the best physical interpretation; similar to the train example given previously, we want variables we can reason about and that are closer to the underlying dynamics of the traffic. So, we use the following observation model:

$$\text{observation} = \begin{pmatrix} \text{horizontal coordinate} \\ \text{vertical coordinate} \\ \text{size} \\ \text{aspect ratio} \end{pmatrix} = \begin{pmatrix} u \\ v \\ s \\ r \end{pmatrix}$$

Here, u and v are the horizontal and vertical pixel locations of the center of the target, and s and r represent the scale (area) and the aspect ratio of the target's bounding box respectively. Since our cars are moving around the screen and are moving further away or coming closer, both coordinates and the size of the bounding boxes will change over time.

Assuming that nobody is driving like a lunatic, the velocities of the cars in the image should stay more or less constant; that's why we can limit our model to the location and velocities of the objects. So, the state we will take is the following:

$$\text{state} = [u, v, s, r, \dot{u}, \dot{v}, \dot{s}]^T$$

 We have used a notation where the dot on top of a variable means the rate of change of that variable.

The **state transition model** will be that the velocities and the aspect ratio stay constant over time (with some **process noise**). In the following screenshot, we have visualized all the boundary boxes, and their corresponding states (the location of the center and the velocity vector):

As you can see, we have set up the model so that what it observes is slightly different from what we receive from our tracker . So, in the next section, we'll go over the transformation functions we need to go from a boundary box to and from the state space of the Kalman Filter.

Converting boundary boxes to observations

In order to pass the boundary boxes to the Kalman filter, we will have to define a transformation function from each boundary box to the observation model, and, in order to use the predicted boundary boxes for object tracking, we need to define a function from a state to a boundary box.

Let's start with a transformation function from a boundary box to an observation:

1. First, we calculate the center coordinates of the boundary box:

```
def bbox_to_observation(bbox):
    x, y = (bbox[0:2] + bbox[2:4]) / 2
```

2. Next, we calculate the width and height of the box, which we will use to calculate the size (that is, the area) and the scale:

```
w, h = bbox[2:4] - bbox[0:2]
```

3. Then, we calculate the size of bbox, that is, the area:

```
s = w * h
```

4. After that, we calculate the aspect ratio, which is done just by dividing the width by the height:

```
r = w / h
```

5. Then return the result as a 4 x 1 matrix:

```
return np.array([x, y, s, r])[:, None].astype(np.float64)
```

Now, since we know that we have to define the inverse transformation as well, let's define state_to_bbox:

1. It takes a 7 x 1 matrix as an argument and unpacks all the components that we need to construct a boundary box:

```
def state_to_bbox(x):
    center_x, center_y, s, r, _, _, _ = x.flatten()
```

2. Then, it calculates the width and the height of the boundary box, from the aspect ratio and scale:

```
w = np.sqrt(s * r)
h = s / w
```

3. After that, it calculates the coordinates of the center:

```
center = np.array([center_x, center_y])
```

4. Then, it calculates the half size of the box as a `numpy` tuple, and uses it to calculate the coordinates of the opposite corners of the box:

```
half_size = np.array([w, h]) / 2
corners = center - half_size, center + half_size
```

5. Then, we return the boundary box as a one-dimensional `numpy` array:

```
return np.concatenate(corners).astype(np.float64)
```

Geared with the transformation functions, let's see how we can use OpenCV to build a Kalman filter.

Implementing a Kalman filter

Now, geared with our model, let's get our hands dirty and write a class that handles all this magic. We are going to write a custom class that will use `cv2.KalmanFilter` as a Kalman filter, but we will add some helper attributes to be able to keep track of each object.

First, let's take a look at the initialization of the class, where we will set up our Kalman filter by passing the state model, transition matrix, and initial parameters:

1. We first start by initializing the class with the boundary box—bbox—and the label for the `label` object:

```
class KalmanBoxTracker:
    def __init__(self, bbox, label):
```

2. Then we set up some helper variables that will let us filter boxes as they appear and disappear in the tracker:

```
self.id = label
self.time_since_update = 0
self.hit_streak = 0
```

3. Then, we initialize `cv2.KalmanFilter` with the correct dimensionality and data type:

```
self.kf = cv2.KalmanFilter(dynamParams=7, measureParams=4,
type=cv2.CV_64F)
```

4. We set the transition matrix and the corresponding process' **noise covariance matrix**. The covariance matrix is a simple model that involves the movement of each object with the current constant velocity in the horizontal and vertical directions, and becomes bigger or smaller using a constant rate:

```
self.kf.transitionMatrix = np.array(
    [[1, 0, 0, 0, 1, 0, 0],
     [0, 1, 0, 0, 0, 1, 0],
     [0, 0, 1, 0, 0, 0, 1],
     [0, 0, 0, 1, 0, 0, 0],
     [0, 0, 0, 0, 1, 0, 0],
     [0, 0, 0, 0, 0, 1, 0],
     [0, 0, 0, 0, 0, 0, 1]], dtype=np.float64)
```

5. We also set how certain we are about the constant speed process. We choose a **diagonal covariance matrix**; that is, our state variable is not correlated, and we set the variance for location variables as `10`, and as 10,000 for velocity variables. We believe that location changes are more predictable than velocity changes:

```
self.kf.processNoiseCov = np.diag([10, 10, 10, 10, 1e4,
1e4, 1e4]).astype(np.float64)
```

6. Then, we set the **Observation model** to be the following matrix, which implies that we are just measuring the first four variables in the state, that is, all the location variables:

```
self.kf.measurementMatrix = np.array(
    [[1, 0, 0, 0, 0, 0, 0],
     [0, 1, 0, 0, 0, 0, 0],
     [0, 0, 1, 0, 0, 0, 0],
     [0, 0, 0, 1, 0, 0, 0]], dtype=np.float64)
```

7. Now that we have set the measurement of the noise covariance, we believe that the horizontal and vertical locations are greater than the aspect ratio and the zoom, so we give smaller values to those two measurement variances:

```
self.kf.measurementNoiseCov = np.diag([10, 10, 1e3,
1e3]).astype(np.float64)
```

8. Finally, we set the initial position and the uncertainty associated with the Kalman filter:

```
self.kf.statePost = np.vstack((convert_bbox_to_z(bbox),
[[0], [0], [0]]))
self.kf.errorCovPost = np.diag([1, 1, 1, 1, 1e-2, 1e-2,
1e-4]).astype(np.float64)
```

After we are done setting up the Kalman filter, we need to be able to actually predict the new position of the object when it moves. We will do that by defining two more methods—update and predict. The update method will update the Kalman filter based on a new observation, and the predict method will predict a new position based on previous evidence. Now let's take a look at the update method:

```
def update(self, bbox):
    self.time_since_update = 0
    self.hit_streak += 1

    self.kf.correct(bbox_to_observation(bbox))
```

As you can see, the update method takes a boundary box of the new location, bbox, converts it to an observation, and calls the correct method on the OpenCV implementation. We have only added some variables to keep track of how long it has been since we have updated the object that we are tracking.

Now let's take a look at the predict function; its procedure is explained in the following steps:

1. It first checks whether we have called predict twice in a row; if we have called it twice in a row, then it sets self.hit_streak to 0:

```
def predict(self):
    if self.time_since_update > 0:
        self.hit_streak = 0
```

2. Then it increments self.time_since_update by 1, so we keep track of how long we have been tracking this object:

```
self.time_since_update += 1
```

3. Then we call the predict method of the OpenCV implementation and return a boundary box that corresponds with the prediction:

```
return state_to_bbox(self.kf.predict())
```

So, now that we have implemented a single-object tracker, the next step is to create a mechanism that can associate a detection box with a tracker, which we will do in the next section.

Associating detections with trackers

In the Sort algorithm, decisions about whether two bounding boxes should be considered to be of the same object are made based on Intersection over Union. Previously in this chapter, you learned about this metric and implemented a function to compute it. Here, we'll define a function that will associate detection and tracking boxes based on their IoU value:

```
def associate_detections_to_trackers(detections: np.ndarray, trackers:
np.ndarray,
        iou_threshold: float = 0.3) -> Tuple[np.ndarray, np.ndarray,
np.ndarray]:
```

The function accepts the bounding boxes of detections and the predicted boxes of trackers, as well as an IoU threshold. It returns matches as an array of pairs of corresponding indexes in the corresponding arrays, indexes of unmatched boxes of detections, and indexes of unmatched boxes of trackers. In order to achieve this, it takes the following steps:

1. First, it initializes a matrix in which the IoU values of each possible pair of boxes will be stored:

    ```
    iou_matrix = np.zeros((len(detections), len(trackers)),
    dtype=np.float32)
    ```

2. Then, we iterate overdetection and tracker boxes, calculate IoU for each pair, and store the resulting values in the matrix:

    ```
    for d, det in enumerate(detections):
        for t, trk in enumerate(trackers):
            iou_matrix[d, t] = iou(det, trk)
    ```

3. Using `iou_matrix`, we will find matching pairs such that the sum of the values of the IoUs of these pairs gets the maximal possible value:

    ```
    row_ind, col_ind = linear_sum_assignment(-iou_matrix)
    ```

    For this purpose, we have used the **Hungarian algorithm**, which is implemented as the `linear_sum_assignment` function. It is a combinatorial optimization algorithm that solves the **assignment problem**.

In order to use this algorithm, we have passed the opposite values of `iou_matrix`. The algorithm associates indexes such that the total sum is minimal. Hence, we find the maximal value when we negate the matrix. The straightforward way to find these associations would be to iterate over all possible combinations and pick the one that has the maximal value.

The problem with the latter approach is that the time complexity of it will be exponential and hence it will be too slow once we have multiple detections and trackers. Meanwhile, the Hungarian algorithm has a time complexity of $O(n^3)$.

4. Then we change the format of the result of the algorithm so that it appears as pairs of matched indexes in a numpy array:

```
matched_indices = np.transpose(np.array([row_ind, col_ind]))
```

5. Then get the intersection over union values of the matches from `iou_matrix`:

```
iou_values = np.array([iou_matrix[detection, tracker]
                      for detection, tracker in matched_indices])
```

6. Filter out matches that have an IoU value that is too low:

```
good_matches = matched_indices[iou_values > 0.3]
```

7. Then, find the indexes of the detection boxes that were not matched:

```
unmatched_detections = np.array(
    [i for i in range(len(detections)) if i not in good_matches[:,
0]])
```

8. After that, find the indexes of the tracker boxes that were not matched:

```
unmatched_trackers = np.array(
    [i for i in range(len(trackers)) if i not in good_matches[:,
1]])
```

9. At last, it returns the matches as well as the indexes of the unmatched detection and tracker boxes:

```
return good_matches, unmatched_detections, unmatched_trackers
```

So, now that we have mechanisms to track a single object and to associate detections with single-object trackers, what's left to do is to create a class that will use these mechanisms to track multiple objects throughout frames. We will do this in the next section and then the algorithm will be complete.

Defining the main class of the tracker

The constructor of the class is given as follows:

```
class Sort:
    def __init__(self, max_age=2, min_hits=3):
        self.max_age = max_age
        self.min_hits = min_hits
        self.trackers = []
        self.count = 0
```

It stores two parameters:

- The first parameter is `max_age`, which specifies how many consecutive times a tracker of a certain object can remain without an associated box before we consider the object to have gone from the scene and delete the tracker.
- The second parameter is `min_hits`, which specifies how many consecutive times a tracker should be associated with a box so that we consider it to be a certain object. It also creates properties for storing the trackers and counting the total number of trackers during the instance lifetime.

We also define a method for creating an ID of a tracker:

```
def next_id(self):
    self.count += 1
    return self.count
```

The method increments the count of the trackers by one and returns the number as the ID.

Now we are ready to define the `update` method, which will do the heavy lifting:

```
def update(self, dets):
```

The `update` method accepts detection boxes and covers the following steps:

1. For all available `trackers`, it predicts their new locations and removes `trackers` with failed predictions right away:

    ```
    self.trackers = [
        tracker for tracker in self.trackers if not np.any(
            np.isnan(
                tracker.predict()))]
    ```

2. We then get the predicted boxes of the `trackers`:

```
trks = np.array([tracker.current_state for tracker in
self.trackers])
```

3. Then, we associate the boxes predicted by the trackers with the detection boxes:

```
matched, unmatched_dets, unmatched_trks =
associate_detections_to_trackers(
    dets, trks)
```

4. We then update the matched `trackers` with the associated detections:

```
for detection_num, tracker_num in matched:
    self.trackers[tracker_num].update(dets[detection_num])
```

5. For all unmatched detections, we create new `trackers` that are initialized with the corresponding bounding box:

```
for i in unmatched_dets:
    self.trackers.append(KalmanBoxTracker(dets[i, :],
self.next_id()))
```

6. We then compose the `return` value as an `array` of the tracker box and tracker ID concatenations of the relevant trackers:

```
ret = np.array([np.concatenate((trk.current_state, [trk.id + 1]))
                for trk in self.trackers
                if trk.time_since_update < 1 and trk.hit_streak >=
self.min_hits])
```

In the previous codes snippet, we consider only those `trackers` that were updated with a detection box in the current frame and that have at least a `hit_streak` consecutive association with detection boxes. Depending on the particular application of the algorithm, you might want to change this behavior to make it a better fit for your needs.

7. We then clean up the `trackers` by removing the ones that have not been updated with a new bounding box for a while:

```
self.trackers = [
    tracker for tracker in self.trackers if
tracker.time_since_update <= self.max_age]
```

8. At last, we `return` the results:

```
return ret
```

So, now that we have completed the implementation of the algorithm, we have everything ready to run the app and see it in action.

Seeing the app in action

Once we run our app, it will use a passed video or another video stream, then process it and illustrate the results:

On each processed frame, it will display the object type, a bounding box, and the number of each tracked object. It will also display general information about tracking in the top-left corner of the frame. This general information consists of the total number of tracked video objects throughout for each type of tracked object, as well as the tracked objects currently available in the scene.

Summary

Throughout this chapter, we have used an object detection network and combined it with a tracker to track and count objects over time. After reading through the chapter, you should now understand how detection networks work and understand their training mechanisms.

You have learned how you can import models built with other frameworks into OpenCV and bind them into an application that processes a video or uses other video streams such as your camera or a remote IP camera. You have implemented a simple, yet robust, algorithm for tracking, which, in combination with a robust detector network, allows the answering of multiple statistical questions related to video data.

You can now use and train object detection networks of your choice in order to create your own highly accurate applications that implement their functionality around object detection and tracking.

Throughout the course of the book, you have made yourself familiar with a background in one of the main branches of machine learning, called **computer vision**. You started by using simple approaches such as image filters and shape analysis techniques. Then, you proceeded with classical feature extraction approaches and built several practical apps based on these approaches. After that, you learned about the statistical properties of a natural scene and you were able to use these properties to track unknown objects.

Next, you started to learn about, use, and train supervised models such as **Support Vector Machines (SVMs)** and **cascading classifiers**. Having all this theoretical and practical knowledge about classical computer vision approaches, you dived into deep learning models, which nowadays give state-of-the-art results for many machine learning problems, especially in the field of computer vision.

You now understand how **convolutional networks** work and how deep learning models are trained, and you have built and trained your own networks on top of other pre-trained models. Having all this knowledge and practice, you can analyze, understand, and apply other computer vision models as well as elaborating on new models once you come up with new ideas. You are ready to work on your own **computer vision** projects, which might change the world!

Profiling and Accelerating Your Apps

When you have a problem with a slow app, first of all, you need to find which exact parts of your code are taking quite a lot of processing time. A good way of finding such parts of the code, which are also called **bottlenecks**, is to profile the app. One of the good profilers available that allow an app to be profiled without modifications being introduced to the app is called pyinstrument (https://github.com/joerick/pyinstrument). Here, we profile the app of Chapter 10, *Learning to Detect and Track Objects*, using pyinstrument, as follows:

```
$ pyinstrument -o profile.html -r html  main.py
```

We have passed an output .html file where we want the profiling report information to be saved with a -o option.

We have also specified how the report should be rendered with a -r option, to state that we want an HTML output. Once the app is terminated, the profiling report will be generated, and it can be viewed in a browser.

 You can omit both options.

In the latter case, the report will be shown in the console. Once we terminate the app, we can open the generated `.html` file in the browser, which will show a report similar to the following:

```
11.989 <module>                                              main2.py:1
  7.843 [self]                                                      :1
  2.739 track                                                main2.py:77
    2.613 update                                              sort.py:178
      2.218 associate_detections_to_trackers                  sort.py:138
        2.014 iou                                             sort.py:124
          ▶ 1.063 product  <__array_function__ internals>:2
            0.950 [self]                                              :124
          0.203 update                                        sort.py:91
            0.173 update      filterpy/kalman/kalman_filter.py:491
              ▶ 1 frames hidden (filterpy)
  ▶ 0.932 <module>                                            sort.py:1
    0.217 <module>                                     numpy/__init__.py:1
      ▶ 1 frames hidden (numpy)
```

First of all, we can note that quite a lot of time is spent on the script itself. This should be expected, as an object detection model is making an inference on each frame, and that it is quite a heavy operation. We can also note that tracking also takes quite a lot of time, especially in the `iou` function.

Generally, depending on a particular application of the app, in order to accelerate tracking, it can be enough to replace the `iou` function with a different one that is more efficient. In this app, the `iou` function was used to compute `iou_matrix`, which stores the **Intersection Over Union** (**IOU**) metric for each possible pair of detection and tracking boxes. When you work on accelerating your code, in order to save time, it might be a good idea to change the code with an accelerated version in place and profile it again, in order to check whether it meets your needs.

But let's take the appropriate relevant code out of the app and analyze the possibilities of accelerating it using **Numba**, which we will cover in the next section.

Accelerating with Numba

Numba is a compiler that optimizes code written in pure Python using the **Low-Level Virtual Machine** (**LLVM**) compiler infrastructure. It efficiently compiles math-heavy Python code to reach performance similar to **C**, **C++**, and **Fortran**. It understands a range of `numpy` functions, Python `construct` libraries, and operators, as well as a range of math functions from the standard library, and generates corresponding native code for **Graphical Processing Units** (**GPUs**) and **Central Processing Units** (**CPUs**), with simple annotations.

In this section, we will use the **IPython** interactive interpreter to work with the code. It is an enhanced interactive Python shell that particularly supports so-called **magic commands**, which—in our case—we will use for timing functions. One of the options is to use the interpreter directly in the console. A couple of other options are to use **Jupyter Notebook** or **JupyterLab**. If you are using the **Atom** editor, you might want to consider the **Hydrogen** plugin, which implements an interactive coding environment right in the editor.

To import NumPy and Numba, run the following code:

```
import numpy as np
import numba
```

We are using **Numba version 0.49**, which is the most recent version at the time of writing. Throughout this section, you will note that we will have to change the code in such a way that it could be compiled using this version of Numba.

Supposedly, in future versions, Numba will support more functions, and some—or all—modifications might be not required. When you work on the code of your app, please refer to the **Numba** documentation for the supported features, available at `https://numba.pydata.org/numba-doc/latest/index.html` at the time of writing.

Here, we cover some important possibilities of Numba and illustrate results on a certain example, so that you will have your vision on how Numba can help you with accelerating the code of your own apps.

Let's now isolate the code that we want to accelerate, as follows:

1. First of all, this is the function that computes the `iou` of two boxes:

```
def iou(a: np.ndarray, b: np.ndarray) -> float:
    a_tl, a_br = a[:4].reshape((2, 2))
    b_tl, b_br = b[:4].reshape((2, 2))
    int_tl = np.maximum(a_tl, b_tl)
    int_br = np.minimum(a_br, b_br)
    int_area = np.product(np.maximum(0., int_br - int_tl))
    a_area = np.product(a_br - a_tl)
    b_area = np.product(b_br - b_tl)
    return int_area / (a_area + b_area - int_area)
```

For now, we have left it as it is from `Chapter 10`, *Learning to Detect and Track Objects*.

2. Next is the part of the code that calculates `iou_matrix` using the previous function, as follows:

```
def calc_iou_matrix(detections,trackers):
    iou_matrix = np.zeros((len(detections), len(trackers)),
dtype=np.float32)

    for d, det in enumerate(detections):
        for t, trk in enumerate(trackers):
            iou_matrix[d, t] = iou(det, trk)
    return iou_matrix
```

We have wrapped up the corresponding loops and matrix definition in a single new function.

3. In order to test performance, let's define two sets of `random` bounding boxes, like this:

```
A = np.random.rand(100,4)
B = np.random.rand(100,4)
```

We have defined two sets of `100` bounding boxes.

4. Now, we can estimate how much time it takes to compose `iou_matrix` of these bounding boxes by running the following code:

```
%timeit calc_iou_matrix(A,B)
```

The `%timeit` magic command executes the function multiple times, computes the average execution time, as well as the deviation from the average, and outputs the result, which looks as follows:

```
307 ms ± 3.15 ms per loop (mean ± std. dev. of 7 runs, 1 loop each)
```

We can note that it takes about one-third of 1 second to compute the matrix. Hence, if we have 100 objects in the scene and we want to process multiple frames in 1 second, there will be a huge bottleneck in the app. Let's now accelerate this code on a CPU.

Accelerating with the CPU

Numba has several code-generation utilities that generate machine code out of Python code. One of its central features is the `@numba.jit` decorator. This decorator allows you to mark a function for optimization by Numba's compiler. For example, the following function calculates the product of all the elements in an array:

```
@numba.jit(nopython=True)
def product(a):
    result = 1
    for i in range(len(a)):
        result*=a[i]
    return result
```

It can be viewed as a `np.product.` custom implementation. The decorator tells Numba to compile the function into machine code, which results in much faster execution time compared to the Python version. Numba always tries to compile the specified function. In the case of operations in the function that cannot be fully compiled, Numba falls back to the so-called **object mode**, which uses the **Python/C API** and handles all values as Python objects, to perform operations on them.

The latter is much slower than the former. When we pass `nopython=True`, we explicitly tell it to raise an exception when the function cannot be compiled to full machine code.

We can use the same decorator with the `iou` function, as follows:

```
@numba.jit(nopython=True)
def iou(a: np.ndarray, b: np.ndarray) -> float:
    a_tl, a_br = a[0:2],a[2:4]
    b_tl, b_br = b[0:2],b[2:4]
    int_tl = np.maximum(a_tl, b_tl)
    int_br = np.minimum(a_br, b_br)
    int_area = product(np.maximum(0., int_br - int_tl))
    a_area = product(a_br - a_tl)
    b_area = product(b_br - b_tl)
    return int_area / (a_area + b_area - int_area)
```

We can note that this function differs slightly from the Python function. First of all, we have used our custom implementation of `np.product.` If we try to use the native implementation with the current version of Numba, we will end up with an exception, as the native `np.product` is not currently supported by the Numba compiler. It's a similar story with the first two lines of the function, where Numba fails to interpret the automatic unpacking of the array into a tuple.

Now, we are ready to time our function, as we did previously, as follows:

```
%timeit calc_iou_matrix(A,B)
```

The latter produces the following output:

14.5 ms ± 24.5 µs per loop (mean ± std. dev. of 7 runs, 1 loop each)

We can note that we already have a huge acceleration (about 20 times), but let's proceed further. We can note that `calc_iou_matrix` is still in pure Python and it has nested loops, which might take quite a lot of time. Let's create a compiled version of it, like this:

```
@numba.jit(nopython=True)
def calc_iou_matrix(detections,trackers):
    iou_matrix = np.zeros((len(detections), len(trackers)),
dtype=np.float32)
    for d in range(len(detections)):
        det = detections[d]
        for t in range(len(trackers)):
            trk = trackers[t]
            iou_matrix[d, t] = iou(det, trk)
```

Again, this function differs from the original one, as Numba could not interpret `enumerate`. Timing this implementation will produce an output similar to the following:

7.08 ms ± 31 µs per loop (mean ± std. dev. of 7 runs, 1 loop each)

We again have an acceleration. This version is twice as fast compared with the previous one. Let's continue with the acceleration and get it as fast as possible, but before doing that, let's first familiarize ourselves with the `vectorize` decorator.

The `vectorize` decorator allows functions to be created that can be used as NumPy `ufuncs` class out of functions that work on scalar arguments, as in the following function:

```
@numba.vectorize
def custom_operation(a,b):
    if b == 0:
        return 0
    return a*b if a>b else a/b
```

The function performs some specific operation when given a pair of scalars, and the `vectorize` decorator makes it possible to do the same operation on NumPy arrays, for example, as follows:

```
custom_operation(A,B)
```

NumPy casting rules also work—for example, you can replace one of the arrays with a scalar or an array with shape (1,4), as follows:

```
custom_operation(A,np.ones((1,4)))
```

Another decorator that we will use to accelerate our `iou_matrix` computation is `guvectorize`. This decorator takes the concept of `vectorize` one step further. It allows `ufuncs` to be written that return arrays with different dimensionality. We can note that, when calculating the IOU matrix, the output array has a shape composed of the numbers of bounding boxes in each passed array. We use the decorator as follows to compute the matrix:

```
@numba.guvectorize(['(f8[:, :], f8[:, :], f8[:, :])'], '(m,k),(n,k1)->(m,
n)')
def calc_iou_matrix(x, y, z):
    for i in range(x.shape[0]):
        for j in range(y.shape[1]):
            z[i, j] = iou(x[i],y[i])
```

The first parameter tells Numba to compile a function that works on 8-byte floats (`float64`). It also specifies the dimensionalities of the input and output arrays with semicolons. The second parameter is the signature, which specifies how the dimensions of the input and output arrays are matched with each other. Once we execute the function with the input, the z output is waiting there with the correct shape and just needs to be filled in the function.

If we time this implementation as we did previously, we obtain an output similar to the following:

```
196 µs ± 2.46 µs per loop (mean ± std. dev. of 7 runs, 10000 loops each)
```

Again, we are about 30 times faster compared to the previous case. In comparison with the initial pure Python implementation, we are about 1,000 times faster, which is quite impressive.

Understanding Numba, CUDA, and GPU acceleration

You have seen how simple it is to create CPU-accelerated code using Numba. Numba also provides a similar interface to make a computation on a GPU using **Compute Unified Device Architecture (CUDA)**. Let's port our IOU matrix calculation function to be computed on a GPU using Numba.

We can instruct Numba to make the computation on a GPU by slightly modifying the decorator parameters, as follows:

```
@numba.guvectorize([' (f8[:, :], f8[:, :], f8)'],
' (m,k),(n,k1)->()',target="cuda")
def mat_mul(x, y, z):
    for i in range(x.shape[0]):
        for j in range(y.shape[1]):
            z=iou(x[i],y[j])
```

Here, we have instructed Numba to make the computation on a GPU by passing `target="cuda"`. We also have work to do on the `iou` function. The new function looks as follows:

```
@numba.cuda.jit(device=True)
def iou(a: np.ndarray, b: np.ndarray) -> float:
    xx1 = max(a[0], b[0])
    yy1 = max(a[1], b[1])
    xx2 = min(a[2], b[2])
    yy2 = min(a[3], b[3])
    w = max(0., xx2 - xx1)
    h = max(0., yy2 - yy1)
    wh = w * h
    result = wh / ((a[2]-a[0])*(a[3]-a[1])
        + (b[2]-b[0])*(b[3]-b[1]) - wh)
    return result
```

First of all, we have changed the decorator, which now uses `numba.cuda.jit` instead of `numba.jit`. The latter instructs Numba to create a function that is executed on a GPU. This function itself is called from a function that is running on a GPU device. For that purpose, we have passed `device=True`, which explicitly states that this function is intended to be used from functions that are calculated on a GPU.

You can also note that we made quite a few modifications so that we have eliminated all the NumPy function calls. As with CPU acceleration, this is due to the fact that `numba.cuda` cannot currently perform all operations that were available in the function, and we replaced them with the ones that `numba.cuda` supports.

Usually, in computer vision, your app will require GPU acceleration only when you are working with **deep neural networks** (**DNNs**). Most of the modern deep learning frameworks, such as **TensorFlow**, **PyTorch**, and **MXNet**, support GPU acceleration out of the box, allowing you to be away from low-level GPU programming and to concentrate on your models instead. After analyzing the frameworks, if you find yourself with a specific algorithm that you think should be necessarily implemented with CUDA directly, you might want to analyze the `numba.cuda` API, which supports most of the CUDA features.

Setting Up a Docker Container

Docker is a convenient platform that can package an application and its dependencies in a replicable virtual environment that can run on different operating systems. In particular, it is well integrated with any **Linux system**.

The replicable virtual environment is described in a **Dockerfile** that contains instructions that should be executed in order to achieve the desired virtual environment. These instructions mainly include the installation procedure, which is pretty much similar to the installation procedure with a Linux shell. Once the environment has been created, you can be sure that your app will have the same behavior on any other machine.

In Docker terminology, the resulting virtual environment is called a **Docker image**. You can create an instance of the virtual environment, which is called a **Docker container**. After the container is created, you can execute your code inside the container.

> Please follow the installation instructions on the official website in order to get Docker up and running on the operating system of your choice: https://docs.docker.com/install/

For your convenience, we are including Dockerfiles, which will make it very easy to replicate the environment that we have used to run the code in this book, regardless of what operating system you have on your computer. First, we describe a Dockerfile that uses only the CPU without GPU acceleration.

Defining a Dockerfile

Instructions in the Dockerfile start from a base image, and then desired installations and modifications are done on top of that image.

> At the time of writing, TensorFlow does not support **Python 3.8**. If you plan to run Chapter 7, *Learning to Recognize Traffic Signs*, or Chapter 9, *Learning to Classify and Localize Objects*, where TensorFlow is used, you can start with **Python 3.7** and then install TensorFlow with pip, or you can pick tensorflow/tensorflow:latest-py3 as the base image.

Let's go over the steps to create our environment:

1. We start from a base image, which is the basic Python image that is based on **Debian**:

   ```
   FROM python:3.8
   ```

2. We install useful packages that will particularly be used during the installation process of OpenCV and other dependencies:

   ```
   RUN apt-get update && apt-get install -y \
           build-essential \
           cmake \
           git \
           wget \
           unzip \
           yasm \
           pkg-config \
           libswscale-dev \
           libtbb2 \
           libtbb-dev \
           libjpeg-dev \
           libpng-dev \
           libtiff-dev \
           libavformat-dev \
           libpq-dev \
           libgtk2.0-dev \
           libtbb2 libtbb-dev \
           libjpeg-dev \
           libpng-dev \
           libtiff-dev \
           libv4l-dev \
           libdc1394-22-dev \
           qt4-default \
           libatk-adaptor \
           libcanberra-gtk-module \
           x11-apps \
           libgtk-3-dev \
       && rm -rf /var/lib/apt/lists/*
   ```

3. We download **OpenCV 4.2** together with the contributor packages, which are required for non-free algorithms such as **scale-invariant feature transform (SIFT)** and **speeded-up robust features (SURF)**:

   ```
   WORKDIR /
   RUN wget --output-document cv.zip
   https://github.com/opencv/opencv/archive/${OPENCV_VERSION}.zip \
       && unzip cv.zip \
   ```

```
    && wget --output-document contrib.zip
https://github.com/opencv/opencv_contrib/archive/${OPENCV_VERSION}.
zip \
    && unzip contrib.zip \
    && mkdir /opencv-${OPENCV_VERSION}/cmake_binary
```

4. We install a version of NumPy that works with **OpenCV 4.2**:

```
RUN pip install --upgrade pip && pip install --no-cache-dir
numpy==1.18.1
```

5. We compile OpenCV using appropriate flags:

```
RUN cd /opencv-${OPENCV_VERSION}/cmake_binary \
    && cmake -DBUILD_TIFF=ON \
        -DBUILD_opencv_java=OFF \
        -DWITH_CUDA=OFF \
        -DWITH_OPENGL=ON \
        -DWITH_OPENCL=ON \
        -DWITH_IPP=ON \
        -DWITH_TBB=ON \
        -DWITH_EIGEN=ON \
        -DWITH_V4L=ON \
        -DBUILD_TESTS=OFF \
        -DBUILD_PERF_TESTS=OFF \
        -DCMAKE_BUILD_TYPE=RELEASE \
        -D OPENCV_EXTRA_MODULES_PATH=/opencv_contrib-
${OPENCV_VERSION}/modules \
        -D OPENCV_ENABLE_NONFREE=ON \
        -DCMAKE_INSTALL_PREFIX=$(python3.8 -c "import sys;
print(sys.prefix)") \
        -DPYTHON_EXECUTABLE=$(which python3.8) \
        -DPYTHON_INCLUDE_DIR=$(python3.8 -c "from
distutils.sysconfig import get_python_inc;
print(get_python_inc())") \
        -DPYTHON_PACKAGES_PATH=$(python3.8 -c "from
distutils.sysconfig import get_python_lib;
print(get_python_lib())") \
        .. \
    && make install \
    && rm /cv.zip /contrib.zip \
    && rm -r /opencv-${OPENCV_VERSION} /opencv_contrib-
${OPENCV_VERSION}
```

6. We link the OpenCV Python binary to the appropriate location so that the interpreter can find it:

```
RUN ln -s \
   /usr/local/python/cv2/python-3.8/cv2.cpython-38m-x86_64-linux-
gnu.so \
   /usr/local/lib/python3.8/site-packages/cv2.so
```

This linking might be redundant or result in an error if you have used a base image that differs from `python:3.8`.

7. We install other Python packages that are used in the book:

```
RUN pip install --upgrade pip && pip install --no-cache-dir
pathlib2 wxPython==4.0.5

RUN pip install --upgrade pip && pip install --no-cache-dir
scipy==1.4.1 matplotlib==3.1.2 requests==2.22.0 ipython
numba==0.48.0 jupyterlab==1.2.6 rawpy==0.14.0
```

So, now that we have composed the Dockerfile, we can build the corresponding Docker image as follows:

```
$ docker build -f dockerfiles/Dockerfile  -t cv  dockerfiles
```

We have named the image `cv` and we have passed a Dockerfile located at `dockerfiles/Dockerfile` to build the image. Of course, you can place your Dockerfile in any other location. The last argument is required in Docker and it specifies a context that might be used; for example, if the Dockerfile contains directives to copy files from a relative path. In our case, we do not have such directives, and it can be, in general, any valid path.

Once the image is built, we can start the `docker` container as follows:

```
$ docker run --device /dev/video0 --env DISPLAY=$DISPLAY  -v="/tmp/.X11-
unix:/tmp/.X11-unix:rw"  -v `pwd`:/book -it book
```

Here, we have passed the `DISPLAY` environment variable, mounted `/tmp/.X11-unix`, and specified the `/dev/video0` device in order to allow the container to use the desktop environment and connect to the camera, where the container is used in most of the chapters of the book.

 If the Docker container fails to connect to the *X* server of your system, you might need to run $ `xhost +local:docker` on your system in order to allow the connection.

So, now that we are up and running with the composed Docker image, let's examine how to support GPU acceleration with Docker.

Working with a GPU

The environment that we create with Docker has limited access to the devices of your machine. In particular, you have seen that we have specified the camera device when running a Docker container and have mounted `/tmp/.X11-unix` in order to allow the Docker container to connect to the running desktop environment.

When we have custom devices such as GPUs, the integration process becomes more complicated, because the Docker container needs appropriate ways to talk to the device. Fortunately, for **NVIDIA GPUs**, this problem is solved with the help of **NVIDIA Container Toolkit** (`https://github.com/NVIDIA/nvidia-docker`).

Following installation of the toolkit, you can build and run GPU-accelerated Docker containers. Nvidia provides a base image so that you can build your image on top of it without bothering about appropriate access to the GPU. The requirement is that you should have an appropriate Nvidia driver installed on your system with an Nvidia GPU.

In our case, we mainly use GPUs for accelerating TensorFlow. TensorFlow itself provides an image that can be used to run TensorFlow with GPU acceleration. Therefore, to have a GPU-accelerated container, we can simply pick the Docker image of TensorFlow and make all other installations on top of it, as follows:

```
FROM tensorflow/tensorflow:2.1.0-gpu-py3
```

This declaration will pick TensorFlow version `2.1.0` with GPU acceleration and Python 3 support. Note that this version of the TensorFlow image uses **Python 3.6**. Nevertheless, you can use the remaining part of the Dockerfile for the CPU that we described in Appendix A, *Profiling and Accelerating Your Apps*, and you will be up and running with a container that can run the code in this book.

Once you are done with creating the image, the only modification that you have to do when starting a container is to pass one additional argument: `--runtime=nvidia`.

Other Books You May Enjoy

If you enjoyed this book, you may be interested in these other books by Packt:

Mastering OpenCV 4 with Python
Alberto Fernández Villán

ISBN: 978-1-78934-491-2

- Handle files and images, and explore various image processing techniques
- Explore image transformations, including translation, resizing, and cropping
- Gain insights into building histograms
- Brush up on contour detection, filtering, and drawing
- Work with Augmented Reality to build marker-based and markerless applications
- Work with the main machine learning algorithms in OpenCV
- Explore the deep learning Python libraries and OpenCV deep learning capabilities
- Create computer vision and deep learning web applications

Learning OpenCV 4 Computer Vision with Python 3 - Third Edition
Joseph Howse, Joe Minichino

ISBN: 978-1-78953-161-9

- Install and familiarize yourself with OpenCV 4's Python 3 bindings
- Understand image processing and video analysis basics
- Use a depth camera to distinguish foreground and background regions
- Detect and identify objects, and track their motion in videos
- Train and use your own models to match images and classify objects
- Detect and recognize faces, and classify their gender and age
- Build an augmented reality application to track an image in 3D
- Work with machine learning models, including SVMs, artificial neural networks (ANNs), and deep neural networks (DNNs)

Leave a review - let other readers know what you think

Please share your thoughts on this book with others by leaving a review on the site that you bought it from. If you purchased the book from Amazon, please leave us an honest review on this book's Amazon page. This is vital so that other potential readers can see and use your unbiased opinion to make purchasing decisions, we can understand what our customers think about our products, and our authors can see your feedback on the title that they have worked with Packt to create. It will only take a few minutes of your time, but is valuable to other potential customers, our authors, and Packt. Thank you!

Index

www.ingramcontent.com/pod-product-compliance
Lightning Source LLC
Chambersburg PA
CBHW080614060326
40690CB00021B/4697